CASH OUT
MOVE ON

CASH OUT
MOVE ON

GET TOP DOLLAR
—AND MORE—
SELLING YOUR BUSINESS

JOHN H. BROWN

WITH KEVIN M. SHORT
EDITED BY KATHRYN B. CARROLL

BUSINESS ENTERPRISE INSTITUTE, INC.,
Golden, CO

Published by Business Enterprise Press,
a Division of Business Enterprise Institute, Inc.
Golden, Colorado

Publisher's Cataloging-in-Publication Data

Brown, John H.

Cash out—move on : get top dollar—and more—selling your business / John H. Brown with Kevin M. Short ; edited by Kathryn B. Carroll.— Golden, CO : Business Enterprise Press, 2008.

p. ; cm.

ISBN: 978-0-9655731-2-2 (hard cover)
ISBN: 978-0-9655731-3-9 (soft cover)

1. Sale of business enterprises—Handbooks, manuals, etc. 2. Business enterprises—Finance. I. Short, Kevin M. II. Carroll, Kathryn B. III. Title.

HD1393.25.B76 2008
658.16—dc22   2007939260

Printed in the United States of America
12 11 10 09 08 • 5 4 3 2 1

DEDICATION

To Jamie, with love and affection.

Acknowledgments

Like many authors, I wish, and need, to thank many individuals for their contributions to this book.

First, I must acknowledge my parents. I dedicated my first book to them, but their actions as business owners are just as important, if not more so, in inspiring this book. I can only hope that readers of this book will learn as much from my book as I did from my parents.

The owners who generously shared their very personal stories enriched this book immeasurably. They recounted their experiences out of a desire to promote understanding that life, post-sale, is filled with possibility. Each owner has moved on in a new direction and illustrates, as only those who have done so can, the importance of having adequate time to make a careful decision to sell and then expertly sell at the right time.

My experience is in helping owners to decide to sell and to prepare their companies for sale, but not in taking the owner through the sale process itself; a transaction intermediary and deal team are necessary for that part of the process. As the principal of one of the leading investment banking firms in this country, Kevin Short, my co-author, has a wealth of experience leading owners through the sale process. As you will read, a properly conducted sale process is the final ingredient in getting top dollar from the sale of your business. It is here that Kevin most generously shares his expertise—and some of his secrets. Many of the owners interviewed for this book were Kevin's clients and they speak more eloquently than I can about Kevin's integrity, his humility, his composure under pressure, and his deep understanding of the sale process.

Three years ago, I cashed out and moved on from the law firm that I founded nearly 30 years earlier. While a number of attorneys helped me to synthesize my thoughts about exiting into a coherent process, I owe Ned A. Minor, Barbara J. Wells, Lisa D'Ambrosia and Elizabeth Mower (now the Project Director for my new company) a debt of gratitude. To Barb and Lisa, thank you for your contributions to Chapters 10 and 11.

In my "post-sale life," I started a new company, Business Enterprise Institute, Inc., to teach advisors of business owners how to help their clients exit their businesses in style. Over the last four years, hundreds of BEI's member advisors have both broadened and refined my thoughts about how to help owners increase value, motivate management, develop a timeline for the sale, stay in control of the sale process, and to imagine a life after the sale.

Finally, I thank Kathy Carroll. Kathy and I have worked together for over 20 years, writing books, articles, newsletters, white papers and more. To this book she added content, forced me to clarify my thoughts, organized my streams of consciousness, turned sentence fragments into paragraphs, interviewed owners and wrote their stories, and, most challenging of all, kept me (for the most part) on track and on schedule. Her efforts make this book possible; her creative and expressive abilities make this book readable. Her involvement is so critical that I have one last request as I write this: Kathy, please review, revise, and rewrite this acknowledgement as needed. And, as usual, can I have it back today? Thanks.

—John H. Brown

DISCLAIMER

This publication is designed to provide information in regard to the subject matter covered. It is sold with the understanding that while John H. Brown is an attorney, and Kevin M. Short a professional investment banker, neither they, their companies, nor the publisher are engaged by the reader to render legal, accounting or other professional service. If the reader requires legal advice or other expert assistance, he or she should seek the services of a competent professional.

The purpose of this book is to educate. The authors and their companies, Business Enterprise Institute, Inc. and Clayton Capital Partners, shall have no liability or responsibility to any person or entity with respect to any loss or damage caused, or alleged to be caused, directly or indirectly, by the information contained in this book.

If you do not wish to be bound by the above, you may return this book to the publisher for a full refund.

To illustrate their points, the authors make liberal use of case studies. Unless otherwise stated, all of these case studies describe fictional characters and situations. Any resemblance to persons, living or dead, is purely coincidental. The owners featured in Chapter 12, however, are real and their stories are used with their permission.

CONTENTS

INTRODUCTION

When my father sold his business in 1970 he relied on his lawyer and accountant to "draw up the papers." Nobody asked why my dad wanted to sell or what he would do after he did sell. Neither Dad nor his advisors asked if it was the right time to sell. No one made any moves to build value in preparation for the sale or even to orchestrate a competitive sale process. Needless to say, the sale failed miserably.

While professional ineptitude played a role in the failure, my father simply didn't realize that he was in a better position to decide the fate of his company than were his advisors. They never told him that there was much he could do to prepare the business and himself for the sale. Things weren't done that way back then.

Well, things have changed for the better. Today Baby Boomer owners are in the driver's seat on every important business decision and they remain there through the sale of their businesses. But how do they stay in charge of the most important transaction of their business lives when they know as little about the process as did my dad?

Some hire advisors and hope for the best. Others, like you, read this book, which shows you how to make informed decisions and stay in control of the process.

I wrote this book for the owners who:

- Understand that orchestrating the biggest financial transaction of their lives requires them to make informed decisions;

- Are running successful, valuable companies; and

- Are part of the Baby Boomer generation.

For Boomer owners, the clock, the demographic clock, is ticking. Boomer demographics, the Law of Supply and Demand, the state of today's Merger and Acquisition market, the current and historically low capital gains rate, and the "Boomer Mindset" constitute the "perfect storm" for Boomer owners. This means that if you and your business are ready to sell, there are opportunities in selling your business now and significant dangers if you delay.

I'll discuss each of these factors at some length below, but briefly, the Boomer generation does not just constitute *the majority* of owners likely to sell in the next several years: this generation represents practically ALL of the sellers likely to sell in the next decade or so.

The Perfect Storm

Demographics And The Law Of Supply And Demand

I'm a Boomer, the business owners I represented for years in my law practice are Boomers, and Kevin Short, investment banker and my co-author, is also a Boomer. There are approximately 78 million members of the demographic group born between 1946 and 1964. This group is larger than any either before or after it. Group size alone has huge implications for Boomer owners as they think about selling or transferring their companies.

The generation following the Boomers is known as Generation X or Baby Busters. This generation is defined by the U.S. Census Bureau as those born between 1968 and 1979. In 2002, the Census Bureau estimated (based on its 2000 Census) that there were 59,802,658 people between the ages of 20 and 34. The direct effect of far fewer potential buyers in the next generation gives additional import to the Law of Supply and Demand.

Various commentators and researchers believe there are more than four million owners of established businesses who are at least 50 years old (Roger Winsby of Axiom Valuation Solutions, 2003) and that the average age of sellers is about 56 (Robert Slee in June 2004 issue Journal of Financial Planning paraphrasing an IMAP survey).

According to a 2005 PricewaterhouseCoopers' survey of 364 CEOs of privately held, fast-growing companies, "nearly two-thirds . . . plan to move on within a decade or less: 42 percent within five years, and 23 percent in five to ten years." ("Wide Majority of Fast-Growth CEOs Likely to Move On Within Ten Years, PwC Finds." January 31, 2005.).

This kind of movement "could result in a glut of companies on the market, driving down valuations and giving new leverage to buyers," said Laura Rich in "Seller's Market" (Inc. Magazine, May 2005).

Interestingly, the largest numbers of Boomers are not yet 50 years old. As these youngsters reach age 50 and 55 they too will be looking to sell their businesses—adding fuel (businesses) to the fire (the glut of businesses for sale by age 50-60 Boomers). Avoiding this added supply means considering the sale of your business sooner rather than later—provided of course that it is (and you are) ready for sale (intrinsic value), the sale cycle is appropriate (extrinsic value), and it is large enough to be sold using the best sale process (promoted value).

The basic Law of Supply and Demand dictates that a glut of sellers will drive down prices. When (not if) this happens, a limited number of dollars will be spent on only those businesses that present the least risk and the greatest potential to the buyer. We'll talk about ways to decrease a buyer's risk and increase your company's potential for future growth in Chapters 6 and 7.

M&A MARKET

Of course, the Merger and Acquisition marketplace is notoriously and historically cyclical. Right now (Fall 2007) it seems to be at a cyclical peak of activity and value, but history tells us it won't stay there long. In fact, the front page of the September 6, 2007, issue of *The Wall Street Journal* trumpeted, "Deals Boom Fizzles As Cheap Credit Fades: Wall Street Mulls End of Golden M&A Era." In Kevin Short's chapter on the M&A cycle, he talks about how, and even if, stories like these relate to the M&A market of the mid-size company. The deals we talk about in this book—generally between $10 and $150 million—are deals that don't make the front page of *The Wall Street Journal,* but do in your community.

THE BOOMER MINDSET

Finally, as Boomers, we want to sell our businesses (cash out), not to retire, but to relaunch—to move on to something else and to do it while we are relatively young and healthy. Boomers are asking, "If the time is right to sell and I can meet all of my goals and objectives, why wait?"

If you have already asked yourself this question, and selling now, or in the next several years, is part of your plan, this book will show you what decisions you must make as you progress through the sale of your business. Make no mistake, the decisions involved in selling your business must be informed, correct, and yours, not your advisors'. After all, this is the biggest transaction in your life; the decisions you make will affect, probably deeply, the course of the balance of your life. Added to this, you have one shot to get this right—and you likely have not sold a business before.

The mindset of Boomers differs markedly from past generations of owners. This means that their post-sale expectations and needs are quite different from earlier generations. You will need to examine your expectations and carefully consider what it will take financially to meet these needs and expectations before you sell.

When Boomers cash out and move on, they not only want top dollar, but they also want more—more activities, more community involvement, more time with family, but ultimately—more freedom to do what they want. This idea of "more" is quite different than that of generations before.

For a look at these differing expectations and needs, let's return to my father's case. My dad sold his business mostly because he was old and wanted to enjoy his "few remaining years." He was 62. Dad lived 30 more years to the day.

Dad had no Exit Plan. Those words were not even in the vocabulary. Retirement meant a life of making do with less, and of having more time but being able to do less. My father never imagined that he would live 30 years after selling his business.

Owners today are not old at age 62. A May 2, 2007, article in Knowledge@Wharton said, "Unlike their parents and grandparents, many baby boomers will never retire in the traditional sense, said [Michael] Milken, who argues that this is all to the good. 'They are young, and they are going to stay young. Medical advances are just one factor,' he noted. In addition, attitudes have changed. Decades ago, the media portrayed women in the 40s and 50s as elderly; now it shows them as young and active. 'So, yes, it's good news. Eighty is the new 60 . . . Sixty is the new 40.'"

Today, Boomer owners have much to accomplish, much to do.

With proper planning, most owners can choose when they want to sell and then sell when business value is sufficient to allow them to do all the things they want to do after they sell.

This very different mindset from our parents has great impact on the decision to sell and on what we will need after we sell. After Boomers sell, they don't retire; they relaunch their lives. That means growing into a new life with a new set of challenges.

When my dad retired, he bought a small fishing boat. Today, former owners buy motorcycles, second homes and new businesses. They carry with them all of the experience gained from years of managing successful companies into new business, charitable or leisure activities. This, in turn, creates a new set of challenges.

THE BOOMERS' UNIQUE CHALLENGE

LONGEVITY COSTS MONEY

Boomers need a lot of money when we leave our companies because we will live longer than our parents did and we want to be active. Living longer and more actively means we need more money than we may have originally thought.

This longer lifespan creates a unique challenge for Boomer owners. Those of us who are 60 today, are of average weight and height, have average blood pressure and cholesterol numbers, drink and exercise moderately, have a reasonably healthy diet and don't drive like maniacs, have life expectancies of 85 years for men and as long as 100 years for women. (If you doubt these numbers or are interested in calculating your own life expectancy (as I did), you'll find free calculators on the Internet sponsored by financial companies, universities and news agencies.)

What this means to you is that you'll likely have decades to live after you leave your company. The challenge is to create a nest egg big enough to (1) cover the expensive medical care, including even more life extending and quality of life treatments, (and if not that, the expensive health insurance premiums) we'll want and need as we age; and (2) last until we die.

We Boomers have a lot of living left to do and we want to live well.

AN ACTIVE SECOND ACT

Not only do we need to finance more years after we leave our companies, we expect the proceeds from the sale of our businesses to finance our next great project. As you'll read, former owners engage in a number of activities after they sell. Here's a short list of what the owners you'll read about have done since they sold their businesses:

- Work for the successor owner without the hassles of ownership

- Take a seven-year break before starting two new businesses

- Sail around the world and engage in charitable activities

- Get away from it all—while staying at home

- Start a consulting business

- Lower the golf handicap

- Volunteer in New Zealand

- Spend time with family

- Take on work-related projects that ownership didn't allow

These activities—starting a new business, buying one or more second homes, travel—cost a lot of money. The message from these former owners is: don't fall for the illusion that there is a way to enhance post-sale life without preparation.

FREEDOM COSTS MONEY

To Boomers, money is by no means everything. This is the group that includes both "Power to the People" and flower children. From activist to pacifist, we share one indispensable essence: we want the freedom *to choose* our lifestyle and *to change* our lifestyle.

To owners, this often means creating a new type of personal significance. (Maybe, as an owner, you've done enough of that already! You are burned out and you just want "to get the hell out of the business." That's fine. It simplifies a lot of the decision-making!) Many Boomers, however, still want to make or continue to make, their mark on the world—for the better. Once they leave their companies, they want to improve the world and through that, themselves. Some pour energy into family, civic or church activities or even new businesses. Some of the owners you'll meet in Chapter 12 have strong feelings in this regard; others don't. One owner gave millions of dollars to his favorite charities; another joined several country clubs. The important lesson is that the owners had the freedom to decide their future because of the decisions they made as they approached the sale and as they sold their businesses.

All of these realities—demographic, physical and perspective—present the Boomer owner with a unique challenge:

> How do we leave our companies for the amount of cash necessary to finance the kind of post-sale life we want (one full of options and opportunities) when there are so many of us and so few buyers?

That's the question that this book attempts to answer. Our goal is not to teach you to write a sale contract or to understand the tax and legal intricacies of selling your business; your skills are needed elsewhere. You are the one—and the only one—who can take your company from where it is today, through a successful sale, and to the post-sale life you desire. Of course, there are advisors (who have helped other owners) who can help you and this book is written by two of them.

WHAT TO EXPECT FROM THIS BOOK

Since you can't expect hints on how to write a sale contract or how to become a business valuation expert, what can you expect for your $24.95?

EXPERT ADVICE

First, Kevin Short (an investment banker) and I (a former lawyer, author of the bestselling book on Exit Planning for owners, and now the owner of a company that educates owners and their advisors about how to exit successfully) will offer you guidance.

Kevin is the co-founder and managing director of Clayton Capital Partners, a St. Louis-based investment banking firm specializing in merger and acquisition advisement. Over the past 25 years, Kevin has become a recognized leader in purchase and sale transactions of mid-size businesses spanning a wide range of industries. He has been involved in more than 150 purchase/sale transactions with an aggregate value of more than $1 billion.

You'll meet several of Kevin's former clients in Chapter 12. He wrote the chapter on the Merger & Acquisition market (Chapter 8), the chapter on controlled auctions (Chapter 9), and contributed numerous comments and insights to this book from his experience with business owners.

I am an attorney, but have retired from the active practice of law. In 1977, I co-founded a Denver law firm where I represented business owners for nearly 30 years. It was there that I became aware of the owner's need for a comprehensive Exit Plan, and for the owner's advisors to have not only an eye on the prize (the successful sale/transfer of the owner's company), but also a means to help the owner reach that prize. I called that means "Exit Planning" and wrote my first book about the subject in 1990.

That book, **How To Run Your Business So You Can Leave It In Style,** has gone through several revisions and numerous printings. It launched my speaking career and prompted me to leave the practice of law to set up my company, Business Enterprise Institute, Inc. to train business owner advisors. If you haven't done any planning for the day you leave your company, I suggest that you pick up a copy of my first book and read it.

Our guidance is based on our experiences in guiding hundreds of owners through the sale process. We've also both owned and exited our own companies and started new ones. As Boomers, we aren't afraid of cashing out and moving on and, in fact, we recommend it.

This book is not a "how to sell your business" manual. You hire professionals to "draw up the papers," but only you can make the decisions that will enable you to get what you want and need. For example, you are not going to conduct the sales negotiations, but you will choose the advisor who will. You are not going to prepare your business for sale, but you must know what needs to be done so that you work with a team of advisors who can decide and implement the necessary actions to maximize value.

DECISION CHECKLIST

We have created two Decision Checklists to help you map a clear path from where you are today to where you are going in the future. The first is for owners who plan to sell their companies in the mid-term (one to two years). The second is for those who plan to exit in the long-term (three or more years). Following each of these summary checklists, you'll find lists of specific actions or decisions you must take or make to reach your goals. These checklists will help you understand what decisions you need to make and when you need to make them. We encourage you to refer back to the lists in this Decision Checklist Appendix as you work through your decisions.

OWNER STORIES

Finally, we offer you the stories of a number of former business owners who have cashed out of their companies and moved on into new lives. We represented these successful Boomer owners as they left their companies and they have agreed to share their stories with you. As you read about them, you will realize that, like you, none of them is perfect, but, unlike you, they've all been through the process. Their experiences offer insight into what you can expect of yourself, of your advisors and of the process as you move through it.

We hope you'll take time to read the stories of these remarkable Boomer owners. Their stories illustrate the points Kevin and I make throughout this book. These owners share their thoughts about their goals and how they achieved them. They talk about what factors—both internal and external—prompted them to sell. You'll see how they orchestrated their sales (both controlled auctions with numerous buyers and negotiated sales with only one), what they did right and what, by their own admission, they did wrong. Finally, you'll see what they are doing in their post-sale lives and what plans they have for the future.

ORGANIZATION

This book is divided into five sections.

- **Section One: Setting the Stage.** What do you need to know before you can embark on the sale process? Can you sell now? What do you want and need from a sale? How can advisors maximize your payday? What is your company worth? How much will the IRS take?

- **Section Two: Creating Intrinsic Value.** What characteristics of a company make it more valuable? How do you prepare a business for sale? How do you prepare yourself for the sale of your company?

- **Section Three: Understanding Extrinsic Value.** What factors outside the business increase or decrease the amount others will pay you for your business?

- **Section Four: Using Promoted Value.** How can the sale process itself increase or promote business value?

- **Section Five: Adjusting Post-sale Expectations.** Former owners share their experiences about the sale process. The information they share can help you make more informed decisions on the sale of your company—and your life thereafter.

To understand why each of these aspects is critically important, let's look at each section in a bit more detail.

Section One: Setting the Stage. This section focuses on the ownership decisions that only you can make. The first question owners generally ask us is, "Should I sell my business now?" so we attempt to answer that question in Chapter 1.

We urge you to figure out where it is you are going before you start your journey of selling your business. Some of the objectives that you must set are common to all owners and others are uniquely yours. All of them are the goals that must be met before answering the first question, "Should I sell my business now?" and before you can begin the sale process.

Once you know what you want out of the sale process, we help you understand who can help you reach your goals. We talk extensively about how each type of advisor should add value to your business. Once you understand what each advisor does and are ready to begin hiring advisors, we hope you'll refer to the Appendix for specific information on the characteristics you should look for in advisors and what qualifications they should have. Finally, we tackle the all-important topic of how these advisors charge and how you can control costs.

Also, in this section we build on the earlier questions of, "Should I sell now?" and "What do I want when I sell?" to ask, "What is my business worth?" Until you know that answer, you can't possibly know if you can cash out for an amount that will allow you to move on. Don't expect a mountain of minutiae about valuation. You'll hire experts to make the valuation estimates. Our job is simply to show you what should be included in those valuations and why.

We conclude the first part of this book with one final, but very common, ownership question: "How can I pay as little as possible to the IRS when I sell my business?" Since the IRS's take can be significant (depending on deal structure as much as 50 percent—not 15 percent or 20 percent), we encourage owners to have a good idea of exactly how big the IRS's piece of the pie will be before they sit down at the closing table.

Section Two: Creating Intrinsic Value. There are measures that you can take to increase the value of your business even when a sale is imminent—within 18 months or so. There are ways to increase your payday, by millions of dollars in many cases. Just as importantly, there are methods of transforming a marginal business into a saleable one.

If you have given yourself more than 18 months to prepare the business—and yourself—for a sale, this section also will describe what longer-term techniques can significantly affect business value. Increased value leads to more money in your pocket, as well as the realization of other dreams and goals. (It also can mean the staying power to wait out a depressed M&A market even if you are too burned out to run the business yourself.)

Section Three: Understanding Extrinsic Value. Picture the television show, "Dancing With the Stars." To win, each dance partner must execute each step perfectly, but also in complete sync with the other partner. Likewise, to maximize and exceed your sale goals, there are two dance partners: your business must be at its peak effectiveness, maximum cash flow and profitability, *and* the Merger and Acquisition sales cycle must be nearing or at its peak. If either partner is weak, the contest is lost.

You must know if the M&A market is favorable as you and your company prepare to sell. The relationship between intrinsic value and extrinsic value is critical. You might make more money selling a business whose value hasn't been maximized if the M&A market is at its peak. Likewise, you might not be able to sell a good business at all if the M&A marketplace contains few or no buyers for your company.

Section Four: Using Promoted Value. The sale process itself can increase the value of your company. Using experienced advisors can increase the value of your company. How? The type of sale process that we usually recommend is called a controlled auction. Several (or many) buyers bid simultaneously for the privilege of buying your company. Rather than paying what you (or some valuation specialist) thinks your business is worth, buyers compete against others and pay what it is worth to them. We'll look at how this is done and the type of advisors skilled in controlled auctions but for now, let's look at an example.

Let's suppose you are selling a parcel of land and three parties express interest. One, unbeknownst to you, needs the land to complete a subdivision while the other two are interested in the property as a standalone parcel for development. The first will pay based on the land's importance to the undisclosed plans to develop all of the surrounding land. The other two bidders view the land as no more valuable than other nearby parcels. If the first buyer was the only buyer interested in the parcel—you would sell for Fair Market Value as determined by an appraiser, never knowing that you could have sold it for much, much more.

Skilled transaction intermediaries (such as investment bankers) conduct controlled auctions, understand the emotions of buyers and bring a number of qualified buyers to the table—including those buyers to whom the business has a greater strategic value.

Section Five: Adjusting Post-Sale Expectations. First, we admit our bias: we think that, given today's M&A market and demographic trends, you should sell. That said, you should not sell today, even if your business is ready and the M&A cycle peaking, *if that sale does not further your personal values and goals.* If you are not ready to sell or you can't envision your life without the business, I ask that you read the last part of this book. Read what owners expected after they left their companies and read about what they are doing since moving on to the next stage of their lives. For those of you who need a bigger motivator, read the story of David Driscoll, an owner who thought he was just too young to sell a company with unlimited potential.

Every owner should be asking, "What do I want to do when I am no longer an owner?" We admit that there is no one-size-fits-all answer. Take this opportunity to learn from many others, just like you—Baby Boomers who sold their companies. See what they are doing now and what they would have done differently. You'll be surprised, as they often were, at the interesting twists, the regrets, the deeper sense of fulfillment, the emotional loss, and the wins.

As Boomers, we face unique challenges and unique opportunities. Unlike our parents' generation, we expect our lives after we sell our companies to be as fulfilling as our lives as owners. If we manage the sale of these companies correctly, we are poised to realize our dreams.

Section One

Setting the Stage

In the first five chapters of this book, we look at ownership decisions—those decisions that only you, as the owner, can make. The first question owners generally ask us is, "Should I sell my business now?" so we attempt to answer that question in Chapter 1.

In Chapter 2, we urge you to figure out where it is you are going before you start the journey of selling your business. You'll see what objectives you must set which may be similar to other owners or unique to your specific situation. These are the goals that must be met before answering the first question, "Should I sell my business now?" and before you can begin the sale process.

Chapter 3, "Using Advisors to Put Money in Your Pocket," is an optional chapter. Whether you read it or not depends on where you are today in the process of selling. If you are wondering why you need advisors to orchestrate a successful sale, read it today. Similarly, if you think you can orchestrate your own sale, I suggest that you read it today and read it very carefully! If, however, you have several years before selling, save it (and the Appendix to Chapter 3) for later. Rely on the checklists found in that Appendix when you are ready to begin hiring advisors.

In Chapter 4, we build on the earlier questions of, "Should I sell now?" and "What do I want when I sell?" to ask, "What is my business worth?" Until you know that answer, you can't possibly know if you can cash out for an amount that will allow you to move on. Don't expect a mountain of minutiae about valuation. You'll hire experts to make the valuation estimates. Our job is simply to show you what should be included in those valuations and why.

We conclude the first part of this book with one final, but very common, ownership question: "How can I pay as little as possible to the IRS when I sell my business?" Since the IRS's take can be significant (as much as 50 percent), we encourage owners to have a good idea of exactly how big the IRS piece of the pie will be before they sit down at the closing table.

SHOULD I SELL MY BUSINESS NOW?
WHY OWNERS SHOULD SELL AND WHY THEY DON'T

CHAPTER HIGHLIGHTS

- Why Owners Should Sell
  Personal Motives
  Objective Conditions

- Why Owners Don't Sell When They Should

- When You Should Not Sell

If you are like many owners, you have spent many sleepless nights staring at the bedroom ceiling endlessly speculating about and weighing the outcomes of the answer to one question: "Should I sell my business now?" If you have finished your deliberations, have resolved all of the questions and are prepared to move directly to the sale process, skip this chapter and move on to the next. But if you are still pacing the floor with the rest of us, read on.

WHY OWNERS SHOULD SELL

Most business owners sell only when two decision paths converge. The first path is the subjective or personal decision to sell: it is time to sell because personal goals can now be met better by selling the business than by staying active in it. The second is the objective or business decision: both the Merger and Acquisition market and your company's readiness make it the right time to sell.

PERSONAL MOTIVES

The personal decision to sell is usually based upon some combination of the following:

- A desire to "take the chips off the table." Your tolerance for risk just isn't what it used to be. (See Bade in Chapter 12.)

- The joy of going to work each day is fading. Not only has the fire in your belly gone out, but it's been replaced by an ulcer or maybe just by a desire to do "something else," known or unknown. (See Berger in Chapter 12.)

- The "Successor Designate" can't or won't succeed. Neither child nor employee is able or willing to fill your shoes. (See McGrath and Braun in Chapter 12.)

- You realize that now is the time to sell because you can attain financial security. We'll talk more about that in the "Objective Motives" section of this chapter. (See nearly every owner in Chapter 12.)

- There are a lot of activities other than running a company that you still want to experience. (See Willerding in Chapter 12.)

If one of these reasons resonates for you, please don't be surprised. We compiled this list after interviewing and working with numerous business owners. Before we look at each of these reasons in more detail, you may want to read the stories of the owners referenced above in Chapter 12.

Taking Chips Off the Table. As we age, our tolerance for risk diminishes and our desire for safety and security increases. If you doubt this observation, compare the typical driver in any Florida retirement community to a driver in your local high school parking lot as the school day ends.

Owning and operating a business places the majority of your assets at risk. Every day these risks might include:

- **Competitive**—from consolidators and others with more money than you;

- **Financial**—the need to constantly keep more money in the business to sustain growth;

- **Personal Health**—owners are not immune from health issues that can (and do) pop up without warning;

- **Liability**—there are hundreds of thousands of practicing lawyers in this country (I've done my best to whittle down that number by one!);

- **Business Conditions**—key employees leave or your industry changes; and

- **The Economy**—when it cycles down will it take your business with it?

For most owners, there is a point at which these risks become overly burdensome, especially when the business itself has become valuable. Owners no longer want to expose their most valuable asset to constant risk. When all of their eggs are in one basket and the basket is now worth a lot of money, it makes sense to lower the risk of losing that basket. The only way to eliminate the risks inherent to owning a closely held business interest is to sell it—for cash. Doing so not only takes chips off the table by converting an illiquid asset to cash, but it also allows owners to eliminate personal guarantees, reduce liability exposure and remove personal collateral (used for business purposes) that was at risk.

No Fire In the Belly. Few owners reading this book are as energetic and enthusiastic about their businesses as they were when they started (or even during the middle years of the business). Owners tend to continue in business beyond an optimum departure date because they don't know what else to do with their time. They continue on and spend months or years in their businesses long after the passion has died. If this description reflects your mental and emotional state, allow me to interject two comments.

First, in my experience, once lost, owners never regain their enthusiasm for, excitement about, or enjoyment of their businesses. The reason is straightforward. Like the first biomedical research scientist, Dr. Frankenstein, entrepreneurs like to create. Once the creature has a life of its own, it is left to wreak havoc or to succeed. When Dr. Frankenstein's job is mostly complete, he moves on to his next project. Making money and all of the other by-products of a successful business are nice, but it is the act of creating, of successfully meeting the challenges, that brings satisfaction to the entrepreneur. The fire in the belly is the passion that gives birth to and nurtures your business. Once the business is on its own, once it no longer needs you, it is time to move on to the next challenge, the next call for your passion and creativity. It is at this point that many owners begin searching for the exit door in order to find the next passion.

Second, the only solution to the loss of fire is to sell the business and get *out*. Your business, which I suspect you still cherish and love, will move to the next level under new ownership for whom moving to the next level provides ample stimulation and challenge.

The Successor Designate Won't Or Can't Succeed. A "Successor Designate" is anointed from within the business (a key employee or usually two) or from within the family (a child or two). If no one has:

a. stepped forward;

b. the talent to take the business to the next level;

c. demonstrated sufficient commitment to the business (at least equal to what yours had been); or

d. enough money now (or through future cash flows from the business) to buy the business;

then the business has become too valuable or too complex to transfer to anyone other than an outsider. (See Berger in Chapter 12.)

Let's look at how one business owner tried (and failed) to lure his desired successor into ownership.

LOOKING A GIFT HORSE IN THE MOUTH

It was the most unexpected outcome imaginable. Dick Langenberg owned a water drilling service (highly demanded in the eastern plains of Colorado) that had prospered for the last 20 years. As a careful, conservative businessman of the "old school," Dick had amassed a significant fortune outside of the business—a business that earned $1 million or more each year. One of Dick's Exit Objectives then, was to reward the key employees who had helped build and sustain his successful company. After much soul searching, Dick decided to give the business to his key employees. They would pay him nothing out of their own pockets.

The mechanism Dick used to give the business away was to have the business contribute money to a separate fund for three years. At the end of that time period, Dick would receive the money in the fund as a down payment for the purchase of the company. The down payment would equal 50 percent of the purchase price. The remaining 50 percent would be paid to Dick over the subsequent six years from the available cash flow of the company. If cash flow was insufficient, Dick was willing to accept a longer pay out period, although if cash flow continued as expected, it would be more than adequate to pay Dick the remaining balance.

*In short, Dick would pre-fund his own buyout with three years of revenues (money he would otherwise be entitled to) and would obligate key employees and the company to provide the remaining 50 percent of the payment—**solely from the future cash flows of the company.** In essence, Dick was giving the company to his employees.*

At the end of six years, without one penny coming from their own pockets, Dick's employees would own a company producing at least $1 million of cash flow per year. Imagine Dick's surprise when their unanimous response was, "Thank you very much, but we don't want to own the company. There's too much risk in this business."

I was not nearly as surprised as was Dick because I've come to realize that many key employees—wonderful, valuable and contributing

> *employees that they are—simply have no tolerance for the risk that is part and parcel of business ownership. In Dick's case, the employees weren't even willing to be given the company. I will admit to being a **little** surprised at that.*

There's More To Life Than Building and Running a Company. Many Boomer owners reach a point where they realize that there are a lot of things "out there" that they want to do while they are young enough to enjoy them. Active vacations, spending time with family and friends, service work, personal growth and development are all items that appear on owners' lists of things to do. These items remain on the list because owners are simply too busy running their companies to pay them more than passing attention.

Many Boomer owners are deciding to pursue a second life or second career full of possibility, activity and involvement. This crowd gravitates toward race car seats, rather than toward rocking chairs. To be strapped into the driver seat, owners need financial, emotional and time freedoms.

If you need convincing that a second act can be as fulfilling as the first, check out what owners say about their lives after the sale in Chapter 12. To a person, they have no regrets about selling, even though some were unsure of what they would ultimately do, post-closing. To track this and other trends among owners, we collect information from former owners through BEI members on an ongoing basis. You can see what former owners are saying at www.BEIBooks.com.

Objective Conditions

Along with personal motives, there are objective conditions that must be present to maximize your chances for a successful business sale. Those conditions must be opportune both in the Merger & Acquisition market and in your company for you to sell for top dollar.

Consider First, Your Company's Business Condition. On a regular basis (no less than annually), you should discuss with your planning team current business value and how best to increase and protect it. If your business has reached a Value Threshold that permits a sale that allows you to realize your financial goals, you have reached a point where you can sell.

If not, you may decide that to keep your business vibrant, you must move it to the next level, a level that requires money, effort and time. At that point, you must decide whether you are able (or more likely, willing) to commit to this plan.

Successful companies are constantly moving forward and constantly growing in:

- Revenues;

- Territory;

- Numbers of employees and customers;

- Profitability;

- And often, risk.

Growth, in turn, creates expansion: new geographic markets, bigger facilities, more equipment and additional personnel. Owners and their businesses may not have the capital necessary to fuel continued growth, especially if market conditions require a large influx of cash. This economic reality combined with an increasing aversion to risk, results in a decision to sell—to take chips off the table.

As one of our BEI member advisors asks his clients, "If you can leave your business today and accomplish all of your financial objectives, why wait?" I would argue that you should not wait, as would David Driscoll—one of the owners interviewed in Chapter 12. After experiencing a significant industry drop he says, "I know now that when times are good and someone makes you an offer for your company, they do so because they see the potential. Let *them* go after that potential and cash out!"

If you decide that your personal objectives (such as keeping the business in the family) are more important than your financial security and you love owning and running your company, then keeping the business makes sense. Or, if you've already achieved your financial objectives and you love owning and running your company, then keeping the business also makes sense. In both these situations, the decision may make sense only to you—but it is your business and your life. Moving on or staying on is your decision to make.

Consider Secondly, Today's M&A Market.   For owners who toil long and hard to overcome the endless challenges that test the survival and success of their businesses, the thought of someday selling out for a lot of money seems, at best, a pipe dream. A typical business owner in this situation thinks, "Who would want to buy my business?"

Yet, as many owners are discovering, the M&A marketplace is receptive to acquiring closely held businesses—businesses just like yours. In some niches, even smaller businesses are able to sell to much larger cash buyers. But the market can be fickle. A number of factors fuel or damper the merger and acquisition mania. These include:

- *Fluctuating interest rates.* Low, stable interest rates provide buyers with inexpensive funds to buy your business. Climbing interest rates increase acquisition costs and dampen buyer enthusiasm.

- *Availability and pricing of financing.* The availability and cost of financing directly impacts deal activity.

> When financing is readily available to buyers at attractive rates, deal activity becomes frenzied because buyers can leverage their equity investment: instead of requiring one dollar of their cash for every $2 of financing (in 2001 time frame) in 2005, they could borrow almost $4 for every $1 of their own. This means they could pay more for businesses and this is the point in the M&A cycle when you must be poised to sell. (Please visit www.BEIBooks.com for current statistics regarding the volume and value of M&A activity in the U.S.)

- *It's the economy, stupid!* A healthy economy encourages investor confidence and a greater willingness to put money in otherwise illiquid businesses. A stagnant or contracting economy depresses valuation. It creates a buyer's market.

- *Corporate earnings overall and in your industry.* Strong earnings provide cash and the promise of future cash; weak earnings portend the opposite.

- *Stock market value.* To keep corporate earnings ever-increasing, it makes sense for publicly owned companies to acquire closely held companies whose price/earning ratios are lower than the acquiring company.

- *M&A currency.* With publicly owned stock trading at high earnings multiples, it makes sense for those companies to use their stock for acquisitions. As the stock market contracts in value, it is reasonable to expect a chilling effect on the M&A marketplace.

- *Supply and Demand.* According to a 2005 PricewaterhouseCoopers' survey of 364 CEOs of privately held, fast-growing companies, "nearly two-thirds . . . plan to move on within a decade or less: 42 percent within five years, and 23 percent in five to ten years." ("Wide Majority of Fast-Growth CEOs Likely to Move On Within Ten Years, PwC Finds." January 31, 2005.) If these owners, and others like them, follow through on these plans, there could be a glut of companies on the market, resulting in lower valuations and a buyer's market.

It is important for owners to be constantly aware of the condition of the M&A market. If it is healthy, owners may have the opportunity to adjust their personal timetables to take advantage of it. When the M&A market is favorable (a lot of buyers offering high multiples), owners need to recognize that adjusting their "ideal" departure date is a whole lot easier (and smarter) than adjusting their financial needs. Conversely, when markets shut down, an owner's personal goals must likewise adjust. (Investment banker, Kevin Short discusses the M&A market and its effect on prices of closely held companies in more detail in Chapter 8.)

Business owners may first become exposed to the M&A marketplace when they receive a letter or unsolicited phone call claiming that someone is interested in buying the business. Often a letter from an out-of-state business broker announces, "We have a buyer for your business!" Most likely there is no buyer in hand, and, if there is, the buyer may well be a "consolidator."

Perhaps you have been contacted directly by an industry consolidator who wishes to acquire a platform company in your region. Consolidators know that the easiest way to establish a presence is to buy a proven company that they can use to make further acquisitions. Buying an existing, well-run, reputable business that already has experienced employees, proven management, contacts in the business community, a diversified customer base, and knowledge of the local marketplace, is the goal of all national consolidators. They are willing to pay a premium (but would prefer not to!) for businesses having those characteristics. (See Visger in Chapter 12.)

If your business is ripe for sale because it possesses those qualities, you need to make a business decision. That business decision, to keep or to sell your business, is best made only after you have completed this book. At the end of the planning and sale process we describe in this book, you may well determine that it makes sense, from both a business and emotional standpoint, to cash out and move on.

In the 1990s, owners of high-tech companies were the perfect example of owners who, to their detriment, ignored the moment when personal motives and market conditions intersect. Even though their wildest financial dreams would be met by a sale to publicly owned companies, they thought they could get more money if they waited for the market to further expand.

One 45-year-old owner was offered one million shares ($90 a share) of a public company in exchange for his company. He declined, secure in his belief that the tech revolution had not yet crested. Eight months later, the offeror's stock was worth $2.25 a share and diving. There was no market for my client's company. This cocktail of market and M&A misjudgment, as well as greed proved nearly fatal. His company barely survived.

Today, he is looking to exit at a much-reduced price based on a multiple of earnings, instead of the multiple of *projected revenue* of years gone by. He is considering a sale—at a much reduced price—because he knows the opportunity may be his last, he doesn't want to work longer, and there are other challenges to meet.

WHY OWNERS DON'T SELL WHEN THEY SHOULD

If you simply are not emotionally ready to sell, if there is still fire in your belly—enough fire to fuel your continued investment in the company—or if you ultimately want to leave the business to family members or employees, then the balance of this chapter, and perhaps even the book, is not for you—yet. If you and the business are ready to sell, but you still hesitate, let's look at typical reasons for that hesitation and what you can do about it.

The premise of the balance of this chapter is that owners don't sell when they should because they procrastinate, or they fear the **unknown** and, perhaps more specifically, they fear losing the **known**.

Procrastination on the part of an owner is not uncommon and can arise for one of several reasons. First, some owners just don't know where or how to start planning an exit. If you are one of those owners, this book will help you immensely.

Second, some owners think that they can sell later, but as we discuss, when most Boomers reach retirement age, the glut of companies in the marketplace may drive prices down. Further, the M&A cycle has a huge affect on the sale price of a company. (See Chapter 8.)

In the third group of procrastinating owners are those who believe that because they have "good" businesses, the process will take care of itself. When they think about selling, they simply assume that there isn't much for them to do. They believe that when the time is right, the right buyer will appear and pay them a great price for their company.

It does happen, albeit quite rarely, that the right buyer appears and pays a great price for a company. However, it can be much better to prepare for the biggest financial transaction of your life. Had I not planned my exit from my business, I'd still be practicing law today instead of writing this book!

The owners who suffer from the fear of the **unknown** usually hold one (or more) of the following opinions:

- I don't think the business is worth enough to satisfy my financial needs and objectives.

- If the employees discover I'm trying to sell, they will all quit.

- Because I'm indispensable to the company, I'll be required to work years for a new owner and I don't like working for anyone!

- The sale process will take too long and cost too much.

The fear of losing the **known** is usually based on the following:

- The business has been my life—or at least it has given my life a great deal of meaning and focus; without it I may feel lost.

- The government will take too much in taxes—it's easier, less risky and more lucrative to stay, enjoy the cash flow and then leave getting paid over time.

- What will I do after I sell and leave the business? This business is my life—it has given me a great deal of meaning and focus. Without it, I may feel lost.

Now let's return to each of these issues.

The Business Isn't Worth Enough To Meet My Financial Needs. You can't know whether your business is "worth enough" unless you know what it is worth, and what value is needed in order to meet your financial needs. (We'll talk more about estimating your financial needs in the next chapter.) That's why obtaining a valuation range for your company based upon current market conditions is so important: Use a transaction advisor, preferably an investment banker (for companies with a likely value of more than $5 million), business broker or other transaction intermediary (for smaller businesses) familiar with what your business can fetch in the M&A marketplace. Do not simply depend on the historical valuation performed by your accountant or the "rule of thumb" used in your industry. (See Chapter 4.) Both "rules of thumb" and traditional valuation approaches rely on what has happened, not on what businesses—businesses just like yours—are selling for in *today's* market, and tend to overlook the importance of current deal activity levels.

This point was brought home to me a number of years ago—near the last peak in the M&A cycle. A client thinking about selling his business asked his CPA for an estimate of value. After some investigation of historical valuation multiples, the CPA ventured an estimate of $14 million. The owner needed significantly more than that just to pay off business debt.

Although inclined to give up the idea of selling, at least temporarily, this owner asked me what I thought his business was worth. My response was, "I have no idea. You need to work with someone who knows what your type of business is selling for in today's marketplace." The investment banking firm that this client hired to answer that question returned with a baseline (or minimum value) sale price estimate of almost $30 million.

With that information, this owner chose to proceed with a sale and eventually sold for more than $40 million. The point of this story is that to determine the value of your business, you don't ask your lawyer or even your CPA. If you are going to dive into the M&A market, ask an experienced professional who makes a living working in that market.

Another way to determine the value of your company is to hire a valuation specialist even if you are a few years (or more) away from selling. Doing so is also helpful if you plan to sell or gift part of your business before the sale in an effort to meet your Exit Objectives (such as transferring wealth to children or employee/s). We discuss this part of the sale process in greater detail in Chapter 5.

The Employees (Or Customers Or Competitors) Will Leave When They Discover I'm Trying To Sell.

While a legitimate concern, the fact is that no one should find out about the sale process until you inform them, provided you adhere to the sale process described in this book. Typically, a potential buyer does not even set foot in your business until you have made a tentative decision to sell the business to that buyer. When conducted by professionals, the sale of a business is highly confidential, and the likelihood of anyone discovering you are selling your business before you inform the public is unlikely. Read Chapter 9 for more information on this element of the sale process.

I Will Be Required To Work Years For A New Owner. If one of your Exit Objectives is to leave the business as soon as possible, make that objective known to your transaction advisors and it will be a prerequisite of any sale. That objective will determine which type of buyer you should seek. There are categories of buyers who typically do not require the former owner to remain with the company beyond a short transition time period—usually no more than a few months—provided your management team is strong.

The Sale Process Will Take Too Long And Cost Too Much. Cost, of course, is a matter of perspective. I don't think the sale process is too expensive. But the only way for *you* to make that determination is to discuss costs and expenses with transaction advisors *before* you hire them. See Chapter 3 for a discussion of expenses involved in the sale process. It usually takes from six to eighteen months to sell your business. One purpose of this book is to explain the sale process so you can minimize costs and time delays. The more you know, the better prepared your company will be for sale. Better preparation on your part means less time and expense on the part of your advisors.

Given The Tax Bite On Sale Proceeds, It Makes More Sense To Stay, Enjoy The Cash Flow And Get Paid Over Time. With proper tax planning (see Chapter 5), Uncle Sam's cut of the sale proceeds is, in my opinion, as low today as it is likely to be for the foreseeable future. Given the structure of the temporary capital gain tax cuts and the unlikelihood of a sweeping Republican victory (60 Senate seats, control of the House of Representatives and the presidency), the current 15 percent tax rate will likely increase to 20 percent (or perhaps more) in the next few years.

What Will I Do After I Sell And Leave The Business? This Business Is My Life! For many of us, the old "fire in the belly" is gone, but there is nothing to replace it. So we hang on to our businesses, willing to accept what we know because the unknown may be even worse. *This is the primary reason owners overstay their usefulness.*

Certainly, the decision to sell the business you created and nurtured is an intensely, personal decision. I am no more qualified to tell you what to do with the rest of your life than is anyone else. Of course, like everyone else, a lack of knowledge will not stop me from offering advice. So, I share experiences of owners who have sold their business and who had the same questions before they sold their business. Read Chapter 12 to gain some appreciation of life after the sale and to learn what other owners have done after cashing out of their businesses and moving on to the next stage of their lives.

The owners you will read about made the decision to sell without knowing exactly life would be like after the sale, but knowing full well that staying in the business was not sufficiently challenging or fulfilling. Selling a business is an act of faith and confidence in your ability to succeed—as you have succeeded as an owner—in the next phase of your life.

When You Should Not Sell

The time gaps between the cyclical peaks in the Merger & Acquisition market are usually about five years. This mean that, as a Boomer, you likely have one or two more opportunities to sell at the peak of a cycle. The rest of the time, the business should continue under your ownership. If you are still enthusiastic about going to work everyday; if you see a bright, financial future for your company; if you want to wait until your children are older, or key employees can take over the business; or the business simply doesn't have enough value to sell now and allow you to reach your financial objectives, then obviously it is time to hang on.

Please don't infer that we think every business should be sold now because of the general financial climate. The assumption we make is that you are reading this book because you are exploring the possibility of selling your company. If you feel the time is not yet right for that sale to take place, continue reading the first few chapters dealing with establishing your objectives and creating more value in your business. These are chapters every owner should read, even if he or she is determined never to sell the business.

A FINAL WORD

Owners make the decision to sell based on a mix of objective and subjective factors tempered by M&A market realities. The purpose of this chapter is to help you make your decision a "mature" one—as it was for Harold Bade, an owner described in Chapter 12.

Selling can make all the sense in the world, but don't sell if you can't reach your objectives or if financial security is subordinate to other objectives. Selling when you can attain financial security and top dollar because of the strength of your company (intrinsic value) and the M&A market is at or near its peak (extrinsic value) is the ideal *but attainable* scenario. Keep in mind too that if your concern is what to do after closing, read the owner stories. Many had no definite plans for the days, months and years after selling, but not one suffers from boredom. Not one has regrets and all look forward to each day.

At the end of the day, the decision to sell is yours.

CHAPTER

2

WHAT DO I WANT WHEN I SELL MY BUSINESS?
DECIDING WHERE TO GO BEFORE YOU ARRIVE

"When a man does not know which harbor he is heading for, no wind is the right wind."

— Seneca (Roman philosopher, 3 B.C.–65 A.D.)

CHAPTER HIGHLIGHTS

O When Do I Want To Sell My Business?

O What Is The Annual, After-Tax Income I Want During Retirement (In Today's Dollars)?

O Who Should Buy My Business?

O Other Objectives

O Using Objectives To Choose A Buyer

Seneca was, indeed, a wise philosopher. Today he would likely become a management consultant and make millions of dollars. His advice is as sound for business owners now as it was centuries ago. Yet, few owners heed that advice or appreciate its implicit warning.

The sale of your business begins with setting your Exit Objectives. Once fixed, your objectives become your homeport and the rest of the planning process is dedicated to ensuring a safe passage. My advice is simple: the journey can be long and trying; do not embark until you are sure of your destination.

The need to fix your Exit Objectives was best explained by Yogi Berra: *"You've got to be very careful if you don't know where you're going, because you might not get there."* Translated, Yogi is saying that you can't *successfully* sell your business if you don't know what that means to you *before* you begin the sale process.

Failing to set goals usually means that an owner will not be able to exit his or her business in style. Many owners do not set Exit Objectives precisely because it is emotionally too wrenching to separate themselves from a business they have created, nurtured, lived with, brought to maturity and in which they have totally immersed themselves. Those owners who are emotionally ready to face leaving often feel confused because they do not know what to do or where to begin. This is precisely the point at which that owner needs clear, simple Exit Objectives. What must your objectives be?

Stop your speed reading for a few moments. This is a vital concept.

> As a general rule, owners begin the sale process in a tentative fashion, in part because they are uninformed and in significant part because they simply do not know what they want.

Until you know your objectives—your homeport—do not set sail. Work with your advisors to set and refine your objectives. This is where empathetic advisors can help you set your compass.

There are three straightforward exit goals that every owner must fix in his mind. Once established, the owner can cut through a lot of muddled thinking that otherwise prevents him from moving forward. Answering the following questions creates your basic exit goals.

- When do I want to sell my business?

- What is the annual, after-tax income I want during retirement (in today's dollars)?

- To whom do I want to transfer the business?

Let's look at your first decision—your first objective.

When Do I Want To Sell My Business?

During my 30-year law career, clients would occasionally ask me when I wanted to sell my practice. My answer, during each of those 30 years before I made my exit was the same, "Five years from today."

When you *want* to leave is inextricably tied to when you are *financially able* to leave the business. It is also tied to when you are *emotionally able* to leave the business. Well, I was certainly emotionally ready but, just as certainly, financially unprepared.

Assuming that you can achieve financial security by selling your business now, as well as in the future, the question you must answer is: Should I sell my business now? Or wait? Provided you have at least tentatively decided to someday sell your business (why else would you be reading this book?), you will usually select one of three paths.

1. Sell the business in the near future—usually two to five years;

2. Sell now, but stay active with the business; or

3. Sell now, and get the heck out.

Selling In The Near Future

Owners who tell us that, despite ideal Merger & Acquisition market conditions, they plan to sell "sometime in the future," usually fall into one of two categories. The first is those who, personally, are not emotionally prepared to sell. They may still enjoy going to work, haven't lost that fire in the belly, and the challenges and rewards of the business still motivate them. Those in the second category don't believe that an immediate sale will satisfy their financial objectives.

If it is the personal joy you take in your business that prevents you from selling now, keep one eye on the state of the M&A market and put your energy into readying your business for sale. Pay particular attention to Chapter 4 on valuation so you know what affects sale price and

Chapters 6 and 7 on Value Drivers, to learn specific ways to increase the value of your business.

Your efforts will certainly please your business planning attorney. Your investment banker, however, will ask you to seriously consider your motives for postponing the decision to sell now when it would meet your other Exit Objectives—specifically your financial objectives.

> If the true reason you are staying in your business is your unwillingness to leave a business you still love, your decision should not be questioned.

If one of your personal concerns, however, is that you are not sure how your life after ownership will look or feel, we often suggest that you step away from the business and let your management team run the show. This may mean leaving, at first, for a few weeks, and then for longer periods. It may mean working half days or two to three days each week, or short days every day. Doing so gives you a chance to discover whether your "new" life could be as emotionally satisfying (or at least not less unsatisfying) than continuing as an owner. It also gives your management team a practice test to determine its ability to run the business without you.

If this strategy isn't practical for you, go on a vacation with an agenda. During that time away from the office, take time to think about something other than business and to become reacquainted with the world beyond your company. Again, I urge you to continue keeping one eye on the status of the M&A market.

If you are postponing a sale because you think that, given a little more time, you can increase business value, thus making more money down the road, beware. The winds of the marketplace are variable and not at all predictable. Even if you successfully increase the profitability of your company by 50 percent over a two-year period (quite a feat), outside factors may halve the earnings multiple valuation formula. The net result is that your business makes more money, but is worth less in the Merger and Acquisition marketplace. Your business or industry climate may change, flattening or cutting your profitability. Suddenly, you find yourself unable to escape. I don't encourage owners to leave before they are ready; nor should you balk at exiting if you are ready and you can meet all of your objectives, including your financial objective.

SELL NOW, BUT STAY ACTIVE

Most owners think they are unique in their desire to sell their businesses yet remain employees—although changing their roles a bit. "I would be happy to sell my business today and take my chips off the table, but I want to continue to work for the company in some capacity." Motives differ but often owners want to return to what first attracted them to the business. As you'll learn in Chapter 12, it is not unusual for owners to sell out completely, take some time off and then return to the work they love best—running a company. (See Dave and Linda Visger.)

I recall the chemist who started a chemical testing business that grew steadily in size. In addition to the financial security to be gained from a sale, he wanted to "return to the bench" doing whatever it is that chemists do. If ever one could have his cake and eat it too, this owner did it. He sold his company, achieved complete financial independence and continued to work in the business he loved, on his terms.

Other owners come to the realization that, for the business to remain vibrant and healthy, it needs to move "to the next level." That movement requires a significant cash infusion at the very time the owner wants to start taking money out of the company. An excellent solution for these owners is to sell the business to a financial or strategic buyer. The owner obtains financial security, the company receives a cash infusion, and the now-former owner continues to work in the same, or even in a specialized, capacity.

While most owners sell *all* of their ownership interest, it is possible to sell less than all of your business. If you keep 10 to 25 percent, you retain your upside potential, maintain your motivation to increase business value, and satisfy those buyers who want the former owner to keep a "skin in the game." This strategy is called "recapitalization." Please see Chapter 9 for more information on this sale strategy.

SELL NOW AND GET THE HECK OUT

Intuitive advisor that I am, I can easily spot the owner who is ready to leave his business. When I ask, "When would you like to sell your business?" and the response shoots back: "Yesterday!" it is a safe bet that the owner wants out sooner rather than later.

In addition to possessing this type of sensitivity, it is vitally important for your advisors to know when you want to sell the business and when you want to leave the business. For example, if you wish to work a few years before you sell, begin working with your CPA, business attorney and investment banker to develop future value for your company. If you wish to sell the business now, *your desire to continue to work or to leave "yesterday" will influence the buyer you (or preferably your investment banker) need to find for your business.* Of course, the timing of the sale might be determined exclusively by financial considerations: if you can't afford to leave now, when you can, you will.

Let's move now to the second objective.

WHAT IS THE ANNUAL, AFTER-TAX INCOME I WANT DURING RETIREMENT (IN TODAY'S DOLLARS)?

According to *The Wall Street Journal*, a 2006 survey conducted by the Employee Benefit Research Institute, found that "fully 55% of surveyed retirees . . . said they were living in retirement on 95% or more of their pre-retirement income." (December 11, 2006, page R-4. "Will More of Us Be Working Forever?" The 2006 Retirement Confidence Survey, Issue Brief No. 292, April 2006; by Ruth Helman, Mathew Greenwald & Associates; Craig Copeland, EBRI; and Jack VanDerhei, Temple University and EBRI Fellow.)

This survey supports our anecdotal findings that business owners (like all retirees) typically underestimate the amount of cash they'll need (or want) after they leave their companies.

This survey also indicated that more than 80 percent of retirees calculated their post-retirement needs in very interesting ways: most (nearly half) guessed. Others made their own estimates, read articles, or used an online calculator. Let me suggest here and now: Join the 19 percent who asked a financial advisor. Let me further suggest that you work with a fee-based planner with a wealth of experience. As you choose a planner, keep in mind the following guidelines:

1. When you are thinking about the post-sale annual income you desire, remember the retirement spending statistics and think carefully about your current spending/lifestyle habits. Statistics and my experience support the observation that people tend to maintain the same lifestyle they enjoyed when they owned their businesses. They may buy a second home or take an extended vacation or two, but overall spending habits tend not to change significantly, and seldom do they decrease.

2. Play "what if" scenarios using various net after-tax sale prices of your company. In this way, you'll discover how much money needs to be invested to yield the *net after-tax, inflation-adjusted, annual income stream needed for the rest of your life.* This is the income stream you must be certain you can achieve in selling your business. *The net after-tax sale price you need from the business sale is the lump sum of money less any available income-producing assets you now own.* Keep this amount in mind as you move through the sale process: you cannot allow yourself to sell for less.

3. Factor in a "safety net" amount that you will never want to dip into, except for income.

4. Realize as you make your calculations that: a) you and your spouse will likely live longer than you might think; and b) health care costs are a real wild card. According to Bernstein Global Wealth Management,

"As of 2000, men who had reached 65 had a 50% change of living past their 85th birthday; indeed, they had a one-in-four chance of living beyond 92. The actuarial data for women were even more striking. And if both a husband and wife reached 65, there was a 25% chance that at least one would see his or her 97th birthday.

Thirty year retirements are no longer rarities, and for early retirees, even four decades are possible." (Retirement: Plan Early and Often, February 2007.)

5.   Decide what you want to leave the kids—if anything.

Please do not rely on your best guess when determining how much income you will need during retirement. Use a fee-based financial planner who will help you to:

- Accurately predict the amount you will need (taking into account your longevity and health, inflation and tax rates, your spending rate, retirement date, and expected market returns);

- Temper your optimism regarding future rates of return;

- More accurately estimate your lifespan;

- Understand market risk; and

- Err on the side of extra cash flow.

Doing so may keep you from having to return to work—as someone else's employee.

WHO SHOULD BUY MY BUSINESS?

The third, and last, major objective is deciding who is an appropriate buyer for your business. The likely cash buyers are:

Insiders With Financing. These are usually small groups of key employees who have the intestinal fortitude, limited financial net worth and limited financing capability to buy your business for cash. Typically, they will need to partner with an investor or a buyout fund with the cash and the ability to obtain financing.

Financial Buyers. Financial buyers typically are private-equity groups (PEGs) or individual financial investors. They invest primarily to obtain a high rate of return on their equity investment. Financial buyers may require ongoing seller involvement and structured or seller financing. Financial buyers do not want to run your business. They don't have the skill, the desire or the management. They need *you* to run the business or at least your management team. If one of your objectives is to ensure that your management and employees keep their jobs or, better yet, improve their prospects, consider selling to a financial buyer. Keep in mind, however, that the financial buyer's own exit objective typically is to resell the business within five to seven years.

Strategic Buyers. "Strategic buyer" is an umbrella term for a variety of buyers (including consolidators, direct competitors, customers, and suppliers) using similar technology or serving the same customer base, and companies with counter cyclical products. All of these entities have several characteristics in common. They purchase businesses in which they will recognize synergistic benefits and add value to existing operations. They have sufficient capital/financing to close a transaction and are *generally willing to pay more than other types of buyers* provided they can be enticed to engage in a controlled auction. They are likely to make operating changes quickly and they facilitate the owner's exit from the business. They may not have as great a need for a strong management team (that includes you) to remain when the business is sold. That said, however, we seldom see a strategic buyer—or any buyer—who doesn't relish the thought of acquiring capable management. After all, don't you?

Buyers Without Cash or Financing. Why would you sell to someone who has little cash and no financing? Because you have no other choice—short of shutting down the company and liquidating the assets. This is the fate of most businesses below a threshold value of $1 million or $2 million whose owners fail to plan. (If you find yourself in this group, I encourage you to read my first book, **How To Run Your Business So You Can Leave It In Style**. (Visit www.BEIBooks.com for ordering information.)

To avoid liquidation, it is especially important for companies in the $1 million to $2 million range to design the post-sale pay-out to minimize the risk of non-payment. You may want to consider other exit paths such as a transfer to key employees or family. If you still want to sell to an outside party, consider modifying your departure date until your business reaches a greater value threshold. Of course, without a well-considered Exit Plan you may end up like me: working in your business for many years beyond your ideal departure date.

OTHER OBJECTIVES

In addition to the top three objectives we've just discussed, (selling *when* you want, selling for an amount that *guarantees* financial security and selling to the party *you choose*) there are others that many owners tackle before deciding to sell. Only by properly communicating your secondary objectives can you achieve the full potential of your company's sale. Chief among these secondary objectives is: to what degree, if any, should the owner provide for or reward long-term employees upon the sale of the business. For a full discussion of this objective, see the section on motivating and keeping key employees in Chapter 6.

Other secondary objectives include:

1.   Desire to stay on as an employee (possibly as CEO);

2.   Desire to continue to own part of the business;

3.   Desire to have a child remain active in the business;

4.   Desire to see the business continue to prosper and to become even more financially solvent and move to the next level;

5.   Desire that the business remain in its current location;

6.   Desire to get *full* value for your company; or

7.   Desire that all employees enjoy continued job security.

Also, many owners want to provide a measure of financial security to their children, who may or may not be active in the business. As you will discover in Chapter 5, the most effective time to transfer wealth represented by your business is NOW, before you sell. If you have an interest in leaving money to the kids, describe to your transaction advisors what you'd like to accomplish. Keep in mind that any assets transferred to children can be controlled and restricted through documents that you design.

USING OBJECTIVES TO CHOOSE A BUYER

So, which type of buyer should acquire your company? For many owners the obvious answer is, "Whoever pays me the most cash." Not a bad response. But sometimes, competing or secondary objectives (as described above) may influence the primary objective of financial security. Competing objectives need to be considered and weighed before you proceed with your Exit Plan. If we assume that the decision to sell your business is a voluntary one, why would you ever sell the business unless you achieve your primary, as well as satisfying your secondary objectives?

Yogi's point is now clear. Don't even begin a difficult, complicated, expensive process unless you know what it is you want and unless you are reasonably satisfied that the process can meet and reach those goals. Once again, this decision is yours.

Using Advisors To Put Money In Your Pocket
Why You Need
Specialized Advisors

"Let us, therefore, decide both upon the goal and upon the way and not fail to find some experienced guide who has explored the region towards which we are advancing; for the conditions of this journey are different from those most travel."

—Seneca, "On The Happy Life" (A.D. 58)

Chapter Highlights

- Why Are Experienced Advisors Of Fundamental Importance To A Successful Sale?

- Exit Planning Team

- Transaction or Deal Team

- A Unique Transaction Outside The Scope Of Your Normal Experience

- A Unique Process Calling For Specialized Advisors

- Level The Playing Field

- Putting It All Together

I will concede that there might be a reader or two who now may be thinking that their deepest suspicions are about to be realized. Here's a book written by a (former) advisor and, surprise! The first thing he tries to sell me is his indispensable value to me and to the sale of my business.

I am certain that you, trusting reader, do not share these skeptical sentiments. Nevertheless, I begin this chapter determined to convince you that advisors, skilled and experienced in Exit Planning and in trans-actions, truly are crucial to the successful sale of your business.

Once you are satisfied that advisors are indeed worth their weight in gold, I'll describe the two advisory teams that you will assemble. The first is your Exit Planning Team and the second is your Transaction or Deal Team.

To learn more about what players make up these teams at each phase of the sale process (Phase I: Pre-Sale; Phase II: Sale; Phase III: Post-Sale) and what they'll do for you during each Phase, please refer to the Appendix, "Finding, Hiring and Using the Most Suitable Advisors."

In that Appendix, one that we hope you will read when you are ready to start hiring advisors, you'll find a detailed discussion of what skills and experience you should look for in your various advisors. At the end of the Appendix we include a discussion about how you can keep their professional fees to a minimum.

Why Are Experienced Advisors Of Fundamental Importance To A Successful Sale?

Presumably, you are reading this book because you are thinking about selling your business and moving on to a new phase in your life. You realize that this critical financial transaction is:

- Unique in that it is outside the scope of your normal experience. It is likely that you have never sold a business before.

- Similarly, it is outside the experience of your normal set of advisors.

For these reasons, even though you are getting out, you really do need expert advice. At the risk of stretching too far to make an analogy, I com-pare the link between the expertise of your advisor and the success of your sale to the expertise of your surgeon and the success of a prostate surgery. According to the July 24, 2007, issue of the *Journal of the National Cancer Institute* and as reported in *Medical News Today* (www.medical-newstoday), "Improvements in patient outcome dramatically increased for doctors once they had done at least 250 operations." While I don't have similar statistics for business sales, my experience in working with owners bears out the same finding: the more experienced your advisor, the better chance you have for closing a sale that meets your objectives.

EXIT PLANNING TEAM

Let's look first then at your "normal" set of advisors. I call these folks the Exit Planning Team (or Planning Team). Planning Teams typically consist of your attorney, CPA, financial/insurance advisor and business consultant. If you read my last book, **The Completely Revised How To Run Your Business So You Can Leave It In Style**, you know how strongly I recommend that owners find and use at least one advisor skilled in Exit Planning.

I do so because preparing to sell your business is a goal that informs an owner's thoughts and actions for years before the actual sale. For example, your CPA should be advising you about how your choice of entity (C corporation, S Corporation or some other pass-through entity) will affect you during a sale. Your CPA also should be keeping your financial statements clean. With one eye on your eventual sale, your business attorney should be working with you to set up plans to motivate and keep key employees. Your business consultant should be working with you to create or enhance your company's Value Drivers. (See Chapters 6 and 7 for a detailed discussion of Value Drivers.)

While each of your advisors has a role in preparing you and your company for eventual sale, *only one of them needs to be trained and skilled in Exit Planning.* (That may be the advisor who gave you this book. Or, you may wish to visit our Web site www.BEIBooks.com to see a list of the advisors in your area that my company, BEI, has trained in Exit Planning. These advisors know how to create individualized Exit Plans that lead to successful sales and they have made Exit Planning a significant part of their practices.)

For years in my law practice, I created Exit Plans for business owners. The other professionals I worked with (CPAs, business consultants, business brokers and investment bankers) had often never heard of Exit Planning. I found that their lack of knowledge in this particular area did not affect the success of my clients' exits as long as the advisors were highly skilled in their areas of expertise and could work productively as part of a team. The most effective teams worked together, saved time and money in both planning an owner's exit and implementing that exit. Their effectiveness was attributable to the facilitation skills and knowledge of the Exit Planning Process of at least one of the advisors on the team.

Once your sale process begins, this primary Exit Planning Advisor will continue to oversee the process even though he or she won't direct it. He or she will help you find the advisors who will get the deal done. Your Exit Planning Advisor's primary purpose is to make sure that your Exit Objectives are met so that you can leave your business on your terms, and that the Deal Team is functioning smoothly so that you *do* leave your business. We will talk more about the Deal Team in a moment.

Let's first look specifically at what you can expect from your Exit Planning Advisor.

Experienced Exit Planning Advisors help fix and quantify realistic Exit Objectives. While the Exit Objectives you fix are your own, experienced advisors have represented dozens, if not hundreds, of business owners who have navigated the same Exit Planning waters and who have grappled with similar issues and concerns. These advisors can serve as guides and as counselors as you work through and modify your objectives. They will help you decide if your objectives are attainable or whether further value creation is needed. They will point out inconsistencies among your objectives and suggest alternatives.

Your Exit Planning Advisor helps keep your Exit Objectives intact as you move through the sale process.

Finally, your Exit Planning Advisor can help you find the best transaction advisors (Deal Team) for you and your business.

From your Exit Planning Advisor and from all the other advisors on your Planning Team, you should expect the following:

- Advisors, if they are to earn their keep, create or augment Value Drivers within your business in order to increase the sale price. Increasing the value of your business through the use of the various Value Drivers (described in Chapters 6 and 7) benefits you and your business, as well as leads to an increased purchase price upon sale. Your advisors (whether CPA, financial advisors or attorney) can help you concentrate on the Value Drivers that are most critical to driving up business value in the shortest amount of time.

- Advisors (primarily your attorney and CPA) perform and complete legal and financial pre-sale due diligence to make certain the business is ready to be sold. Pre-sale due diligence can best be compared to a comprehensive pre-flight checklist for NASA's Space Shuttle. Every possible issue must be addressed and, if necessary, corrected before all systems are "go." Once the sale process (or Shuttle) takes off, it is too late to locate and correct problems. The process and the flight must be aborted (if possible) and it usually takes years, not months, for the company to reenter the market. Occasionally, the problems are so severe that the flight ends in disaster or the business is never sold for fair market value.

- Advisors minimize or eliminate the tax bite through proactive tax avoidance planning well in advance of the actual sale. This can spell the difference between post-closing financial security and having to stay active in the business.

- Your advisors should, early in the process, design and implement wealth transfers between family generations to potentially avoid millions in estate taxes.

The most important reason that advisors are crucial to your success is that they increase business value. Used prudently, planning advisors increase and protect the value of your company. Good Deal Team advisors package that value, find the right buyer and induce that buyer to pay top dollar for your company.

The problem we see too often is owners bumping along with advisors who do everything they are asked to do, but who do nothing they are not asked to do. They don't work in concert with others. If you recognize your advisors in this description, first read this chapter. Then realize that some advisors can be energized by a good Exit Planning Advisor. Finally, only you can decide if the advisors you currently retain are the right ones to guide you through the most important transaction of your life.

TRANSACTION OR DEAL TEAM

When you sold your home, you did not hesitate to use a real estate agent. The sale of a business is much more involved (and financially more significant) and requires sophisticated, experienced transaction intermediaries. A lawyer and CPA are not enough, just as they were not enough in the sale of your home. Why use a real estate agent to sell your house, but not use an investment banker to sell your business? If your answer is, "Cost!" remember that the banker's fees (typically 2 percent to 4 percent of the purchase price) are less than 50 percent of the 5 to 7 percent that realtors charge. Remember also that investment bankers do much more in vastly more complicated and complex transactions.

WHO NEEDS ADVISORS ANYWAY?

Dale Baird and his son, James, did not agree on much, but they finally did agree that James was not the right person to take over the family business. So, Dale approached several business brokers seeking their assistance. The brokers confidently assured Dale that his business was certainly saleable—for cash. (Have you ever met a business broker or an investment banker who lacked confidence?)

But Dale balked. Not at selling out, but at the fees of the broker, attorneys and CPAs estimated to be 5 to 7 percent of the total deal. Besides, like many self-made entrepreneurs, Dale was comfortable in his ability to act on his own initiative. In fact, would-be buyers already were contacting him on what seemed to be a daily basis. Dale knew he could locate a buyer himself.

I learned these facts two years after Dale located his buyer. Dale had allowed the buyer to take over the business before the final financing was approved. Two years hence financing had yet to be secured. The problem when we finally met was that the business was not doing as well and Dale and his accountant had discovered that, according to the contract, Dale could not kick out the would-be buyer for another 18 months. To add insult to injury, Dale had not been paid a dime.

Let's look in more detail at the reasons (as illustrated by Dale's story) for using qualified Transaction Advisors from the very outset of the Exit Process.

A UNIQUE TRANSACTION OUTSIDE THE SCOPE OF YOUR NORMAL EXPERIENCE

In your day-to-day business activities, do you buy businesses? Are you knee-deep in transactions? Waist-high in tax law? Up to speed on the Merger & Acquisition marketplace and its current trends? The strategic or financial buyer, (such as an industry consolidator) who will be sitting across the table from you is. Savvy buyers know how to buy your business. We all like to root for the underdog, but few of us want to be one. You will be hopelessly mismatched if you don't use advisors who understand the process and how to manage that process to your benefit.

So, resist that temptation to be a do-it-yourselfer. This is the largest and most important transaction of your life. The financial and tax consequences can be quite complex. Worse, if you mess this up, there are no Mulligans, no second chances. Using experienced advisors (investment bankers, transaction attorneys, tax professionals and audit CPAs) will cost money. But experienced advisors should *make you money*. This book will show you how they do that for you.

A UNIQUE PROCESS CALLING FOR SPECIALIZED ADVISORS

As comfortable as you may be with your existing advisors, comfort is not what you need right now. Receiving top dollar may not be everything, but it certainly brings its own sort of comfort. To receive top dollar from your company, first you must sell the company. Recall the old maxim: "To finish first, first you must finish." Countless obstacles and pitfalls crop up in every business sale. I like to say, "A deal isn't a real deal unless it has been in the ditch at least five times before closing." Experienced advisors not only know that, they know how to pull the deal out of the ditch and put it back on the track toward the checkered flag.

LEVEL THE PLAYING FIELD

Your advisors will cross swords with the buyer's advisors so level the playing field by hiring the most experienced advisors you can. Just as you should not take this opportunity to learn from your mistakes, don't give your advisors that chance either.

In mid-market deals, the buyers almost always have experienced, capable advisors who cost as much, or more, than yours will cost you. Why would you not want to be on the same playing field?

To cite a simple example, the final purchase contract can be 100 pages or longer. It is full of warranties and representations you will make and have to live by. It is a document prepared by the buyer's law firm. Do you not want your law firm to be as capable as the buyer's?

The buyer's advisors do Merger & Acquisition work for a living. It's all they do. Their role is to find reasons to reduce the purchase price, and not just during the initial negotiations. After the initial documents (such as the Term Sheet or Letter of Intent) are signed, due diligence and negotiation of escrow amounts begin. This is where M&A advisors earn their money: if they can reduce the purchase price by 5 or 10 percent, they may save the buyer—and cost you—millions of dollars. This is why you hire the best talent you can find to represent you as you sell your business.

Again, let's look at specific ways your transaction advisors will make money for you.

Transaction advisors determine not just the fair market value of your business but, far more importantly, the likely *sale price*. Determining the likely sale price and the marketability of your company is central to all efforts to sell your business. The early involvement of your investment banker or business broker is the best means of determining sale price and marketability. It is also an opportunity for you to judge the skill, experience and compatibility of transaction advisors before you commit to using their firms to sell your company. That's right. Consider taking your investment banker or business broker on a "test drive." This gives you an opportunity to judge their promptness, professionalism, your compatibility with their company, their personality and their ability to work with other members of your Planning and Deal Teams.

- Transaction advisors are prepared to tell you when **not** to sell your business—especially if your Exit Planning Advisor continues in an oversight role.

- Transaction advisors expedite the sale process by avoiding mistakes and solving deal problems before they become deal killers.

- Investment bankers create value by forming and directing a "controlled auction" process—causing multiple buyers to offer more, hopefully far more, than they would if there was a single buyer.

- Transaction advisors negotiate the sale to minimize your financial exposure and bargain with the buyer to limit your post-sale liability for the representations and warranties you will make to the buyer.

PUTTING IT ALL TOGETHER

Using transaction advisors is like "using" your doctors. The more you know, the better your questions and the quicker your cure. You are the biggest factor—positive or negative—in your health. In a transaction, what you have done—or haven't done—to build your business is the biggest factor in a successful sale. Your advisors offer expertise, alternatives and answers. Let your advisors worry about the deal. You worry about the business.

Who is going to help you find, interview and select all of these advisors? It is a significant time burden and it is vital to the success of your exit that you use the best advisors available. I suggest you use an advisor whom you trust and who understands the planning process and the sale process to find appropriate advisor. Your trusted advisor can interview possible advisors and then present final candidates to you and perhaps other trusted advisors (in particular your CPA) for a decision.

Again, if you are ready to begin hiring advisors, please see the Appendix to Chapter Three for a complete list of advisors, their roles in each phase, the expertise they should bring to the table and guidelines on how each charges fees.

WHAT IS MY BUSINESS WORTH?

BEAUTY IS IN THE EYE
OF THE BEHOLDER

I make one promise about this chapter: you will not be confronted with arcane valuation theory or formulae. You will learn how your company's value affects not only when you sell, but also your ability to sell for cash.

—John Brown

CHAPTER HIGHLIGHTS

○ Elements Of Value
Marketplace
Intrinsic Value
Promoted Value: Skill Of Your Transaction Intermediary

○ Valuation Answers Your Questions
Can The Sale of My Company Support My Financial Objectives?
Does The Expected Sale Price Satisfy My Wishes To Get Full Value
   For My Company—As I Define Full Value?
Is My Company's Value Above The Threshold Necessary For A
   Cash Sale?

○ Obtaining A Valuation For Your Business
What Will This Valuation Cost?

VALUATION

Chances are, you've had your business valued in the last several years. Perhaps your motive was estate planning or buy-sell driven, or perhaps you wanted to gift ownership to children or sell stock to employees. Whatever the reason, doing so was good planning and using a low value—a value based on historical information—was smart planning.

The question now is whether using that value—one based on historical information—makes sense when considering a sale to a third party. The simple and obvious answer is, "No." Basing value upon historical earnings fails to consider the current and future earnings strength of the business, as well as the climate of the marketplace. To determine the value of a business in an active Merger & Acquisition market, you need to consult with someone who plays in that market everyday. To rely on a traditional valuation ignores what the marketplace is doing **today**, what it is expected to do in the near future, as well as the value that a transaction intermediary adds to the sale process.

In the late 1990s during the rash of consolidations, it was not uncommon for consolidators and others who wanted to compete in the M&A marketplace, to pay an abnormally high earnings multiple—higher than even the buyer expected. In this environment, Merger and Acquisition activity was at an all-time high, for the expectations of the sellers were easily met and often exceeded. Contrast that with 2001. Seller expectations caught up with the valuation multiples that reigned in 1998 and 1999. Unfortunately, those multiples were as much as 50 percent higher than the multiples buyers were willing to pay in 2001. The cycle bottomed out between 2001 and 2004, while steadily improving through 2006.

> Consider this: Relying solely on historical information when valuing the business cannot take into account that the same business producing the same EBITDA might be worth 50 percent less—or more—in a matter of two years or so *solely due to market fluctuation*.

A review of the chart on the following page confirms the fluidity and significant impact the M&A cycle has on sale prices.

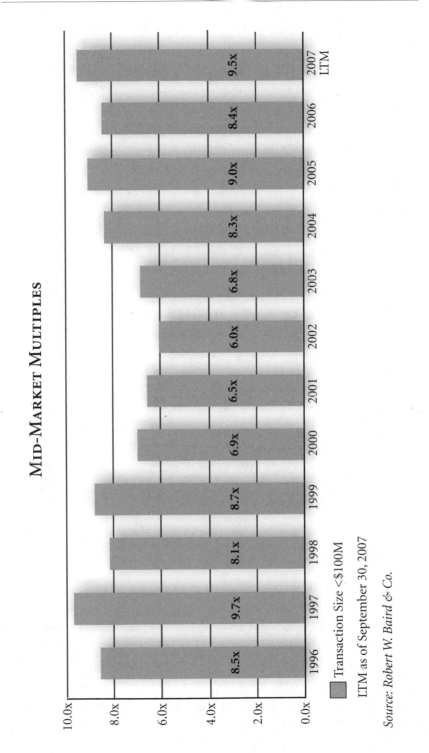

MID-MARKET MULTIPLES

Transaction Size <$100M

LTM as of September 30, 2007

Source: Robert W. Baird & Co.

If we simply compare 1998's multiple of 8.1 to 2002's multiple of 6.0, we see that the multiple in 2002 was only about 74 percent of what it was only four years earlier. Then, if we compare 2002 (6.0) to 2005 (9.0) we see that the multiplier has rebounded in that three-year period by 50 percent.

The point of this comparison is that valuation for sale purposes does not lend itself to easy formulation. Instead, the underlying market conditions shift almost weekly, and certainly monthly, with changes in the economy, in interest rates, with the availability of bank financing, and with the level of acquisition interest in your industry and geographic area. All of these factors considered, determining the sale price and marketability of your business is not a simple task.

Having said this, determining the value of your company is not a mere guess. Instead, it is the careful evaluation of changing facts, circumstances and even emotions. To value a business for imminent sale requires the services of not just a technically savvy valuation expert, but a valuation expert with his or her moistened finger raised high in the wind of the marketplace, ever alert to the smallest changes in the market's direction.

It is not unusual for owners to be unaware of how high (or how low) multiples are as they operate in a world where sale prices are closely guarded secrets. In Chapter 12, you'll read about Dave and Linda Visger who received an offer that preempted their Exit Plan.

Elements Of Value

I promised at the outset that this chapter would not delve into the minutiae of various valuation techniques. I do, however, want to provide a quick overview of the factors that determine the sale price of your company. (For those who would like a more in-depth explanation, please see our Web site, www.BEIBooks.com.) There are three primary elements of value in a third-party sale. They are: 1) the marketplace; 2) the intrinsic worth of your business (including Value Drivers specific to your business); and 3) the skill of your transaction advisors.

MARKETPLACE

An estimate of deal value or the likely sale price tells you what businesses similar to yours have sold for, but doesn't tell you what your business will sell for. As a starting point, comparable sales provide you with the likely range of value. To obtain this information, talk to a transaction intermediary who has access to current databases and recent M&A experience in your industry. Read Chapter 8 on the Merger & Acquisition cycle to learn more about how the market affects the value of your company.

INTRINSIC VALUE

Formula Or Typical Methodology. The most important component of formulas used to determine a range of value is cash flow. Valuation is typically a multiple of available cash flow. You hear of businesses being sold for a "three multiple of cash flow" or "six times cash flow." The natural question to ask is, "What is cash flow?" Depending on how cash flow is defined, one person's value of four times "cash flow" can be far more than another person's valuation of the same company using ten times "cash flow." The first person may use earnings before interest, taxes, depreciation and amortization (EBITDA) while the second refers to net after-tax income. Consequently, be cautious when someone—an industry consolidator or perhaps an advisor you hear at a seminar or workshop—starts tossing around market values based on five times cash flow, etc. Ask first what they mean by cash flow.

> One of my former investment banking partners often said, "Owners are always asking me what kind of multiple of cash flow I can get when I sell their businesses. I tell them, 'If you let me define cash flow, I'll get you any multiple of cash flow you want.'"

The two most commonly used definitions of cash flow or earnings are "EBIT" and "EBITDA." EBIT stands for Earnings Before Interest and Taxes, while EBITDA stands for Earnings Before Interest, Taxes, Depreciation and Amortization. To determine EBIT, take your recast earnings (more about that in a moment) and add any interest expenses and income taxes paid. To determine EBITDA, add back depreciation and amortization, as well as taxes and interest to your recast earnings.

When we refer to recast earnings we mean the process of restoring the mountain of pre-tax earnings your business had before you and your CPA reduced it to a molehill of taxable income. You did this, in part, by taking a salary and bonus higher than the salary you would pay your replacement. Most owners also receive higher than normal lease payments if the company leases facilities, buildings or equipment from them. There are a myriad of other tax planning techniques (such as imaginative inventory adjustments) used to adjust income downward. (Refer to the Vince Diamond case study contained in the Appendix.) Recasting income adds back your clever income adjustments to earnings for EBIT and EBITDA purposes. (Just remember not to be *too creative*: buyers are skittish around owners who seemingly skirt the tax law.)

This recast cash flow is commonly projected forward using a discounted cash flow (DCF) analysis to arrive at the business value. This is a somewhat complicated, but popular method likely to be used by both buyers and sellers. (If you don't believe me, take a quick look at the mathematical formulas used for calculating discounted cash flow at Wikipedia: http://en.wikipedia.org/wiki/Discounted_cash_flow.)

PROMOTED VALUE: SKILL OF YOUR TRANSACTION INTERMEDIARY

The third component in getting the best sale price for your company is the skill of your transaction intermediary. As valuable to you as are your other advisors, (attorney, CPA, financial planner and business consultant) they are not in the business of buying and selling companies. This is the realm of a highly specialized group of experienced business brokers, transaction intermediaries and investment bankers. These are the men and women who dream about business valuation at night and spend their days thinking up ways to convince a buyer to pay top dollar for their clients' companies. The good transaction intermediaries have loads of invaluable experience and I cannot overstate their value. For a more complete description of what they do, please see Chapters 9 and 10.

VALUATION ANSWERS YOUR QUESTIONS

Let's look now at three reasons why smart owners have independent business valuations for their companies in hand before deciding to sell.

"CAN THE SALE OF MY COMPANY MEET MY FINANCIAL NEEDS?"

When thinking about your exit, one of the first questions you must answer is, "How much will I need from the sale of my company to maintain the lifestyle I want for me (and for my family) in retirement?" (Please see Chapter 1 for a discussion of determining this Exit Objective.) The next question should be, "Is my business worth enough (on an after-tax basis) to support those needs?" You must know this answer before you proceed down any exit path.

"DOES THE EXPECTED SALE PRICE SATISFY MY WISHES TO GET FULL VALUE FOR MY COMPANY—AS I DEFINE FULL VALUE?"

Your expected sale price may be more than enough to provide total financial independence to your family, and satisfy every financial and charitable goal you have. *But is it enough?* The answer for many owners is, "No, I think my business is worth more. I don't want to sell my business unless I can get $X million more." If this is the case, you need to find a different investment banker or delay the sale of your company until either the M&A market is paying a higher earnings multiple or until your company increases its performance.

Experience tells us that once a business can be sold for more than about $10 million, after tax, the decision to proceed with the sale is not dependent upon the owner's financial security needs, but is tied to more subjective or personal "wants." Perhaps a more tactful way of saying this is: owners who have spent lifetimes creating successful businesses want full value—as they assess it—and are unwilling to settle for anything less than their idea of the value of the business.

I once represented an owner who wanted $35 million for her business, but the investment banker who looked at the company anticipated a $30 million sale price, at best. At the time, the M&A market was at or near its peak. This owner chose not to sell, even though the $30 million sale price would yield the financial security she desired. She wanted the amount she thought her business was worth.

Four years later, poor health forced this owner to sell her company. The company had experienced a slight decline in EBITDA, but the owner did not have the luxury of time to turn things around. This owner's timing could not have been worse. The year was 2003, the M&A cycle was at its lowest point. The company sold for $12 million.

Be sure that the expected sale price is an amount you can live with— happily. If it is, beware of being reluctant to sell simply because you think you can get a bit more in a year or two. The marketplace may prove you wrong.

"IS MY COMPANY'S VALUE ABOVE THE THRESHOLD NECESSARY FOR A CASH SALE?"

Let's assume that you have decided to sell your business to an outside party. You would prefer an all-cash deal even though you know that most business sales are not all-cash sales.

In the M&A world that you plan to enter, there is a threshold business value that separates those owners who will likely carry back significant promissory notes from the buyer and/or "earn outs" (meaning the business must meet future performance targets—after it is sold—before the owner receives the full purchase price) from those owners who will likely sell for all, or substantially (85 percent) all cash.

As we will discuss in greater detail in this chapter (as well as in the Appendix to this chapter), the current the Value Threshold is no less than $5 million and can be as high as $10 million. As you might guess, the Value Threshold fluctuates based on market conditions. Therefore, it behooves you to determine whether your business meets the then prevailing threshold.

In mid-2007, we could safely assume that a company worth $10 million met the Value Threshold. In other words, its owner could expect (to the extent that owners can expect anything during the sale process) to command an all-cash or nearly all-cash price. That's not to say that a company worth nearly that amount couldn't attract a cash buyer **if** it offered the buyer very little risk or was in a particularly promising industry. Companies with strong Value Drivers in place (see Chapters 6 and 7) offer the lower levels of risk that buyers seek.

For more information on the Value Threshold in today's market, you should contact an experienced investment banker.

Ask your transaction advisor for information on the range of values of recently sold businesses similar to yours. He or she can provide information on sales of businesses (with similar earnings histories, sales volumes, and other relevant factors) in your industry. An investment banker also can describe the current M&A activity in your industry.

If the value of your business is within reach of the threshold, I urge you to consult with an appropriate transaction intermediary (probably an investment banker) to provide you with information about how industry conditions, your location, and your company's unique value proposition affects not only the value of your company, but also its relationship to the threshold.

Most Boomers simply don't have to sell today. Some of us are young enough to spend more time growing business value and/or waiting for the next upturn in the M&A cycle. If that is the strategy you choose, however, do so armed with the information we've provided in this book: demographics are not in your favor, the M&A market is not predictable and if your financial needs can be met by a sale, you need to think long and hard about exactly how motivated you are to manage your company through the tough part of the cycle.

At the risk of diverting you completely from this chapter's important discussion of business value, allow us to spend just a moment on the important issue of Value Threshold. Meeting the Value Threshold is critical in attracting an all-cash buyer. But owners of profitable companies willing to accept less than all cash wonder why their companies can't catch the eye of larger buyers. Kevin's answer to this important question highlights the following issues:

- **Companies worth less than $5 million lack management teams.** "These companies are almost always dependent upon the owner. In the rare cases where there is a management team, it has no depth. These companies can't afford to hire a Vice President of Sales, a Vice President of Manufacturing and a Vice President of Human Resources," said Kevin. As we discuss in this book, buyers look for a skilled, motivated management team poised to stay with the company and make it profitable for the new owner. (See Chapter 6.)

- **Companies worth less than $5 million reflect the strengths and limitations of their owners.** "These companies are lead by entrepreneurs who are generally independent thinkers, street smart and good with people. Further, their strongest suit, be it as a general manager, sales person or technician, tends to define the strength of the company. Sophisticated buyers understand that these businesses grow to the limits of each owner. For example, the owner whose strong suit is sales may cultivate a diverse and loyal customer base, but fail to put adequate resources into upgrading his product. Or, not being the greatest manager, he has not put into place adequate financial controls or operational systems. He's so busy filling the bucket that he doesn't see the leaks."

- **Companies under $5 million in value generally have weak financial systems.** "Most of these companies have no reviewed or audited financial statements. I'm lucky if they have sent their numbers to an accountant at year-end for compilation. Worse yet is the fact that whatever statements there are have little accuracy and even less credibility. Buyers are risk averse creatures who have no interest in unsupportable financial records."

- **Owners of companies under $5 million often engage in "creative" bookkeeping.** "Owners sometimes under-report inventory in an effort to lower profits. In doing so, they pay less tax in the short term but when they want to sell, they face a difficult choice. If they correct the under-reporting, they may face charges of tax fraud. If they let the under-reporting stand, their EBITDA is so low that no buyer will be interested. Some owners fail to realize that for every $1 lost to EBITDA, they lose about $4 of sale price."

- **Companies worth less than $5 million typically lack Value Drivers.** "Their owners are so focused on survival that they have not had time to install (much less enhance) the Value Drivers that not only increase the value of their companies, but also attract the notice of buyers. We call this working *in* the business rather than working *on* the business. These owners have created a good standard of living for their families, but they have not grown their companies to a large enough size to attract the buyer who is looking to make a sizeable impact on its own bottom line."

If your company falls short of the Value Threshold, it does not mean that you shouldn't sell. It does mean that you should proceed with eyes open and well aware of the risk that you may not be fully cashed out in a sale to a third party.

Investment Banker Kevin Short tells owners in this position to return to their Exit Planning Team of Advisors. If owners don't already have an Exit Plan, they need to create one that concentrates on Value Drivers. If, for example, a company must increase its sales, the owner and his or her advisors must determine how to do so organically (internal changes) or through acquisition.

OBTAINING A VALUATION FOR YOUR BUSINESS

Ask yourself this question: If you were to transfer ownership to a sophisticated outside buyer, would that buyer acquire your business without first determining its worth? Of course not—nor should *you* sell it to anyone without *first* determining its worth.

Assuming a third-party sale is imminent or definitely contemplated, it makes sense to use a transaction advisor—investment banker or business broker—to value your company. They are suited to value businesses for sale by training, background and experience. Engaging them to perform the valuation is also a good way to determine whether you wish to use that firm for the sale of your business.

On the other hand, if you do not plan to sell the business for a number of years, consider using a business valuation specialist.

One note of caution: If you use your existing business valuation created by a valuation specialist, ask that specialist if the stated valuation adequately accounts for current market conditions, the presence or absence of factors (other than earnings) within a business that drive the value up or down (called "Value Drivers" and described in Chapters 6 and 7), and the upward pressure on the sale price generated by a well-conducted sale process (which will include strategic buyers as potential acquirers of the business.)

Getting top dollar for your business means getting substantially more money than the amount that generally is predicted by relying solely on historical valuation methodology. It involves extracting real-time values from today's marketplace, enhancing value within your business, and wisely using the strongest transaction intermediary you can find and hire.

WHAT WILL THIS VALUATION COST?

For purposes of a third-party sale, you'll likely use a transaction intermediary to determine value. The cost of that valuation depends on what you want. If you only need a range of value based on current market conditions for your industry and based on your EBITDA, most transaction intermediaries will not charge for this service. The transaction intermediary will assess market conditions and activity, review your EBITDA and provide a range of value. This is a great way to see if your company's value is "in the ball park" of what you want or need.

If you want a more accurate determination of value that requires a closer analysis of your business, expect to pay a transaction intermediary for his or her time. If you engage this advisor, he or she often will credit this fee against the commission they charge for a successful sale.

Turning again to Kevin Short, we asked what valuations typically cost. "The cost often depends on the reputation of the firm performing the valuation, but the range is usually from $5,000 to $20,000," said Kevin. "Even then, the result is the valuator's best guess. Owners need to keep in mind that a business is not a piece of real estate. Business value changes on a daily basis and, most importantly, the controlled auction process is the only way to learn what price the market will bear."

If you need a valuation for planning purposes, (such as gifting ownership, selling part of your company to one or more key employees, or as the basis of cash-based key employee incentive planning) you'll need to hire a valuation specialist. I say that because valuations in these situations will have to hold up under IRS scrutiny. Don't stint on hiring an experienced valuation specialist if you wish to use a conservative value on ownership to be transferred shortly in advance of the sale. The IRS may well look at per share value disparity in stock gifted shortly before a sale at a much higher per share value. If this is your objective, you need to contact your Exit Planning Advisors before proceeding further.

5

How Can I Pay As Little To The IRS As Possible When I Sell My Business?
Paying The IRS Exactly What It Deserves

Chapter Highlights

O What Do You Really Need To Know About Taxes And When Do You Need To Know It?

O The Best Tax Structure
C vs. S Corporation: What Difference Does It Make?

O Charitable Giving
How Does A CRT Work?
   Advantages Of A CRT
   Disadvantages Of A CRT

O Wealth Preservation Via Pre-Sale Transfers Of Business Interest To Children

O Saving Taxes Via Deal Negotiations

O The Bottom Line
Technique 1: Choice Of Entity
Technique 1.5: The C Corporation And Personal Goodwill
Technique 2: Charitable Remainder Trust
Technique 3: Pre-Sale Transfer Of Business Interest
Technique 4: Ongoing Tax Considerations

WHAT DO YOU REALLY NEED TO KNOW ABOUT TAXES AND WHEN DO YOU NEED TO KNOW IT?

The most important thing you need to know about taxes is that if you don't work with your advisors on strategies (legal ones, of course!) to minimize the amount you pay, you will send the U.S. Government more dollars when you sell your company than you would have had you planned. The second most important thing that you need to know about taxes is that the more time you have to plan and implement your strategies, the more money you will save. The final point about taxes flows from the second: start planning now. It is almost never too late to start some type of tax minimization planning.

Not convinced? Read our case study, "A Stitch In Time Saves $1.2 Million" later in this chapter to see how a simple tax election, made on a timely basis, could have saved that owner over $1 million. Also, see the last section of this chapter, "The Bottom Line," for a comparison of various tax saving techniques.

Tax planning and prompt action can save you literally millions of dollars. Be absolutely certain you've done everything you can before you enter the fray of the sale process.

Owners universally share one financial goal when it comes to the sale of their businesses—to leave the closing table with as much cash as possible. Naturally, these owners focus almost exclusively on achieving this goal through selling their companies for top dollar. They imagine themselves as all-pro wide receivers catching 75-yard financial touchdown passes as the clock ticks down. But they often forget that to score the points they have to out-maneuver the defense and keep possession of the ball. Owners, like wide receivers, need to pay as much attention to hanging on to their cash as they do to making it in the first place. In the case of the business owner, the "defense" that must be beaten is the "now friendlier" IRS. In a football game, the bottom line is the score. In the sale of a business, the ultimate financial bottom line is how much money you keep—*after tax* (or after the IRS is finished with you).

Experience tells me that the more owners know about the severity of taxation upon the sale of their businesses, the more motivated they are to learn to "read" the defense. They quickly realize that without a plan, they will be sacked by the taxman for a significant loss.

In my last career as an Exit Planning attorney, it was not uncommon for clients to save millions of dollars in unnecessary taxes using prudent tax planning. It was not that I was a genius; rather, we achieved significant savings for two reasons: 1) Most owners had done no tax planning because their advisors had never mentioned the topic; and 2) We had sufficient time to implement planning techniques—some of which needed years to bear fruit.

Given your instinctual aversion to tax law, (after all, that is why you hire CPAs and tax attorneys) who can help you start planning?

First of all, smart owners do hire tax professionals to provide the answers to the difficult tax issues likely to be encountered in the sale of a business. These tax professionals will figure out what needs to be done, once the deal is underway, to minimize your tax liability. Be sure you have a skilled expert on your team—one fully versed in the tax consequences surrounding the sale of a business.

This chapter is not about what these tax professionals do once the deal is moving forward.

> Once the deal is in motion it is usually too late to save significant dollars through creative tax planning. There is a simple reason for this. Whatever planning you do to reduce the nature or delay the timing of taxes at this stage of the transaction will likely have the offsetting effect of creating tax costs for the buyer—resulting in a lower purchase price.

For example, if you want to convert your ordinary income tax treatment to capital gains treatment, the buyer will lose a tax deduction and instead will have to use after-tax dollars to buy a capital asset—so it likely won't pay as much.

This point is too important to gloss over: *If owners wait to begin tax planning until the sale process commences, they have lost the tax battle. The IRS will take more, perhaps much more, of your money than necessary, or the buyer will pay you less.*

This chapter assumes that, for whatever reason, you have not taken full advantage of planning your departure with tax professionals. If you had, what is it that they would tell you to do now?

They would consider the following tax saving possibilities: 1) the most tax efficient business structure (C Corporation, S Corporation etc.); 2) charitable deduction considerations; 3) transfer of business value to children prior to a sale; 4) ongoing tax considerations present in the sale process; 5) installment sale; 6) personal goodwill; and 7) tax-free merger. Why aren't owners like you aggressively pursuing these tax savings ideas? Usually because:

- Your current advisors (because they have not asked you) are not aware of your desire to exit the business (and when you want to do so) and therefore cannot appreciate the need to begin tax planning in anticipation of a sale. (Engaging experienced professionals in the early stages of the Exit Planning Process puts them to work thinking and planning for you.)

- Your current advisors are not experienced in sophisticated tax planning for business owners who are selling their companies. Their inexperience means that they really don't appreciate the potential of reducing or avoiding taxes through early tax planning beginning years before an owner sells his business.

Let's look at each of the tax planning issues mentioned above in more detail.

THE BEST TAX STRUCTURE

If you are operating your business as an S corporation (or other flow-through tax entity such as an LLC or partnership), and have been for at least 10 years, congratulations. You have potentially saved yourself a lot of money. Unless you want your brilliance confirmed, you also have saved yourself the time necessary to read this section of the book.

If your business is *not* a Sub-Chapter S Corporation, LLC or partnership—in other words if it is a regular or C Corporation—converting your C Corporation to an S Corporation as far in advance of a sale as possible is critical to maximizing terrific tax savings.

Selling your company as an S Corporation instead of as a C Corporation can save you millions of dollars. It could enable you to keep up to an additional 30 percent or so of the total sale price of your company. Generally, there are few disadvantages to converting from a C Corporation to an S Corporation (with a couple of major possible exceptions discussed below).

C vs. S Corporation: What Difference Does It Make?

Every business is conducted, for income tax purposes, as either a regular corporation (C Corporation) or as some type of flow-through tax entity. Selecting the wrong entity when you start your business can result in the payment of additional taxes during the operational years, thereby restricting the capital available for expansion. Having the wrong entity in place when you ready the business for sale can more than double the tax bill upon that sale.

The best entity for tax purposes during a business's start up and operational years is often a C Corporation; yet the C Corporation is the worst entity (causing most of the tax problems) when it comes time to sell the business. Conversely, the best tax form at the time of sale—an S Corporation or other pass-through entity—is often a poor choice for tax purposes during the operational and growth years of a company.

One of my clients, Chuck Ramsey, found paying Uncle Sam an additional 25 to 35 percent of the proceeds from the sale of his business a bitter pill to swallow. This pill is so bitter that, for many owners, it often spells the difference between selling and staying. Chuck Ramsey's problem, then, was typical of many businesses and business owners.

A Stitch In Time Saves $1.2 Million

"I need at least $3 million from the sale of my business, Ramco." That was the conclusion Chuck Ramsey and his financial advisors reached after careful analysis. Given that Ramsey's accountant conservatively valued his software design and consulting company at about $4 million, Chuck's goal was realistic. Chuck anticipated 20 percent capital

gains tax (15 percent federal and 5 percent state) netting him $3.2 million. He was ready to sell when we first met.

I reviewed Ramco's financial statement and noted two significant items. First, there were not a lot of hard assets. As a service company, most of the purchase price would be paid for "goodwill" (an asset without any basis). Second, I found that Ramco was organized as a C Corporation. I suggested to Chuck that this entity choice would prove to be a major stumbling block because any buyer would want to buy the assets of Ramco, not the stock. As a C Corporation, he should expect the total tax bill to be closer to $2 million than to the $1 million that he anticipated.

Chuck immediately responded, "How could we have been so wrong?" Wondering whether he referred to me, to his accountant or to himself, I offered him the following explanation.

"Chuck, most buyers of your company will want its assets (for the two reasons explained below). Since Ramco is a C Corporation, there is a tax imposed, at the corporate level, on the sale of those assets. When Ramco receives the $4 million, it is taxed on the difference between that $4 million and its basis in the assets being sold. At most, Ramco's basis in its assets is about $1 million, so the tax will be levied on the gain of $3 million. Because the effective tax rate is approximately 35 percent federal and 5 percent state, the tax paid by Ramco will be about $1.2 million. When you, in turn, receive the $2.8 million left in Ramco there will be a second tax—a capital gains tax—on that gain. That 20 percent capital gains tax (federal and state combined) equals about $550,000, since you have very little basis in your stock. (A situation most owners face, I might add). The net to you is not $3.2 million, but a little over $2 million—well short of your goal."

On the other hand, if Ramco were an S Corporation, most of the $3 million gain ($4 million sale price minus $1 million basis) on the sale of assets would be taxed once at capital gains rates, and there would not be an additional tax when the money was distributed to Chuck. Chuck would have received $3.4 million, not $2,250,000.

Buyers Want To Buy Assets For Tax Reasons. The *tax* reason that buyers want to buy assets rather than stock is that they can depreciate or amortize assets—but not stock.

In Ramco's case, a 15-year amortization produces $200,000 of deductions a year—which provides $80,000 of tax savings, each year, over 15 years, and a total of $1.2 million of tax savings. If a buyer is to give this up, the business will sell for less.

Let's assume that a buyer purchases the assets of your company, and the basis of those assets is the price paid. When he or she resells those assets, the buyer has no gain to the extent of the original price paid for the assets (assuming no subsequent depreciation or amortization is taken by the buyer). This again illustrates the major tax advantage of an asset sale: when the buyer purchases the assets—there is a "step-up" in basis equal to the price paid for each asset—such as goodwill. "Goodwill" is basically the difference between what a company paid for the acquisition and the book value of the net assets of the acquired company. Goodwill is the major component of gain when most businesses (especially service companies) are sold. The buyer will amortize (deduct) the goodwill over 15 years or so.

The exception to this—and it is a major exception—is that publicly owned corporations, in particular, are not as concerned with tax savings as they are with being able to state pre-tax income. This type of buyer often will want to purchase stock—their eyes are on the stock price, not the tax consequences.

Buyers Want To Buy Assets To Avoid Liability. Several years ago, I represented Fritz, the owner of a manufacturing company. Fritz had purchased the stock of the company from the former owner. Years later, he received a letter from the EPA informing him that it was about to include his company in a Superfund lawsuit because of his company's dumping of toxic waste—all prior to Fritz's acquisition of ownership. It was the first Fritz had heard of it. The company was being held responsible for its previous liabilities, even though Fritz was not individually responsible. The problem could hardly have been worse: the liability was far greater than the value of the business. The company faced financial disaster. The EPA was sympathetic with Fritz and understanding, but insisted upon payment of a significant portion of the clean up costs. Fritz's company bled a lot of money, but stayed alive.

Most would-be buyers are far too savvy to buy stock. They want assets, but not unknown liabilities. Had Fritz bought only assets, the liabilities would have remained with the original corporation—not attached to the goodwill and other assets it sold to Fritz.

As I've already mentioned, however, the entity choice that best suits doing business may not be the best form for selling the business. How, then, does a business owner decide? May I suggest that he or she ask his or her planning advisors—both tax and Exit Planning—today?

Should you question most CPAs as to what business form they suggest for their business clients, they typically answer, "A C Corporation— at least in the early capital formation years of the business."

Ask any investment banker or other transaction advisor what entity form they prefer and you will likely hear, "An S Corporation or LLC (Limited Liability Company), or perhaps partnership or a sole proprietorship. Anything, *anything*, but a C Corporation."

Buyers Want To Buy Specific Assets, Not The Entire Company. An asset sale allows you greater flexibility in exactly what you sell. For example, an industry buyer may be interested in acquiring your customer list, equipment, proprietary technology, etc., but not the assets of a subsidiary business also owned by your corporation. Selling assets accommodates buyers who want to pick and choose in a way that the sale of company stock simply does not.

Converting From C Corporation Tax Status To An S Corporation. Unfortunately, the IRS doesn't shine its benevolent smile upon owners who wish to convert their C Corporation to an S Corporation shortly before (actually for ten years before) a sale of its assets. The IRS frowns on this activity because allowing business owners to do so would cost the IRS billions of dollars every year. For this reason alone you should switch to an S Corporation, if you can and if there are no other tax consequences. (Again, I caution you to make certain you discuss any proposed conversion with your tax and Exit Planning Advisors).

This IRS-imposed ten-year time frame cannot be avoided, but much can be done to minimize its effects. The more time you put between the conversion date and the sale date increases the possible tax savings. We've seen companies and their owners save millions of dollars in taxes when the conversion was made only two or three years in advance of a sale.

Before making a conversion, you must have the assets of the business valued—as of the conversion date—by an experienced business valuation specialist. Converting from C to S is a complex area. We suggest that you read BEI's white paper "C vs. S Corporation" if you now have a C Corporation and consult with an expert in your community. To request a copy of this white paper, please visit www.BEIBooks.com. If you are considering converting to an S Corporation, talk to your planning team NOW.

Allocation Of Purchase Price To Personal Goodwill When An Asset Sale Of C Corporation Looms. If your company is a C Corporation and you must sell assets, ask you advisors about a specialized technique that can, in some cases, save 30 cents on the dollar.

The most common variation of this technique involves allocating the goodwill of the company, typically the biggest asset, to you. For example, the founder of an architectural firm who is responsible for all of the creative designs or for bringing in (through his contacts and reputation) all of the company's business may be in a position to sell that "personal goodwill" directly to a buyer. The owner will pay a capital gains tax on the value of the goodwill.

The alternative is to treat the goodwill as a corporate asset taxed at the C Corporation level—35 percent federal rate (plus state taxes)—and then have the remaining proceeds taxed yet again, at the personal federal capital gains rate of 15 percent (plus any state taxes). This is an interesting planning idea with some support in case law. Can it work for you? Your valuation specialist, tax advisor and Exit Planning Advisor must advise you.

CHARITABLE GIVING

Given the opportunity, tax professionals will jump at the chance to discuss the transfer of ownership to a Charitable Remainder Trust (CRT) when an owner is contemplating the sale of a business. Like the tax savings gained from the conversion from a C Corporation to an S Corporation, the up-front dollar savings can be substantial. *In this case, owners can keep up to 20 percent (or more) of the total sale price of their companies out of the grasp of the IRS because the capital gains tax can be advoided or, at least, deferred.* As with most tax planning strategies, there is a downside (which we will discuss).

That said, there is a huge exception. If one of your sale objectives is to provide money to a charitable cause, then you should be knowledgeable about how to do that in the most tax effective way—giving some ownership to an irrevocable CRT (and getting a partial income tax deduction when doing so) *before* the sale process begins. By anticipating the sale, ownership interest owned by the CRT is *not taxed* upon the sale of the business. You then can serve as the trustee of the Charitable Trust after the sale and receive annuity payments for the rest of your (and your spouse's) life based upon sale proceeds received by the CRT, unreduced by capital gains taxes. Upon your death or the deaths of you and your spouse, the money is distributed to the charity of your choice. That, in a nutshell, describes the workings of a CRT.

I've provided a quick sketch below on how the CRT works, and its advantages and disadvantages. If, after reading that summary, you think the CRT fits your objective of giving money to charity and your objective of enjoying a nice tax deduction, I encourage you to visit our Web site, www.BEIBooks.com to read more about this planning tool.

How Does A CRT Work?

A CRT is an irrevocable trust that you, the business owner, fund with the stock of your company. There is a *designated payout*, or annuity rate, which you fix (irrevocably) when you establish the trust and which is paid to *designated individuals* (usually you and your spouse) for a *specific time period* (usually the joint lives of husband and wife). After the end of the specified time period, the assets remaining in the CRT are distributed to the charity of your choice.

Advantages Of A CRT

1. Avoidance or deferral of capital gains and consequently an increase in investment return of at least 15 percent (or more, if state taxes apply) because there is at least 15 percent more capital to invest.

2. Creation of a partial income tax deduction.

3. Avoidance of estate taxes on the value of the CRT assets.

4. The charities of your choice ultimately receive a large bequest; the IRS gets nothing.

5. Ongoing diversification of investments inside the trust without tax consequences (because the trust is not a taxpayer).

Disadvantages Of A CRT

1. Distributions from the CRT are limited to the original designated payout rate—usually a percentage of the trust principal. The biggest reason owners don't use a CRT is the loss of access to all of the money whenever they desire.

2. Trust investments generally must be in publicly traded securities, not in new business ventures.

3. Children receive nothing from business assets after parents die.

4. "S" election is revoked.

5. Ownership of stock stays inside the CRT if the business doesn't sell.

The bottom line: If capital gains rates are, in your mind, modest, the tax savings are usually not sufficient to outweigh the disadvantages. Most owners therefore don't use this planning technique unless they have a strong charitable bent.

> Before you even consider a Charitable Remainder Trust, look back at your objectives. Does charitable giving appear on that list? If so, it may pay to examine the tax benefits of charitable giving in advance of a sale. Although some advisors disagree, my feeling is that the tax savings alone, in today's low capital gains tax environment, are usually outweighed by the advantages of having free and unfettered use of the net after-tax proceeds after paying a 15 percent federal capital gains tax (and state tax, if any).

Just as with S Corporation conversions, time and valuation issues must be resolved as early as possible or the IRS will shine its malevolent smile upon you. If you are considering using a CRT, talk to your planning team NOW!

WEALTH PRESERVATION VIA PRE-SALE TRANSFERS OF BUSINESS INTEREST TO CHILDREN

The third tax planning element that a tax professional will discuss with owners planning to sell their businesses is the possibility of giving part of the business interest to loved ones (typically children—no matter how undeserving) *before the sale.* The idea here is that if you're going to do it, do it now. Giving your children ownership now rather than later can eliminate estate taxes, *with respect to the transferred property.* With proper planning, valuation and sufficient time to implement the planning before a sale, gift taxes can also usually be avoided. And that's just on the portion of the business that is gifted now. If you consider the benefit of post-sale growth in value of the asset gifted, the savings can be far greater.

To see how one fictional business owner transferred significant wealth to his children well before the sale of his business commenced, please see our Web site, www.BEIBooks.com.

SAVING TAXES VIA DEAL NEGOTIATIONS

In the previous elements, what the business owner gained, the IRS lost. In this discussion of ongoing considerations, what the business seller gains, the business buyer loses, and vice versa. As a seller gains a tax benefit, a tax cost is created for the buyer and that buyer will typically want a reduction in the sale price, or some other benefit. Said another way, discussions of tax benefits become discussions of deal points—and no deal point is without cost of some kind. In short, long-term tax planning creates far more benefits to you than does waiting until the sale process begins.

THE BOTTOM LINE

What affect do all of these methods have on the business owner who wants to get top dollar from the sale of his or her business? Let's put some dollar amounts on the potential tax savings of each of the above tax planning techniques, using a business sale of $10 million.

TECHNIQUE 1: CHOICE OF ENTITY

On the asset sale of a business worth $10 million:

- Owner of C Corporation: Net after-tax proceeds as little as $5.5 million.

- Owner of S Corporation: Net after-tax proceeds approximately $8 million or more.

- Tax savings: As much as $2.5–$3 million.

TECHNIQUE 1.5: THE C CORPORATION AND PERSONAL GOODWILL

- Tax consequences similar to Technique 1 *may* be possible.

TECHNIQUE 2: CHARITABLE REMAINDER TRUST

On the sale of the stock of a business worth $10 million:

- Owner who sells stock outright to buyer: Net after-tax proceeds are $8 million.

- Owner who transfers stock to CRT, which then sells stock: No tax; proceeds are $10 million (in trust).

- Capital Gains Tax savings (deferred): $2.0 million.

- Estate Tax savings: (depends on estate tax law at time of death): $2–$4 million.

Technique 3: Pre-Sale Transfer Of Business Interest

- Owner who makes no gifts before the sale incurs an estate tax (the exact amount depends on tax law at time of death) of approximately 50 percent on all assets passing to children.

- Owner who gifts stock before the sale of his or her business saves children the tax liability on the gift at the time of the owner's death. A pre-sale gift (using a Grantor Retained Annuity Trust) may save millions in estate taxes.

- Estate Tax savings: $2+ million.

Technique 4: Ongoing Tax Considerations

- The amount of tax savings one can achieve through deal negotiation is much more difficult to predict or to quantify than the other three techniques. As noted earlier, buyers always seek some advantage when sellers achieve a tax benefit. For our purposes here then, let's assume that any tax negotiations create a neutral result (although good advisors usually can squeak out positive gains by spinning your tax benefits as a win for buyer as well).

If we assume that your company is a C Corporation, you don't want to incur the adverse tax consequence described earlier in this chapter. Therefore, to induce a buyer to acquire the stock of your company (rather than its assets), the purchase price may be negotiated downward, perhaps by a million dollars or more.

The decision to save millions of dollars in taxes is an easy one. Surprisingly, the planning and implementation necessary to achieve huge tax savings are similarly easy—provided you give knowledgeable advisors the necessary time to implement the plan, in *advance* of the sale.

SECTION TWO

CREATING INTRINSIC VALUE

There are measures that you can take to increase the value of your business when a sale is imminent—within 18 months or so. There are ways to increase your payday, by millions of dollars in many cases. Just as importantly, there are methods of transforming a marginal business into a saleable one.

If you have given yourself more than 18 months to prepare the business—and yourself—for a sale, this section also will describe what longer-term techniques can significantly affect business value. Increased value leads to more money in your pocket, as well as the realization of other dreams and goals. (It also can mean the staying power to wait out a depressed M&A market even if you are too burned out to run the business yourself.)

CHAPTER

6

What Every Buyer Wants And What You Need
A Motivated, Experienced Management Team

Chapter Highlights

O Stable, Motivated Management And A High-Performing Workforce

O Multiples, EBITDA And Value Drivers

O Key Employee Incentive Plans
   Short-Term Key Employee Incentive Plans—The Stay Bonus
   Long-Term Or Non-Qualified Deferred Compensation Planning

What makes buyers pay top dollar for your business? More to the point: If you decide to sell your business what can *you* do to get top dollar for *your* business? Buyers pay premium prices for businesses that have characteristics a buyer perceives to be valuable. Buyers look at more than EBITDA; they look for attributes they believe reduce risk and increase return. In short, the business must have a good story—in both past and future tenses.

In other words, **prior** to a sale, you, the business owner, must create value within the business and then conduct a sale process that compels the buyer to pay top dollar for it. This chapter discusses how to create intrinsic value for your business. Chapter 8 describes the two variants of the sale process and what needs to be done during the process to ensure that you receive top dollar for your company.

In the Merger & Acquisition marketplace, your company will undergo intense buyer scrutiny. Therefore, it pays to know, in advance, what it is that will cause buyers to pay a premium price for your business. These qualities or, "Value Drivers," drive the value of the business upward. The absence of Value Drivers can mean that your business has no value to a third-party buyer.

Once the sale process begins, your transaction advisors, principally your investment banker, are responsible for effectively telling the story of your already successful business. Prior to the sale, however, there is much you can do to contribute to a successful future for your company. What you can do proactively to increase business value is the subject of this chapter and the next.

The Value Drivers we will discuss are:

- Stable, motivated management and a high-performing workforce

- Systems that sustain the growth of the business

- Established and diversified customer base

- Appearance of the business facility consistent with asking price

- Realistic growth strategies

- Effective and documented financial controls

- Growth in cash flow, profitability, revenue and sales

- Presence in an attractive business sector

- The existence of protected proprietary technology

Before we look at each Value Driver individually, I want you to be aware that Value Drivers do more than increase the amount of cash in your pocket at closing. Value Drivers also can increase the marketability or saleability of your business. For example, if you lack a capable management team, many buyers will have no interest in your company. Imagine that, instead of selling your business, you decide to keep it, but back away from any active participation. Perhaps you really are interested only in the strategic planning aspect of running your company. What has to be in place in the business for you to successfully realign your involvement in your company? The same Value Drivers that any buyer insists upon, and the stable, motivated management team is a first among equals.

We devote this entire chapter, then to that premier Value Driver—a stable, motivated management team and high-performing workforce. We do this because none of the other Value Drivers (so necessary to maximizing business value) can be achieved through your efforts alone. It takes a team—a strong management team—to accomplish all of them.

As any reasonably sophisticated buyer appreciates, the absence of a management team means that other vital aspects of a business also are deficient. That's why management is so important to you and to your future buyer. Buyers want to be sure the management team extends beyond you and that they will stay when you leave.

STABLE, MOTIVATED MANAGEMENT AND A HIGH-PERFORMING WORKFORCE

We'll begin our Value Driver discussion with the most important one: your management team. This team includes people who are responsible for setting and implementing the company's strategic direction, aligning strategic objectives with the company's mission and vision, monitoring and controlling high-level activities with the business plan, and motivating and supervising other employees.

In many small companies, this "team" consists of one person, generally the owner. To build a championship organization, however, the management team should include people with a variety of skills. Many football teams have a star quarterback or running back. Unless the team is well-coached and has other strong supporting players, it cannot put together a winning season. Surrounding yourself with quality people whose skills are different than yours is a necessary preamble to a successful sale.

In a supporting role, though no less important, is the workforce in general. Paula Cope, a business consultant, often asks owners, "If no one came to work tomorrow, what would the company produce?" The answer, of course, is, "Absolutely nothing." Her question brings home the point that having the best products and services, the most innovative

strategies, and even cutting-edge operating systems alone cannot produce revenue. People do. Selecting your workforce with care, training it
well, and creating the right mix of talent and potential are essential when
increasing the value of your business.

In addition to talent, you need a management team with staying
power—and that's what the balance of this chapter will discuss. One of
the first questions prospective buyers ask is, "Who runs the company
and are they willing to stay?" If the answer is, "The owner is in charge,
likes to manage everything, and wants to leave soon after closing," the
value of the company plummets and most buyers look elsewhere.

MULTIPLES, EBITDA AND VALUE DRIVERS

As we discussed in Chapter 4, the shorthand method for determining the
sale price of a business is typically: EBITDA x some multiple = sale price.
Naturally, owners are very curious about the unknown: the multiple
they can get for their companies. What they can quantify is EBITDA so
they tend to focus on how much EBITDA or cash flow their companies
have. While we applaud that focus, we alert owners to the fact that they
also should focus their efforts on increasing that "unknown" multiple.

We acknowledge that, to a large extent, the multiple for companies
in your industry is determined by market forces (discussed in Chapter
8). The multiple that applies to your company, however, also is based on
the existence and strength of your company's Value Drivers. Let's look
at an example.

> *Business A and Business B each have $3 million of EBITDA, are
> located in the same city and are in the same business.*
>
> *Business A has a strong management team motivated by an eco-
> nomic incentive to both improve company performance and remain
> through any ownership transition. Business A has developed and
> documented various systems designed to sustain the growth of the
> business apart from its owner. It has carefully diversified its customer
> base in the years leading up to the sale process: no customer represents
> more than 8 percent of its revenue.*

> *Business B has a good management team, but they are the same age as the owner and have expressed a desire to leave the business when he does. The company's systems are not documented; rather they are "between the ears" of the management team. Business B has six customers.*
>
> *Which company is worth more? Which would you pay more for? Developing Value Drivers is vitally important . . . and it is your job as an owner.*

It is not only desirable, it is *necessary,* to install Value Drivers, if you are to sell your business at the highest possible price. How do you motivate your key employees both to increase the value of your company and stay through any transition to a new owner?

Key Employee Incentive Plans

Any key employee incentive plan that you, as an owner, install must achieve these three results:

1.   *Motivate* employees to increase the company's cash flow during the crucial sale process;

2.   *Keep* employees on board *before, during,* and *after* the transition; and

3.   *Reward* employees when the business is sold (provided that the award is not so great and so immediate that there is no incentive to continue working with the new owner).

To achieve these results, you must create sound and thoughtful incentive-based plans for key employees. These plans include the following attributes:

•   Earmark a "significant" slice of the future value to the key employees who helped create that value. If the company is to be sold in the near future, management will expect its "share" of the windfall you receive. A strong reason to plan ahead for this expectation is to implement incentive plans combined with covenants not to compete.

- Incentives that "handcuff" the key employees now, during the actual sale process, and through any earn-out period that may be imposed by the buyer.

- Incentives are perceived as win-win situations for both company and key employee.

Begin key employee-based planning now—before a business transfer occurs and ideally before the key employees are aware of a possible sale.

The issue of "now" brings me to my next point. The exact nature of the incentive plan depends on the amount of time between "now" and your eventual sale. For our discussion here, we'll define short term plans as those for companies with two years or less before a sale. Longer-term plans are for those companies with three or more years.

SHORT-TERM KEY EMPLOYEE INCENTIVE PLANS—THE STAY BONUS

If you anticipate a sale within the next two years, you must take every reasonable step to ensure that your key employees remain at their posts even as you begin leaving yours. Their efforts to maintain and increase cash flow are key to maximizing the business's eventual sale price. These same employees may need to shoulder extra duties as your attention wanes or is diverted. For these reasons, it is not uncommon for owners to offer key employees a portion of the "spoils" when the business is sold.

When I discuss incentive plans, owners always ask, "Do I really need to do this? My management team has been with me for years. They're loyal and already highly motivated. I pay them well—more than they can earn elsewhere." The short answer is yes, you really do need to provide additional incentives when selling your business.

Remember, you are leaving and taking a pile of cash with you—money these employees (especially in their minds) helped you create. As long as you were active in the business, all was well. You earned your money and so did your management. But now you are leaving, financially well-off (some would say, with more than you deserve), and management is staying. Members of your team know it is important for them to stay if you are to get full value for your company. Once you leave them behind, they have no loyalty to the new owner. They worry about their positions, their compensation, and the future direction of a company that until now, they had thought of as *their* company. Can you imagine that they might be a bit resentful that you are taking off with money they helped you earn?

Key employees want a share of the "windfall," and if that expectation isn't met, they can, and do, leave. We've witnessed key managers threaten to walk out before closing, refuse to sign covenants not to compete desired by the potential new owner, and demand a bonus to stay.

> *Kevin remembers one deal in which the actions of a disgruntled key employee not only threatened the deal, but cost the selling owner almost 10 percent of the deal's value. In this case, the buyer told the seller that it wanted the seller's best salesman to sign both an Employment Agreement and Covenant Not to Compete. When presented with these documents, the salesman threatened to leave. After protracted negotiations, the seller paid the salesman nearly $300,000 to sign the contracts in order to close the deal. There was some justice: aware that the salesman had held up the transaction, the buyer fired the salesman after closing.*

Lessons Learned. This owner (and all others) would do well to remember the following key employee incentive lessons:

- First, don't give your key managers a reason to leave; give them a reason to stay.

- Second, creating the type of short-term incentive plan (stay bonus) we describe below can increase business value, thus increasing the amount of money you are paid at closing.

- Third, in addition to providing a carrot for enticing management to stay, some owners also provide a stick: covenants not to compete that prevent your key managers from leaving before or after the sale (usually for about two years post-sale) and from taking vendor relationships, employees, clients or customers, or trade secrets. Expect key employees to object to signing such a covenant. After all, it restricts their value in the marketplace. That's why they won't sign covenants unless they are combined with lucrative stay bonuses (or other incentives). Even with such incentives, they may not be willing to sign.

> At the risk of being redundant, let me assure you that the more important your management team is to the success of your company, the more important it is to the buyer that they stay (or at least don't compete if they leave).

Finally, when you reward your management team for its dedication and value, you will feel good. Most likely, it is something you want to do. Too often owners realize, at the eleventh hour, that they need to do something for their management or they risk management rebellion at the sudden announcement of the planned sale. It doesn't look good, or feel good, to institute a stopgap, incentive plan as an afterthought—implemented only days before the potential buyer's first visit to the company and the consequent unveiling of your decision to sell the business. Rather than wait until the last moment, incorporate your good wishes into a plan now that benefits both you and your employees.

Let's look at the fictional case of Chase Ewing, owner of Ewing Lubricants, Inc. to see how these incentive plans work in the real world.

CHASE EWING, OWNER OF EWING LUBRICANTS, INC.

Business value: $10+ million
Number of employees: 48
Number of key employees: 3
Exit Objectives:
    Timing: Leave as soon as possible—sell today.
    Financial: $8 million cash—net of taxes at closing.

We weren't 60 seconds into our meeting when it became clear that, while Chase Ewing may have not formally launched the process of selling his company, he had mentally checked-out months ago. Ewing Lubricants was being maintained by the efforts of its three key employees— all of whom were well aware of, and increasingly nervous about, Chase's desire to sell the business. In fact, his relationship with these employees is what brought him into my office. In a sound effort to retain these employees during an eventual sale process, Chase had "sort of unofficially, informally promised" them a "piece of the pie" upon a successful sale. In addition, his "promise" reflected his desire that they benefit should he sell the business for his asking price.

Further, Chase knew that if anyone from his management team left before, or immediately after, the sale, the deal would be in jeopardy. He was especially worried about his sales manager, who increasingly controlled many of the customer relationships as Chase began to back away.

Chase's problem is typical. As he thinks about how to exit the business, he must give equal thought to discouraging his key employees from doing the same. Key employees are never so "key" as when the owner begins exiting his business. There are several reasons for this.

1. **Owners often lack motivation—"the fire in the belly"—to enhance the success of the business on a daily basis.** They are either tired of slugging it out in the trenches every day, or they have become bored with the daily activities of the business. In order to keep the business successful and on track, owners need a properly motivated, strong management team. Chase Ewing was acutely aware of the need to motivate his key employees. Somebody had to propel the company forward and it was all he could do to go to work each morning.

2. **Buyers buy cash flow—and they pay top dollar for cash flow that they expect to increase after they buy the company.** Think like a buyer. Owners cannot allow cash flow to stagnate simply because they are planning their escapes. Once again, it falls to the key employees to drive cash flow growth.

3. **Key management is as vital to a new owner as it was to the exiting owner for its role in maintaining and increasing cash flow.** Sophisticated buyers in particular will pay far more for a business if key management will stay with the company after it is transitioned. In fact, a potential buyer may have little or no interest in acquiring a business, at any price, without assurance that the key employees will continue under new ownership. Remember, the buyer knows you are going to leave the business—that's why you are selling it. Unless you have a strong management team willing to remain—motivated and excited to take the business to the next level—you may not be able to leave at all.

4. **Key management should stay after the sale so your earn-out is achieved.** One method for bridging the gap between a seller's expectation of the purchase price (based in part upon the company's continued growth and strong future performance) and the buyer's unwillingness to pay a premium for projected future performance (which exceeds historical results) is to pay the seller the difference if the business performs post-sale as predicted by the seller. If performance fails to meet these projections, the value difference disappears—thereby limiting the buyer's exposure to overpayment. You'll increase positive future performance by making sure your management stays after the sale.

5. **Key management provides an owner with an alternative exit strategy.** If a sale to a third party fails or is unworkable for some reason, the management team may be willing to purchase the business.

6. **The Quid Pro Quo.** Management receives money to stay and in return, agrees not to compete.

Although Chase Ewing may have checked-out emotionally, he was still a quick study. He readily understood that his key employee incentive plan must pay out quickly and assure the key employees that their benefits were secure. Because Chase wanted to exit as soon as possible, his key employee incentive plan had to cover only two to three years from inception to *total* pay out. During that time frame the business would be marketed and sold, while the key employees would work for the new owner for one to two years.

Second, Chase needed to assure his key employees that, even though the ownership of the company would change, their benefits would not be affected. He realized that when employees think about their employer selling out to a larger and possibly (especially in their minds) less employee-friendly company, they are naturally apprehensive.

The only thing employees fear more than the unknown is the "loss of the known;" namely, their job security and their roles within the company. They trust the direction and mission of your/their company and suspect that everything they've known will evaporate overnight only to be replaced by promises made by an unknown and more remote owner. Many key employees act on these suspicions with their feet: they leave to seek other employment.

Rather than lose key employees at the very time your company needs them most, consider providing a formal incentive plan to handcuff and motivate management. This plan is also helpful if (for some reason) the sale is not completed; the company and its key management team will remain intact.

If you neglect to provide an incentive, talented management has little reason to remain employed by a new owner it did not choose. Peak performers leave organizations in times of change simply because they can: they have options. On the other hand, if you promise key employees a "share of the windfall" upon a sale, they will certainly accept, but may leave shortly after you do. To avoid this scenario, create a short-term stay bonus plan.

The short-term bonus plan must provide the key employees with what they need to continue with the new ownership. What they need is a promise—a promise that comes not from the new organization but from the existing owner—you. And that promise is for *cash*. For these reasons, we call these plans "stay bonus plans."

Part of Chase Ewing's Exit Plan involved installing a stay bonus plan for his key employees. To determine the amount of a stay bonus, look at: (i) either the unvested benefits of any existing key employee benefit program, (ii) the percentage of the anticipated purchase price that you wish to give to your employees, or (iii) a specific cash amount. In Chase's case, he had already "informally" promised his three key managers a total of 10 percent of the anticipated sale price. Using that as our basis, we began to design a plan. If you have no existing plan, the method to create a stay bonus is still the same.

Formulating The Stay Bonus.

Step 1. Upon the sale of the company, Chase agrees to *escrow* an amount equal to 10 percent of the net, after-tax purchase price. The escrow will be outside of the acquiring company's ownership. In effect, Chase will own the monies in the escrow account, subject to the three key managers vesting in that money.

Step 2. Each manager will be entitled to a *stay bonus* equal to his *pro-rata share of the escrow amount*, as he or she becomes *vested*. The vesting schedule provides for vesting at the rate of 33 percent per year for each of three years.

Step 3. Unlike typical key employee compensation plans, the vesting schedule is also the payment schedule for this stay bonus plan. This plan provides that a manager becomes vested in one-third of his share on the sale closing date and receives payment of that amount at that time; one-third at the first anniversary, and the remainder at the second anniversary. If a manager chooses not to remain with the new company for the entire two years, he or she will not receive the full amount of the stay bonus. Any funds remaining in the escrow after two years will revert to Chase.

This stay bonus program accomplishes several vital objectives for Chase's management team. These include:

1. **Cash, A Lot Of It!** In Chase's case, three key employees will each receive about $300,000. This amount is about twice their annual salary and is certainly appealing to them. How do you determine an equally appealing amount for your management team? Since every business is different, I suggest working with an advisor who has experience in this area. Just make sure the bonus, in the mind of the key employees, is substantial.

2. **Accelerated Vesting And Pay Out.** Payments will be made from the escrow account when the key employee vests in that portion of his account. Unlike most incentive plans that vest over an extended period of time and pay only after vesting is completed, this program provides a rapid reward for the key employees—provided they remain with the new organization.

3. **Minimizes Risk: Yours And The Employees'.** Because the money is held in escrow (controlled by you) for the exclusive benefit of the management team and is not controlled or owned by the acquiring company, the chance that key employees will leave the new organization is minimized. Their stability and motivation markedly improve your chance of both receiving a better price and of fulfilling your earn out.

    From the key employees' perspective, their economic reward is divorced from the rise or fall in the value of the acquiring company's stock. Rather, it is based upon the value of your company at the date of sale. Further, the payments that your key employees receive for remaining employed for a period of only two years are paid in cash—not in stock of the new company.

4. **Outside Of New Employer Control.** Because the stay bonus plan is completely separate from the acquiring company, it is easier to negotiate the management team's participation in the acquiring company's stock option program, or other program, provided for its key employees. The employees may feel more comfortable with *your* promise to pay than that of a new (and unknown) employer.

This stay bonus program meets Chase's Exit Objective of creating a saleable and valuable company. What benefits does the program provide for his prospective buyer?

1. **Management Continuity.** Key employees have a significant reason to remain with the new organization; namely, the cash benefit to be paid by the existing owner as they stay with the new company. This benefit provides an acquiring company the assurance

that the individuals who have been instrumental in the purchased company's success will remain with the new company for a substantial period of time.

2. **Simplification Of Key Benefit Programs.** Attempting to require the buyer to continue any existing plans—formal or informal—for the seller's key employees would make the acquisition of Ewing Lubricants unnecessarily complex. By assuming these plans, the acquiring company would incur not only administrative costs, but also redundancy or competition with its plans for its existing employees. Additional complications never make a company more attractive to a suitor and often lead to delays in the closing.

For everyone involved—buyer, seller and key employees—the short-term bonus program is a win-win-win situation. The last critical issue is to make sure that your investment banker (or Exit Planning Advisor) present the program to key employees properly.

It is best that you do *not* present the plan. Let any employee dissatisfaction, concerns or issues be directed at your advisor, not at you. If an employee is upset because the plan does not seem sufficiently generous or fair, let the advisor take the heat. They are trained (and paid!) to deal with this common situation.

Your advisor will communicate the details of the plan so that key employees understand that:

1. You have installed a well-conceived, financially appealing incentive plan as far in advance of a sale as possible;

2. The incentive plan is intended to protect their financial interests if the business is sold;

3. You have taken them into your confidence by raising the possibility of an eventual sale; and

4. If a buyer has already appeared on the scene, the successor owner offers more opportunity for career advancement and financial reward than can your smaller company.

LONG-TERM OR NON-QUALIFIED DEFERRED COMPENSATION PLANNING

A longer-term incentive plan (three plus years before a sale) shares many of the same characteristics of a short-term plan. Common characteristics of these plans are that the benefit to the employee increases as the value of the business increases, they are substantial and they financially "handcuff" the employee to the business—there is a financial disincentive if the key employee leaves too soon. In a long-term plan, this disincentive feature takes the form of vesting in a cash-based plan and "risk of forfeiture" if ownership-based.

In addition, the long-term plan has the benefits of: 1) not disclosing intent to sell now; and 2) motivating the key employees to grow business value (and to stay) even if the owner does not sell.

To see how a long-term plan works in a real-life scenario, read the story of Ed Wekesser in Chapter 12. Ed describes how his company's management team worked to achieve the owners' goals. Ed and his partners used the dollar amount that they would need from a sale as the basis for their incentive plan. Under this plan, as the managers built the company, they would share (in an increasing percentage) in the proceeds.

If your expected sale date is three or more years away, consider a longer-term incentive plan in lieu of, or in addition to, a stay bonus. Stay bonus plans are used when the business is to be sold in two years or less. Longer-term incentive plans, such as Stock Option, Purchase or Bonus Plans, or Non-Qualified Deferred Compensation Plans are usually designed to last five, or more, years—but can work well within a shorter time frame. Their purpose is to motivate key employees to create more value and to stay long term regardless of an owner's ultimate exit strategy. Of course if a sale occurs more quickly than anticipated, these plans can be effectively converted to or combined with a stay bonus plan.

Key employee incentive planning is a vital element to building and sustaining business value. If your anticipated departure date is more than two to three years away, (making Non-Qualified Deferred Compensation Plans more appropriate) I suggest you visit www.BEIBooks.com to read about key employee incentive planning and to download a white paper on the subject.

Ideally, you and your Exit Planning Team Advisors created and funded long-term incentive plans for management years ago—as part of your comprehensive Exit Plan. These plans are either cash-based, such as Phantom Stock Plans, Stock Appreciation Rights (SAR) Plans, and Non-Qualified Deferred Compensation (NQDC) Plans, or ownership-based such as Stock Bonus Plans, Stock Purchase or Stock Option Plans.

If you have done this type of planning, now is the time to re-examine those plans and consider increasing their benefits. You also might consider modifying the vesting schedule to further enhance the likelihood that management will remain through your departure. If you wish or need to remain as the owner of your business for longer than a few years, longer-term incentive plans such as these may make a good deal of sense. (If this is the case, I suggest reading **The Completely Revised How To Run Your Business So You Can Leave It In Style**.)

If, however, your exit horizon is more immediate, and richer plans are called for, ask yourself, "If my top management left as I began the sale process, what would it mean to my ability to sell for the price I want and on the terms I need?" Your answer, I expect, might be, "My ability to sell the business disappeared when my management did."

I've spent a lot of your time telling you about motivating and keeping your management team through your exit. I've done so because this is the single most important Value Driver for your business.

CHAPTER

7

WHAT BUYERS LOOK FOR
AND HOW YOU HELP
THEM FIND IT

CHAPTER HIGHLIGHTS

O Systems That Sustain The Growth Of The Business

O Established And Diversified Customer Base

O Appearance Of Facility Consistent With Asking Price

O Realistic Growth Strategies

O Effective And Documented Financial Controls

O Financial Growth: Cash Flow, Profitability, Revenue And Sales
   Growth Through Acquisition
   Reinvigorate Yourself
   Hire A Management Consultant

O Attractive Business Sector

O Protected Proprietary Technology

SYSTEMS THAT SUSTAIN
THE GROWTH OF THE BUSINESS

If your objective is to sell your company for the highest possible price, you must build reliable systems that can sustain the growth of the business. Paula Cope, a business consultant, contributed to the following section on business systems.

Before we get started, here are a few quick definitions:

- *Systems* refer to a group of related processes.

- *Processes* have purposes and functions of their own and are components of a system. Taken independently, a process alone cannot do the work of a system.

- *Procedures* are the approved way we do things and often include a sequence of steps.

- *Steps* are the actions we take to get something done.

An important Value Driver then is the *development and documentation of business systems that either generate recurring revenue from an established and growing customer base or create financial efficiencies.* For most businesses, this includes all the core processes that generate revenue or control expenses. These *systems* may include *processes* related to production or service delivery, but also may include people-related processes such as a succession planning or a performance management approach.

Look at your business from a buyer's perspective. If you leave shortly after a sale, what remains? If the answer is top management and highly efficient business systems, you can be more confident that you will be able to get top dollar for your business.

In addition to the business systems related to revenue and expense, some systems are related to customers, such as tracking systems, and the delivery of your products and services such as distribution systems. The documentation of these systems and their related processes and procedures is important to ensuring that quality and consistency can be maintained after the sale. They also signal to the buyer that everything is in place for their future success. Some examples of items worthy of documentation are:

- Financial control systems and accounting policies.

- Policies to ensure compliance with legal and regulatory matters, especially those related to employer/employee relationships and safety.

- Data management and information systems that tie the company together.

Again, put yourself in the shoes of a would-be buyer. Buyers want assurance that the business will continue to move forward after new ownership and that operations will not break down if and when the former management leaves. This assurance can best be obtained when there are documented systems in place that will enable the buyer to repeat the actions of the former owner to generate income and grow the business.

An easy way to show a process is by using a process map. The following page shows an example of a finance process of a typical business. Process maps are not only useful in orienting your buyer to how things are done, you can use them now to orient and train new employees.

The process map illustrates the process of invoicing a client, which is just one piece of a small business financial management system. The map shows the flow of steps and procedures, as well as the number of people involved, and the dependencies inherent when there are multiple steps and people. In its entirety, the company's financial management system might include separate processes for: creating projections, invoicing clients, processing payments, processing vendor bills and processing queries. Each process shows the same level of detail and allows you, your employees, and the buyer to understand how to maximize efficiency and avoid breakdown or bottlenecks in the system.

There are several business systems, which, once in place, enhance business value whether you plan to sell your business now or decide to keep it. These systems are:

1. Human capital management including: recruitment, selection, hiring, and retention; performance management; training and development; compensation and benefits.

2. Production including product or service quality control and improvement.

3. Product or service research and development.

4. Inventory and fixed asset control.

5. Sales, marketing and communications.

6. Procurement including the selection and maintenance of vendor relationships.

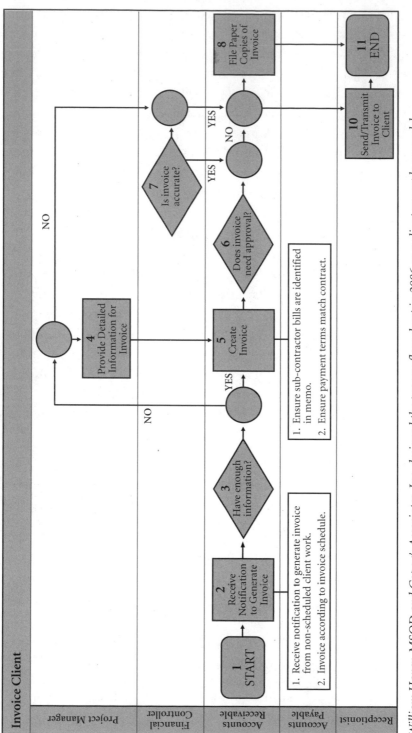

Invoice Client

| Project Manager | Financial Controller | Accounts Receivable | Accounts Payable | Receptionist |

1
START

2
Receive Notification to Generate Invoice

3
Have enough information?

NO

YES

4
Provide Detailed Information for Invoice

5
Create Invoice

6
Does invoice need approval?

YES

NO

7
Is invoice accurate?

NO

YES

8
File Paper Copies of Invoice

10
Send/Transmit Invoice to Client

11
END

1. Receive notification to generate invoice from non-scheduled client work.
2. Invoice according to invoice schedule.

1. Ensure sub-contractor bills are identified in memo.
2. Ensure payment terms match contract.

William Hancy, MSOD and Cope & Associates, Inc. designed the process flow chart in 2006 as a client example or model.

Obviously, appropriate systems and procedures vary depending on the nature of a business, but at a minimum, those resources and activities necessary for the effective operation of the business should be documented.

Document and enhance your company's systems now. Business consultants can assist you in process mapping and other Exit Planning team members can help you document related policies and procedures. To find a skilled advisor in your area, you can search our Web site www.BEIBooks.com.

Finally, remember that if for some reason your business doesn't sell as expected—creating and enhancing Value Drivers—such as this one—make your business far stronger and more manageable—and more enjoyable to continue to own.

ESTABLISHED AND DIVERSIFIED CUSTOMER BASE

Put on those buyer's shoes one more time and you'll find yourself shuffling past companies with great management teams and excellent systems, but whose cash flow is dependent on one or two customers. Why spend millions of dollars on a business only to have those customers go elsewhere after you've acquired the company? At the very most, a prudent buyer will structure a buyout to protect against the loss of a key customer, probably by making much of the purchase price contingent or requiring the seller to carry a note for the bulk of the purchase price. As a seller, risking your financial security (for several years) to the ability of the new owners to retain customers is to be advoided, if at all possible.

Another Value Driver, then, is the development of a customer base, in which no single client accounts for more than approximately 10 percent of total sales. A large customer base helps to insulate a company from the loss of any single customer. Talk to your investment banker or other advisor for customer concentration information specific to your industry.

Achieving this objective can be problematic when you are building a business with limited resources and one or two good customers are willing to pay for everything you can deliver. If this is the situation in which you find yourself, it is important to begin now to: (i) reinvest your profits into additional capacity that will make developing a broader customer base possible, and/or (ii) acquire customer diversification by buying smaller competitors.

High customer concentration can prevent a third-party sale of an otherwise attractive company. Witness the situation with Double L Boilers, a profitable fabricator and installer of commercial heating systems.

Double L's EBITDA exceeded $3 million per year, a strong management team was in place and all systems were "go." So thought Lloyd and Larry, its owners, until the investment bankers analyzed the company's customer base and discovered that more than 85 percent of the company's revenues and profits derived from eight customers.

The owners didn't quite understand why that fact presented a problem. After all, those eight customers were long-time customers and provided a steadily increasing cash flow to the business. Lloyd asked, "Why should we try to diversify when it is all we can do to keep up with the new business from our existing customers?"

Double L's most attractive buyer (a Fortune 100 company) provided the answer. It insisted on meeting with each of the eight customers to determine their willingness to remain with the company after it was sold.

Lloyd and Larry objected vehemently. "What will our loyal customers think—and do—if they assume that we're selling our business? Will they stay as customers? What happens if we don't end up selling and they leave anyway?" These owners realized that losing even one customer would be a financial set-back and losing two or three spelled disaster. Not only would the sale fall through, but the company might be thrown into a financial tailspin.

These same insights prompted the would-be buyer to demand the interviews. It was not prepared to pay $20 million for a business whose customer base and cash flow might well decrease by 15 to 45 percent overnight—simply because the business was under new ownership.

Lloyd and Larry faced a true dilemma: the only way to pursue the sale was to allow this buyer to meet with their customers. If they refused, the sale process was over and their dreams of cashing out and moving on into new lives would be destroyed. If they allowed the buyer to meet their customers, the sale might fall through for totally unrelated reasons, but Double L's relationships with its customers might be irretrievably harmed. Even if the sale did close, their customers' potential loss of confidence might cause them to bolt and jeopardize Larry and Lloyd's earn outs. Had this business had even 20 customers, the situation would not have surfaced.

In the end, Lloyd and Larry did allow the prospective buyer to meet with their customers. All indicated that they would remain customers if the service level remained high. As expected, the buyer's terms included that the sale price would be reduced on a percentage basis if any customer left within 30 months after the sale. Tough terms, but the only ones that the buyer would accept.

APPEARANCE OF FACILITY CONSISTENT WITH ASKING PRICE

Although matching the business's face to its asking price is not usually a problem for business owners, some owners can be, shall we say, "economical" when devoting financial resources to the physical appearance of their places of business. This is most often true of businesses whose facilities are not visited by the general public. Examples are the offices of a phone-based or off-site sales organization, or a manufacturing or warehouse type business. Although many would argue that those facilities should be as beautiful as possible in order to benefit the work force, owners can be reluctant to expend cash flow for an item that does not directly translate to increased profitability, especially when considering the sale of the company. However, for the same reason that your retail facility is top notch, your other "hidden" facilities must also appear first class. When you meet with vendors or large customers at your facility, these folks may well be potential buyers. A good looking physical plant can convey your company culture, extend your brand image, and provide an opportunity to market your products. A picture is worth a thousand words and maybe tens of thousands of dollars!

Some owners ask me if there is a reason why the new owner of their companies would need better appearing facilities than the ones that have gotten them where they are today. I often respond that if they intend to ask the new owner to pay millions of dollars for the company, they should expect that buyer to want the business to "look like a million dollars." A good-looking facility shows buyers that you are proud of your business in every respect and that you have made the necessary investments to keep it going. It also indicates that you have not deferred necessary capital investments only to create future capital investment requirements for the buyer.

A clean, well-organized facility communicates the message that the business is also clean and well organized. It is amazing how a few thousand dollars of improvements improves the marketability of your business, strengthens its brand, and increases the interest of potential buyers.

Before you dismiss this Value Driver as not as important as other Drivers that directly impact cash flow, let me point out that businesses are sold to private equity buyers for millions of dollars. These sophisticated buyers base their decisions on more than just cash flow projections, business plans and the like. They consider subjective factors. just as you did when you bought your last house. I expect that you haggled a bit over purchase price, but your decision to purchase was strongly influenced by how you felt about the house. Something made it the "right" house for you and your family.

Similarly, businesses are acquired—or not acquired—for many seemingly insignificant reasons. Rarely do numbers alone tell the story. Impressions always play a role. You can build value, or at least not destroy it, by having a favorable looking facility.

REALISTIC GROWTH STRATEGY

Buyers pay premium prices for companies that have developed realistic strategies for growth. This growth strategy must be communicated to a potential buyer so that the buyer can see specific reasons why cash flow (and the business itself) will grow after it is acquired. The growth strategy is illustrated in pro forma statements that are used by buyers (and their investment bankers) to create a discounted future cash flow valuation of your company. Since future cash flow is based on estimates of future growth, having a realistic growth strategy is vital to reaping top dollar for your business. This strategy can be based upon:

- Industry dynamics;

- Historical growth;

- Increased demand for the company's products (due to population growth or other factors);

- New products and new product lines; and

- Expansion through augmenting territory, product lines, manufacturing capacity, etc.

Don't expect buyers to appreciate the growth opportunities your company offers unless you speak convincingly about them. First, a buyer will not understand your business as well as you do, and will not likely see its hidden opportunities. Also, if a buyer does discover an opportunity that it believes you have ignored, the buyer will likely attempt to take advantage of that knowledge during purchase price negotiations. You need to demonstrate that you are aware of the opportunity.

Even if you plan to sell tomorrow, you need to have a written plan describing future growth and how that growth will be achieved based on the areas listed above, as well as any other catalysts for future growth unique to your business. It is that growth plan, properly communicated, that will attract buyers. If you're not a short-timer; meaning that you and your business have a few years or more before an expected sale, it is worthwhile to create more than a growth plan: consider creating a strategic business plan.

Again, I asked Paula Cope, an experienced business consultant, to comment here about strategic business plans. She graciously provided the following comments.

Growth plans come from strategic plans, which form the foundation of a solid business. They provide the road map for growth and sustainability.

A strategic plan is based on data usually gleaned from your customers, ven-dors, trade journals and other data you collect. Strategic plans, when done right, align an organization's vision (fuzzy yet compelling future), mission (the reason your business exists), values (your guiding principles) and goals (wishes with deadlines). They lay out the strategies and action steps a busi-ness must take to achieve those goals, and tie those steps to the budget.

The Organizational Clock Model (see at right) depicts the notion that building a high-performing and self-sustaining organization means not being dependent on one person (typically the founder) for long-term success.

An organization is an array of interconnected elements. One way to think of these interconnected elements is in terms of process, people and strategy. Strong strategy supports the right people who accomplish work with good processes. Overall business value links processes, people and strategies. These three areas can be separated to examine each facet, but are inextricably linked in actual execution. They are easy identifiers for figuring out where you need to focus to build organizational value.

The detail behind process, people and strategy are like the different parts of a clock. Foundational elements create the organizational base that remains steady. Strategies are firm enough to drive forward, yet flexible enough to be able to change when necessary to stay competitive. These are like the works behind the clock face. Enabling elements are either people or processes that link the foundation to the overall organization. If enabling

ORGANIZATIONAL CLOCK MODEL

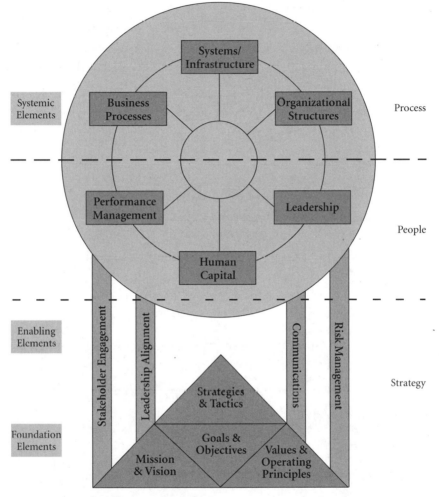

The authors of the Cope Clock Model for a Systems Approach to Succession Planning & Management are: Paula Cope, MEd., William Hancy, MSOD; and Mary Vargas, MBA. Cope & Associates, Inc. 2007. Our influences were: Marvin Weisbord's "Six Box Model" and Jim Collins, author of "Good to Great."

elements work smoothly, the organization can concentrate on real work, rather than on time-consuming distractions like bottlenecks in production due to a lack of communication or dissatisfied customers due to a lack of focus on stakeholder priorities or dependencies. These are like the weights of a grandfather clock that keep accurate time. Systemic elements are all

the moving parts of the organization, like the face of the clock, that accom-
plish the work of the company. Systems that support process and people are
dynamic and interconnected. For example, does organizational structure
reflect core process or is it the result of 30 years of the organization grow-
ing up around its original members? Are the right technology systems and
infrastructure in place to support the organization's core business? Do per-
formance management systems reflect and support business process and
how people produce work? By considering foundation, enabling, and sys-
temic elements as a whole, you develop organizational capacity throughout
the organization and not only in a localized leader or team.

Most business owners have difficulty developing comprehensive strategic plans that really drive business and align all of the essential elements. They confuse strategic plans with marketing plans or take the time to write a great plan without knowing how to get it off the paper and into action. This is a great opportunity to draw upon the expertise of a management consultant. The key actions owners must take to develop a strategic plan include:

1. Collect data: including industry projections, financial performance, customer data, employee satisfaction, sociological, technological and economic development data.

2. Develop vision.

3. Affirm mission.

4. Articulate corporate values.

5. Develop goals and objectives.

6. Draft an inventory of strategies.

7. Prioritize the strategies.

8. Develop action plans for each strategy naming an "owner" for each action and tying each plan to resource allocations and budgets.

9. Develop a set of measures to monitor progress.

Any opportunity you have to include your management team and employees in developing any part of this written plan will pay large returns. With proper planning, most owners can choose when they want to sell and then sell when business value is sufficient to allow them to do all the things they want to do after they sell.

EFFECTIVE AND DOCUMENTED FINANCIAL CONTROLS

Another key Value Driver is the existence of reliable financial controls that you use to manage the business. Documented financial controls are not only a critical element of business management, but they also safeguard a company's assets. Most importantly, however, effective financial controls verify (for the buyer) the financial condition of your company.

During the sale process, the buyer will conduct an extraordinarily detailed examination of your company's finances known as financial due diligence. If the buyer's auditors are not *completely* comfortable when reviewing your company's past financial performance, there will be *no deal* (or, at best, a lowball offer).

Remember that buyer who wanted your business facility to look like the million dollars he's paying for it? He's the same buyer who is purchasing a company he probably had not heard of three weeks before. The owner of that business tells him that the company has been making $5 million per year for the past three years and expects it to make even more in the future. Are you really surprised that the buyer's first thought is, "Prove it!"? If a seller then produces financial information that proves incorrect, insupportable or incomplete, the buyer will be highly skeptical or, more likely, simply gone. You would never pay millions of dollars without complete confidence in the company's financial information. Should your buyer?

The best way to document that the company (1) has effective financial controls and (2) its historical financial statements are correct is through a certified audit by an established CPA firm.

Business owners universally perceive financial audits to be an unnecessary expense, or, at best, a necessity required by their banks. In reality, an audit is an investment in the value and the marketability of your business. *The lack of financial integrity is one of the most common hurdles encountered during the sale process.* In addition, the best way to demonstrate the sustainability of your company's earnings is to have its historical financial statements audited by an independent, certified public accounting firm. An audit demonstrates to potential buyers that the historical information can be relied upon when making judgments about buying the company based on historical cash flows.

Given that audited financial statements will be necessary, when should you begin compiling them? You can probably wait until you have begun the sale process described in Chapters 9 and 10.

It is very important to have your CPA review your current financial statements *and practices* so that any financial irregularities or inadequacies are immediately exposed and corrected.

One common "irregularity" is the shifting of income. Everyone, buyer included, understands that for the years prior to the sale, owners will naturally handle the company's finances from a perspective of minimizing tax consequences. This is good tax planning and is anticipated by the sophisticated buyer—the kind with whom you are likely to deal.

Unfortunately, some owners go one step too far in an effort to reduce tax consequences. They shift income from one year to the next and shift expenses from one year to the next—neither the expense nor income shifts relating to each other, or to the actual services or manufacturing activities that give rise to the income or expense item. Hopeless confusion, inconsistency and a sea of uncertainty are created.

Or, the business performs services for the owner at a considerable, but unrecorded expense that goes beyond normal and proper tax schemes—a game many owners play. For example, a construction company builds a vacation home for its owner or a service type company buys and maintains an owner's racecar and passes off the costs as marketing. (In the interest of full disclosure, I do have to admit that using my race car as a marketing expense did work for me for several years!)

Other owners improperly report inventory or lack sufficient inventory controls. (For an example, see fictional owner Vince Diamond in the Appendix.)

If you recognize yourself as an owner who has been overly aggressive in shifting income and expenses, (or, more likely, have given the financial controls insufficient attention over the years) it is of fundamental importance to the entire sale process that your past aggressiveness be diligently reviewed and corrected where appropriate.

FINANCIAL GROWTH: CASH FLOW, PROFITABILITY, REVENUE AND SALES

Ultimately, all Value Drivers contribute to stable and increasing cash flow. It is cash flow that determines what a buyer will offer to pay. Buyers buy cash flow—and they pay top dollar for cash flow that they expect to increase after they buy the company. Think like a buyer for a moment. Which earnings chart looks better?

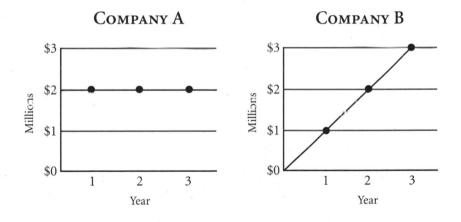

Notice that the total cash flow for each company is the same, $6 million over three years. Yet company B has a better story to tell because its immediate past and present cash flow has improved and continues to improve.

It is important, especially in the year or so preceding the sale of the business that cash flow be substantial and on an upswing. The buyer also will look for earnings of the company to continue to increase through the sale process itself (which can take a year or more). Perhaps I've just stated the obvious to you. In any case, the critical question is: How do you go about increasing *your* company's cash flow?

GROWTH THROUGH ACQUISITION

Prudent growth through acquisition is one of the best ways we know of to increase cash flow. Assuming that you choose your acquisition candidate carefully, acquiring another company not only can increase cash flow, revenue and profits, it can also:

- Give your company a healthy shot of intrinsic value in the form of:
  - A more diversified customer base;
  - Independence from reliance on your existing market sector;
  - Presence in an attractive business sector; and/or
  - New protected proprietary technology.

- Elevate your company into a range of value that:
  - Attracts more and better qualified buyers; and
  - Improves the multiple sellers will pay.

- Rejuvenate yourself—and your employees—as all of you earn more, learn more, and manage a more complex operation.

- Give you invaluable experience as a buyer before your big (and final) debut as a seller. In growing through acquisition, you will experience all of the following critical aspects of the sale process:
  - You will look for a target acquisition with intrinsic value that complements your own;
  - You may use the services of a trained transaction intermediary giving them the opportunity to audition for the role as the transaction intermediary who handles your eventual sale;
  - You will be the one asking for and examining documents in the due diligence process; and
  - You will gain a gut-level appreciation for the fact that, for a deal to succeed, both parties must gain.

Just as there is no one better to tell you about life after the sale than those who are living it, so too, the best way to describe the growth through acquisition strategy is in the words of an owner who has done (and is doing) it. Meet Kevin's client, Harry Mueller.

Harry Mueller is the 56-year-old co-owner of Delta Group Electronics, Inc., (DGE) a high-mix, low volume electronics manufacturing services provider. (Harry's brother-in-law is the other owner.) In 1987, Harry's involvement in the Albuquerque company was as an investor while his childhood friend, Steve Klein, ran the company. "For five years," Harry recalls, "we struggled like any other start-up business."

In 1996, DGE made its first acquisition, Quality Components, Inc. in Florida. "Our purpose in that purchase was to establish a Southeast Division," Harry explains. Shortly after (1997-1998), DGE began to experience huge growth. "We had a relationship with Cymer, Inc. in California," Harry recalls, "and when they took off, so did we. We broke into Inc. 500's list of the Fastest Growing Companies in America."

In 1999, Harry left his job in banking to split management duties at DGE with Steve. "Steve handled the day-to-day side of things, and I handled the corporate side—legal, accounting, human resources and banking relationships," Harry explains.

Harry and Steve continued to acquire companies. "In 2000, we purchased Northstar Electronics in San Diego so we'd have a presence in the West," Harry recalls. "In 2001, we made another Florida purchase so we could strengthen our presence in the Southeast."

Having made these acquisitions, DGE dug in for the 2001-2003 downturn in the business cycle. Those years were difficult in more ways than one. In 2002, Steve died of cancer and Harry was left holding the reins. "We didn't make a whole lot in those years but we did learn important lessons," says Harry. "In 2001, we did about $5 million worth of business with Cymer. In 2003, that business was only worth $1 million." In addition to a wider geographic presence, DGE needed a more diverse customer base.

Diversification became Harry's goal. "I saw how the fortunes of one customer affected us and I decided to limit the ability of any one customer to hurt us." Harry went further and decided to expand the number of industries DGE served. "I didn't want a downturn in any one industry to hit us with any more than a glancing blow."

With those goals in mind, Harry spearheaded the acquisition of another San Diego company in 2005, a Dallas company in 2006 and another Florida company in 2007. With each of these purchases, DGE acquired more customers in a wider variety of industries.

Obviously, Harry's acquisitions satisfied his diversification goals, but did they improve profitability, revenues and cash flow? In 2001, DGE had annual revenues between $17 million and $20 million. For 2006, those numbers were in the $48 million to $49 million range.

"My goal has never been to reach a certain dollar amount," explains Harry. *"In our Mission Statement's first phrase, 'To be a growing, profitable electronic manufacturing services company,' we talk about growth and profitability. I love growing something. It is fun for me and great for my employees. It infuses us all with a new level of excitement."*

As for profitability, Harry explains, "We must make money. Growth without profitability makes no sense."

Making Acquisitions. Any owner considering a growth through acquisition strategy should consider the following guidelines:

1. **Start small.** Your current cash flow must finance all or most of the acquisition, so don't bite off more than you can chew.

2. **Be picky.** Given all the Boomers looking to get out of their companies, choose a company with a strong management team. You want to improve your bottom line, not spend more hours at work. Also, make sure the acquisition is a good fit, both financially and personally. As Harry explains, "I look for a company with similar values and mission. Honesty and integrity are hugely important to me. Even if all my other requirements for the acquisition are met, if the two cultures don't sync, the deal won't be successful."

3. **Don't pay too much.** If you are willing to pay cash to a seller who has few options, (his management team can't or won't buy him out, his family members aren't interested and his company is too small to attract the attention of the big boys) you shouldn't have

to offer a premium. We recommend that, like Harry, you work with an investment banker who knows your industry to make sure that you are paying only as much as you should. We also recommend that you use the negotiated sale process instead of the controlled auction process. While you want to use the latter to sell your company for the highest price; when buying, you don't want to compete against other buyers.

Finding Acquisition Candidates. There are several ways to identify appropriate target acquisitions. First, you know your industry better than anyone else. Attending your trade association meetings is a great way to start looking for candidates. The second way is to retain a transaction intermediary to both identify targets and to negotiate the purchase. We return to Kevin's client, Harry Mueller.

"Kevin's firm, Clayton Capital Partners, uses my target criteria to identify potential acquisitions. It then approaches the target using my company's name and lets it know that we are interested in a purchase," explains Harry. Both Kevin and Harry reiterate that using DGE's name when approaching a candidate for acquisition is hugely important. *"Unlike the unsolicited calls owners constantly receive mentioning 'an interested buyer,'"* says Kevin, *"my firm always identifies DGE as the interested buyer. Doing so gives our inquiry credibility and gives the target a chance to check out DGE."*

"Clayton Capital Partners stays active through the Letter of Intent stage," says Harry, *"but I conduct the negotiations and the due diligence. In the acquisitions we've done, I'm a hands-on guy."* Harry's strong financial background and experience in acquisitions allows him to take on these roles that Kevin plays for most other owners.

REINVIGORATE YOURSELF

Pay greater attention to increasing cash flow through operating the business more efficiently. Sit down for 30 minutes and think about all of the ways your company can improve its cash flow. Concentrate on the methods that you've declined to pursue because you and the company are comfortable with "the way things are." Your business is probably operating at less than peak efficiency simply because you are thinking of selling it. Owners who have decided to sell tend to exhibit less enthusiasm for the company, for going to work each day, and for giving it their best. If you are not giving the business your personal best, the performance of the business suffers. You cannot allow this to happen if you wish to get top dollar for your company. Realizing this and acting upon it is vital.

HIRE A MANAGEMENT CONSULTANT

If you simply lack the drive or the skill to move the business forward, hire a management consultant. One of my clients decided to sell his business because he felt he just couldn't move it forward any longer. Revenues were barely keeping pace with inflation, EBITDA was stagnant at about $2 million per year, and the industry was outperforming his company. While he certainly was tired, he did not want to exit with a whimper. It was evident that there was a lot of opportunity for growth and greater value and that this owner truly loved his company. The suggestion, to simply "reinvigorate yourself," however, was worthless. Instead, we hired a consultant.

Lest you think I sound like a typical consultant (you know, someone who takes the watch off your wrist and tells you the time) trying to convince you to hire one, let me reveal a dark secret of my company: we hired a consultant when BEI was less than a year old (and at a time when the consultant's monthly retainer exceeded 10 percent of our gross revenues!). We continue to this day to retain him. His initiative and experience (which I lacked) have helped BEI move forward at a vigorous, yet controlled pace.

Of course, your financial situation is vastly different and for you, a consultant is much more affordable, but no less valuable. The consultant's primary task will be to quantify the Value Drivers discussed in this chapter, prioritize them, develop action plans to achieve each Value Driver bench mark and then measure progress. Review Paula Cope's discussion earlier in this chapter. If you don't take the recommended actions, hire someone who will.

Additional suggestions on what must be done to increase your company's cash flow include:

- If you have become a semi-absentee owner, spend more time at the office. You, better so than anyone else, will discover many ways to increase productivity, decrease costs and increase cash flow.

- If you are still working *in* the business, step back. Remember, your goal is to leave your business by selling it. If your work is still indispensable, you won't be able to leave.

- Implement procedures to increase cash flow. These may include tightening the reins on the accounts receivable department or perhaps changing the method and timing in which you handle payables. Do you have the best people possible in charge of these areas? Have you provided them the economic incentive to maximize cash flow for the business?

- Stop using the business as your personal pocketbook (if applicable). Many owners seize the opportunity to use the business to pay for all kinds of hidden perks. I will never forget the business in the middle of the Mojave Desert that listed, as its largest asset, a yacht. Since the business was a motorcycle shop, it was clear that the owner had used the business, in a large part, to maintain his lifestyle. All kinds of money, employee time and effort went into maintaining a yacht that served no business purpose whatsoever. These are the types of expenses that are difficult to recast because they are not actual out-of-pocket expenses, but are "soft costs" (using employees or materials owned by the business for personal benefit). These activities depress and deplete cash flow and simply cannot be factored back into the sale price via recasting earnings.

- List the ways you benefit financially from the company. This list will help your investment banker "recast" the cash flow to account for cash diverted to you that would be available to a purchaser, thereby increasing the purchase price. Your list should include excessive compensation for you, family members, close friends and relatives. It may also include: cars, vacations, recreational vehicles, or excessive rental payments for a building or equipment you rent to the company.

- Don't play games with the balance sheet, particularly in inventory and accounts receivable.

- Carefully scrutinize employee benefits, including discretionary compensation items, such as bonuses and qualified retirement plans. Look for opportunities to provide "free benefits" such as casual days, free guest speakers on hot topics, or time off to reward increases in sales, decreased expenses, or improvements in safety.

- Avoid unnecessary capital expenditures immediately prior to the anticipated sale date. We recently sold a capital intensive, manufacturing company whose owner was an "equipment junkie," always buying the latest and best machinery. During the sale process, we recommended that the owner stop making all non-essential equipment purchases. The company deferred the purchase and payment of approximately $300,000 in machinery—machinery that would have required significant time and money to install and yet additional time to train personnel in its use. As a result of deferring this outlay of time and money, the company's bottom line and cash flow increased, and since the business was sold primarily on a multiple of cash flow basis, the purchase price increased by over $1 million.

ATTRACTIVE BUSINESS SECTOR

"Owning a company in a business sector that the market considers 'hot' certainly never hurts value," says Kevin Short. "The problem is predicting what will be hot when you are ready to sell." Generally, companies that enjoy healthy growth expectations due to forecasted changes in the economy attract buyers. "Infrastructure, such as road building or bridge building are currently in vogue," Kevin explains. "Immunity from foreign competition used to be a plus for companies," Kevin says. "But as the cost of outsourcing has fallen dramatically, that benefit has disappeared." At the risk of boring you with repetition, the only way to find out what buyers are looking for is to talk to someone who knows: your investment banker.

PROTECTED PROPRIETARY TECHNOLOGY

To illustrate how control of proprietary technology can make the value of a business far greater than the capitalization of historical earnings would indicate, let's look at the case of Will Rogers.

Will owned a small systems engineering firm that designed and installed cellular networks. Like many small service businesses, Will's company had a sporadic earnings history. The most recent three years' profit and cash flow had been declining and Will had been told by his CPA that the business did not have much value.

On the surface, I would have agreed with Will's CPA. When I probed further, however, and asked why the company had lost money in the past three years, I learned that Will had been investing heavily in the research and development of a new switching device. This device could revolutionize cellular and wireless switching networks technology and was particularly applicable in the development of wireless networks, which were just beginning to emerge. Through further inquiry, I learned that this technology was patentable and that Will was certain that it would greatly enhance the services his company could provide. Supporting Will's assertion was a multi-million dollar contract from an international wireless communication company.

To capitalize on the significant potential for the device, Will had to greatly increase the size of the company and invest at least $1 million into the company. Will's recent heart attack convinced him that life was too short to purse this strategy and that he wanted to sell the business. He recognized that the switching device technology would be attractive to larger companies in his industry. In fact, Will had been approached by a major competitor interested in buying his business.

Buyers were more interested in Will's company's protected, proprietary technology for its potential to significantly increase the value of their other, compatible products than they were in the "stand alone" value of the technology. The fact that Will's company had little or no positive cash flow was unimportant. Companies like Will's often sell to buyers who can use the technology to increase the value of their own products and technologies.

CONCLUSION

To review, the Value Drivers that drive up the value of your company are:

- Stable, Motivated Management And A High-Performing Workforce

- Systems That Sustain The Growth Of The Business

- Established And Diversified Customer Base

- Appearance Of Facility Consistent With Asking Price

- Realistic Growth Strategy

- Effective And Documented Financial Controls

- Financial Growth: Cash Flow, Profitability, Revenue and Sales

- Attractive Business Sector

- Protected Proprietary Technology

Getting a premium price for the sale of a business depends, in large part, upon your efforts to adopt and implement the Value Driver techniques described in this chapter. Concentrating on developing and enhancing each Value Driver will position you to get a premium price for your business.

Section Three

Understanding Extrinsic Value

Picture a dance contest, something akin to the television show "Dancing With the Stars." To win, each dance partner must execute each step perfectly, but also in complete sync with the other partner. Likewise, to maximize and exceed your sale goals, there are two dance partners: your business must be at its peak effectiveness, maximum cash flow and profitability, *and* the Merger and Acquisition sales cycle must be near or at its peak. If either partner is weak, the contest is lost.

To get top dollar, you must sell when you and your company are both prepared to sell. You might make more money selling a business whose value hasn't been maximized if the Merger & Acquisition market is at its peak. Similarly, you might not be able to sell a good business at all if the M&A marketplace contains few or no buyers.

Your ability to cash out and move on requires you to understand the cyclical nature of the M&A world and to be prepared to sell when the market is hot. You must know how the market views *your company*, *today*, in *your industry* and *your geographic region*. Then you can decide if it is your time to cash out and move on.

THE MERGER & ACQUISITION CYCLE
WHEN SELLING YOUR BUSINESS TIMING IS EVERYTHING AND THE TIME IS NOW

KEVIN M. SHORT
MANAGING DIRECTOR, CLAYTON CAPITAL PARTNERS

As I've explained in the previous chapters, exiting your company is best accomplished when: 1) your personal Exit Objectives can be met by the cash that a sale will yield, 2) your company is well-positioned to sell (it possesses the characteristics buyers look for), 3) you've located skilled advisors to navigate the exit process, and 4) the Merger and Acquisition market is in a favorable phase. I have asked investment banker, Kevin Short, to explain how that last variable—the state of the M&A market—affects every business seller.

—John Brown

CHAPTER HIGHLIGHTS

- What You Can Do About Timing Your Sale
  Wait And Watch
  Move Quickly

- Non-Market Variables
  Your Personal Situation
  The Health Of Your Company
  Skilled Advisors

O   The M&A Market Climate
    Positive Market Influences
    Negative Market Influences
    More Unpredictable Influences
    Fluctuations In The M&A Cycle

THE COST OF SELLING AT
THE BOTTOM OF THE M&A CYCLE

I first met Geraldo Limon in 2002. He was not a happy man. He arrived in my office one week after his doctor had blind-sided him with an ultimatum that he had not expected, "Get rid of that company or get your affairs in order. The stress is killing you." Geraldo had seen his doctor after experiencing chest pains. Subsequent tests revealed that Geraldo's heart had aged much faster than he had.

Geraldo had planned to sell his company in 2007, at age 50. When I met with him, Geraldo was only 45, his company was growing and he was definitely not ready to retire. Geraldo's wife, however, sided with the doctor. Because his "retirement" was to come sooner than expected, Geraldo needed every dime from his company.

Geraldo's company had an EBITDA of $5 million, a great management team and a growing customer list. Unfortunately, his timing could hardly have been worse. In 2002, companies in his industry (like most others) could only command an EBITDA multiple of 3.0 or so, and there just were not many buyers in the market.

We did sell Geraldo's company for the multiple we had expected and Geraldo happily left the closing table with $12 million, after taxes.

Early in 2007, I ran into Geraldo again. This time, we were in a social setting and he quizzed me about current market conditions and multiples. When I told him that companies like his were selling at multiples in the 7.0 range, Geraldo quickly did the math and had to sit down. Selling at the low point in the M&A market cycle had cost the-now-very-unhappy-Geraldo $16 million. Luckily, Geraldo's heart condition had improved enough to endure the stress of hearing the news.

W e often hear the adage that, in business, timing is everything. Does this adage apply to selling your company? At the risk of sounding like a lawyer, I answer, "Yes and no."

If you've read this book, chapter-by-chapter, you realize by now that there's a little bit more to selling your company than timing. Multiple variables (your personal timetable, the existence of a skilled management team, steadily increasing profits and a team of experienced advisors come to mind) not only take time to develop, but must be in sync in order to complete a successful transfer. Not only must they be in sync with each other, they must coalesce when the Merger & Acquisition (M&A) market is favorable.

Even if you are ready to leave your business, (one loaded with Value Drivers and poised for growth) you should know that the state of the M&A market will determine how much cash will change hands. The state of that market can, in some situations, determine if your company is marketable at all.

Just as the M&A market moves through cycles, so does M&A activity in your specific industry and geographic area. As we write this book in the Fall of 2007, pundits herald the end of the M&A boom. While the mega-deal market that they refer to and mid-sized deal market where we work are often in sync, you need to verify that with an investment banker who can evaluate the M&A activity and pricing *in your regional or metropolitan area and in your industry.* To learn more about M&A activity in your industry and area, please visit our Web site www.BEIBooks.com.

If the mid-sized M&A market does falter due to threats posed by buyer uncertainty, the sub-prime mortgage scandal, and weakness in the mega-deal M&A market, what can owners in the mid-sized market expect? First, the bad news: multiples will drop. Multiples always drop when buyers perceive their risk as increasing. All-cash deals may disappear as buyers (feeling uncertain) demand more earn-outs and promissory notes from sellers. The vultures that seek to take advantage of difficult times will take to the skies looking for the weak and the desperate.

There is good news, however. First, companies with strong Value Drivers in place rise to the top like cream on milk. If any company is going to sell, it will be one of those. Second, we've never gone through a down cycle with Private Equity Groups holding extraordinary amounts of cash: cash they must invest. There's no reason to think that PEGs won't continue to purchase the companies that fit their strategic plans.

As we Boomers become increasingly anxious to move on with the rest of our lives, we have to ask ourselves if we are willing to remain as owners for another five years in what may be difficult business conditions. The M&A market waits for no owner. Future market conditions may be more favorable or less so. Waiting to sell involves risk: you may reap a bigger windfall or you may not. There is nothing wrong with taking risk: as owners we do it every day. Just make sure that the risk you take is an informed, calculated one.

WHAT YOU CAN DO ABOUT TIMING YOUR SALE

First, understand that there is a Merger & Acquisition cycle and that, historically, the time between peaks of this cycle is about five years. Second, you need to understand where in the cycle your company is today. Third, waiting is not a passive activity.

As we have discussed, the M&A market tends to mirror general economic activity. If you try to delay your sale in order to make the most money at the very peak of the cycle, should you miss that peak, you will have to wait about five years. As you calculate how much the loss of value will "cost" you, (the drop in company value simply due to market conditions) remember to factor in the profits you will earn during those "waiting" years. The chart on page 43 illustrates, from a value perspective, the cyclical nature of the M&A market.

When faced with a less than favorable M&A market, what can an owner do?

WAIT AND WATCH

First, engage in the Exit Planning that John describes in this book. Concentrate on creating "intrinsic value." Establish your personal exit goals, and create a company that is ready for sale (install as many Value Drivers as possible into your company and focus on profitability). As you do all this, you'll find that ownership becomes more enjoyable and the wait can be more pleasant. Also, start trying out some post-retirement activities. Wise sellers ride the tide until the end of the difficult part of the cycle, raising their own profits and boosting their balance sheets.

Historically, the time period between peaks is about five years and peaks—or plateaus—last longer than a few months. (Remember the peak of 1999, 2000 and the first three quarters of 2001?) Boomers attempting to predict how long a current trough or plateau may last, or how long they'll have to wait until the next peak, would do well to consult an investment banker with experience watching the cycle.

Second, learn to recognize the middle years of the M&A cycle. Watch for banks to make capital more available, look for corporate profits to go up and you'll soon see that strategic acquisitions are the name of the game.

> Time your sale to occur before the end of the favorable portion of the cycle. Once the market starts to turn, deals become harder to initiate as nuggets of economic bad news begin to hit the airwaves.

Finally, this period of waiting should be quite active. In addition to working with your advisors to install and enhance the Value Drivers described in Chapters 6 and 7, we encourage owners to initiate pre-sale due diligence. In this process, your attorney will review all of the documents that your eventual buyer will review. Your transaction intermediary will review all of your financial records, visit your facilities and (if appropriate) talk to some of your employees. To view a sample Pre-Sale Due Diligence Checklist, please visit our Web site: www.BEIBooks.com.

Briefly, the purposes of this legal and financial pre-sale due diligence are:

1. Provides you the opportunity to clean up your company's records well before a buyer's professional advisors go through them with a fine-tooth comb. (For a true story of how squeaky-clean records speed the sale process, see Harold Bade's story in Chapter 12.)

2. Gives your advisors the opportunity to identify and to correct and issues that could delay or block an eventual sale. It is critical that

you be candid with your advisors and remove all the skeletons from the closet. It is far better to evaluate the impact of these skeletons *before* the buyer discovers them.

3.   Increases the value of your company. Up-to-date financial and legal records demonstrate to a buyer that you run a clean ship. This helps increase the buyer's confidence about the future success of the company and reduce the perception of risk. You will recall that the buyer's perception of risk is one of the key elements in negotiating a sale price.

MOVE QUICKLY

No matter how many indicators we watch, we can never predict with certainty the course of the economy. Without a crystal ball, we certainly cannot predict terrorist attacks or corporate scandals. So how can you neutralize these uncertainties when selling your business?

Your best weapon is speed.

You might not be able to predict what the market will do, but you should be able to recognize when your personal situation is right and both your company and the market are strong. Once those two factors align, you must move with all possible speed to enter the market and close the deal.

Owners committed to "speed" favor the controlled auction process over a negotiated sale (see Chapter 9) because they can exercise more control to keep the process moving forward. They discriminate among potential buyers based on the speed with which a buyer can complete a deal (the fewer financial contingencies the better, for example). Finally, they use an experienced Deal Team—especially an investment banker who can negotiate land mines, ever-present in every deal, quickly and efficiently.

If the market is favorable, it will not remain so forever. It can change overnight, but usually moves take months. Closing quickly helps minimize the potential for closing after the market has entered a trough. If the market is less than ideal, closing quickly puts more money in your pocket faster.

Dave and Linda Visger (see Chapter 12) were able to close on the sale of their company in only 30 days. This was only possible because their planning advisors had deal experience and their business was prepared for sale (both key elements of intrinsic value).

NON-MARKET VARIABLES

As a business owner, you are quite capable of assessing the non-market variables that affect your decision to sell. These include: 1) your personal situation, 2) the general health of your business, and 3) the skill of your advisors. In fact, you are likely able to determine (or at least sense) whether the business climate is favorable or unfavorable for business sales. Therefore, the purpose of the remainder of this chapter is three-fold:

- To demonstrate how the health of the M&A market directly affects the number of dollars you put in your pocket;

- To highlight the issues that cause a shift—positive or negative—in the M&A market; and

- To describe what you can do if you find yourself poised to sell but the market is less than favorable.

Armed with that information, your job is to decide whether you can meet your financial goals if you sell during the current business climate. We suggest you use an investment banker to research the current business climate, and help you to determine what your company is worth today (considering your industry and your geographical location). His or her job is to evaluate these issues and determine how they affect your timing when entering the M&A marketplace. (I encourage you to re-read the story of Geraldo Limon earlier in this chapter.)

YOUR PERSONAL SITUATION

Are you ready to retire? Have you found something else you'd like to do? Idle retirement appeals to few hard driving entrepreneurs who have successfully grown their own businesses.

Are you physically and mentally prepared to endure and to consummate the transaction? Studies indicate that younger owners are far more likely than older owners (age 70-plus) to complete a sale. Older owners, especially those who have not invested in a quality Exit Plan, do not sell. Some are "addicted" to the business and are simply unable to let go. Others fall ill before the transfer can close, and the company suffers as much as the owner.

It bears repeating that *you must be emotionally prepared to proceed* with the sale of your business when the M&A market climate is positive. Likewise, during market downtimes, you must be emotionally committed to continuing ownership, unless, of course you can sell your business (during a market trough) and still attain your objectives.

THE HEALTH OF YOUR COMPANY

A company is most attractive to buyers when it has at least one to two years of good performance. Buyers use past performance to predict future performance and the multiple they pay reflects the risk that they'll be able to match or improve that performance. (High risk equals low multiple and low risk equals a higher multiple.) If your company has experienced recent performance hiccups, this may not be the best time to put it on the market. You want to put your company on the market when you can persuasively argue that the company's performance can be expected to continue.

Finally, you want your company to be ready for sale when *you* are ready to sell it. To ready your company, review the Decision Checklist (at the beginning of this book) and begin the pre-sale due diligence process. You must do both well in advance of any sale so that you (and your advisors) have time to discover any skeletons in the closet and take corrective action.

SKILLED ADVISORS

John is a strong advocate of owners using skilled advisors to navigate the Exit Planning Process successfully. He's created a business that trains advisors to do exactly that. Investment bankers are in the trenches with owners on a daily basis. We work with those who tried to do it alone and those who have a team of skilled professionals working for them. We know what value skilled advisors can add to the owner's bottom line.

If your plan is to sell when the M&A market is on the upswing, you can't be exactly sure when that will be. Just as it is important to have your other non-market variables ready (your company poised to sell and yourself prepared emotionally for a sale) you must select, at least on a preliminary basis, those advisors who will help you throughout the entire sale process. This is especially true of your Planning Advisors, as even under optimal circumstances there is ordinarily much work to be done to ready a business for sale.

· Let's look now at those issues that can trigger marketplace climate change.

THE M&A MARKET CLIMATE

First, let's define what a "good" M&A climate includes. From the seller's perspective, in a good market, we see vigorous buyer activity, low interest rates, low capital gains rates and high prices. A lot of buyers with deep pockets are chasing a limited number of companies. To sellers, a good climate translates into higher value and greater marketability to more interested buyers and more favorable deal terms.

Conversely, a "bad" M&A market or climate, from the seller's perspective, is one in which there are few buyers picking and choosing among a lot of companies. To a seller, an unfavorable market means, in the best case, less value, more tax at closing, and less cash (as a percentage of the purchase price) paid at closing. In many cases, however, it means no sale at all. Just ask some of the dot-com survivors of the late 1990s.

Forecasting the M&A market is much like forecasting any economic trend or predicting where the stock market is going to be in six or twelve months. Realistically, you just can't do it with any degree of certainty.

As you read the balance of this chapter, keep in mind that there is one critically important action or decision that you can take. That is: ask your investment banker to periodically reassess the market for your business. Use those periodic reports to plot a marketability and valuation trend for your business. This way, you will know when it is time to go to market.

The health of the M&A market has a significant impact on your future financial health. Let's look at the key market influences that trigger either a market slump or a market rebound. These are the issues you and your investment banker will be watching as you determine the best time to put your company on the market.

POSITIVE MARKET INFLUENCES

Underlying Economic Strength.   When market fundamentals are strong, the M&A market tends to flourish. When we evaluate economic strength, we look at several key indicators. These include:

- Gross Domestic Product. By measuring the country's total output of goods and services, the GDP is the most general barometer of the economy's health. When GDP grows, the economy tends to follow suit.

- Job Growth. If the job market is expanding, consumers tend to feel confident and spend discretionary income.

- Consumer Confidence. High consumer confidence is an indication of a strong market. The Conference Board measures consumer confidence on a monthly basis.

- Retail Sales. Weekly and monthly retail sales figures provide another way to evaluate consumer confidence. When consumers feel the economy is strong, they spend more money. Consumer spending in turn helps the economy grow and stay strong.

- Manufacturing Data. The Institute for Supply Management compiles manufacturing data from more than 400 companies. An index reading of about 50 percent indicates that the manufacturing economy is expanding.

- Construction and new home sales. High levels of new home construction frequently accompany a strong economy.

Company Profitability. Strong and consistent profitability across a spectrum of companies creates confidence in the marketplace. Confidence helps keep the stock market stable.

Positive Public Relations. Investors are affected by what they see and hear in the media about the general economy. When the news is generally optimistic, it bolsters consumer and investor confidence and drives spending and investment.

Low Interest Rates. Low interest rates in 2005, 2006 and into 2007 drove consumer spending to help the economy. Low rates also make it easier for investors to finance acquisitions and expansions. Buyers generally consider rates to be low when they are able to finance the deal within the current multiples. Obviously, rates in the 2 percent to 5 percent range are low. Once rates reach about 8 percent to 8.5 percent, buyers begin to feel the strain.

Big Business Credibility. As we saw with the Enron debacle, scandal affects not only other companies, but the economy as well. When business misdeeds become headline news, consumer confidence diminishes and the subsequent enhanced regulations can stifle economic conditions. This problem is exacerbated if banks are involved in scandals. As we write, the sub-prime mortgage loan "scandal" has the potential to affect the M&A market for mid-sized companies ($10 million to $150 million). High levels of bank credibility may not single-handedly cause growth and prosperity, but the absence of it can trigger economic slowdowns and poor market conditions.

Well-Funded Private Equity Groups (PEGs). In a prosperous economy, people invest in traditional securities as well as in PEGs. These PEGs must provide those investors with a good return and do so by purchasing small to mid-sized companies. The presence of active, well-financed PEGs indicates a strong Merger and Acquisition market.

Low Capital Gains Rate. Sellers often assume that low capital gains rates are better for them than high rates. They reason that low rates allow them to sell their companies for more money (because buyers can borrow more) and they then put bigger checks in their pockets. True, but let's look at how higher rates also may work in the seller's favor. When rates are high, many sellers back out of the market. They do so because as interest rates climb, prices fall and owners decide that the prices they'll be able to command are simply too low to support their retirement objectives. (These sellers should, however, weigh the lower prices against the higher returns they'll earn on their invested proceeds.)

The few sellers who do not pull out typically own the most solid and profitable companies. Buyers have fewer choices and compete fiercely for the handful of companies on the market. If your company has a strong balance sheet and a healthy outlook, high capital gains rates may benefit you in the long run.

Looking ahead, experts expect capital gains rates to remain low (barring any market catastrophes) until they are phased out on December 31, 2010. While some speculate that Congressional Democrats may raise rates to 30 or 40 percent, no one can be sure. It is entirely possible that the undeniable positive affect low rates have on the economy will persuade lawmakers to maintain (or at least, not drastically increase) current rates. Owners should watch activities in Washington, D.C. to anticipate how and when rates may change.

NEGATIVE MARKET INFLUENCES

The same law governs both gravity and the M&A market. What goes up must come down. As we've seen time and time again, neither boom nor bust lasts forever. The normal business cycle includes both ups and downs. Weak markets can stumble over a single boulder or a series of smaller obstacles. When markets are vulnerable (especially near the end of a boom) conditions can deteriorate within weeks and months.

Just as there are signs that the economy, and by extension, the M&A market, is healthy, so too are there indicators that the market is ailing. Let's look at those issues that can jeopardize a healthy market.

Underlying Economic Strength.   When market fundamentals are weak, the M&A market tends to falter. As we mentioned earlier, there are a number of elements to consider when we evaluate economic strength. Let's quickly review the major ones.

- Gross Domestic Product. When GDP slows, becomes stagnant or even shrinks, the economy tends to follow suit.

- Job Growth. Slowing job growth may be an indication of a looming economic slowdown.

- Consumer Confidence. Faltering consumer confidence, as measured by The Conference Board, indicates a weak market.

- Retail Sales. When weekly and monthly retail sales figures fall, consumers are spending less. Less spending often indicates a lack of consumer confidence. When consumers feel uneasy about the future, they spend less and the economy slows.

- Manufacturing Data. If the Institute for Supply Management index indicates that manufacturers are pulling back, this can be a sign of an economic slowdown.

Construction Activity And New Home Sales. When the construction and new home sales markets are stagnant, the economy, and the M&A market, may follow suit.

Rising Capital Gains Rates. When the capital gains tax rate rises, owners must sell their companies for more money (than they would have under lower tax rates) to meet their personal financial Exit Objectives. As we discussed earlier, however, rising rates do not harm all sellers. High rates weed out the weakest sellers, thus leaving buyers to compete (usually quite aggressively) for the few remaining sellers in the market.

Rising Interest Rates. When interest rates rise, borrowing becomes more expensive and buyers feel the pinch. They are much less willing to pay premium prices when the cost of doing so becomes prohibitive.

Private Equity Group Instability. PEGs have become major purchasers of small and mid-sized businesses. They often involve numerous investors and are bound by contracts and bylaws. A well-publicized violation of these bylaws or fraud on the part of a major PEG could wreak havoc on the entire M&A marketplace.

MORE UNPREDICTABLE INFLUENCES

While events of the magnitude of September 11, 2001 are hopefully few and far between, other events can damage national confidence and hurt the market. Terrorist attacks, wars, corporate or government scandals, and global instability undermine consumer confidence and can cause tremendous market uncertainty. When these events occur, governments often take steps to bring markets back into equilibrium.

Traumatic or Terrorist Events.   The events of September 11, 2001, provide a powerful example of how influences, not intrinsic to the market, can affect the M&A market. Companies that were worth $20 million on September 10, 2001, were suddenly worth only $5 million one day later. Why? To say that the business climate "changed" during those terrible days following the tragedy is a stunning understatement.

When the New York stock markets reopened after the longest closure since 1929, the Dow Jones Industrial Average (DJIA) fell 684 points (or lost 7.1 percent of its value) to 8920, its biggest-ever one-day point decline. By the end of the week, the DJIA had fallen 1369.7 points (14.3 percent), the largest one-week point drop in history. U.S. stocks lost $1.2 trillion in value in one week. Consumer confidence plummeted; and at the most basic level, people's trust in the world around them shattered. It took a full five years for the Merger and Acquisition climate to return to its former robust levels.

Boom Or Bust In One Sector Affects The Entire Market.

Remember the late 1990s? Investors were making money in many sectors. Stock prices rose sharply through the last part of the decade and peaked in 2000. At the peak of this business boom, the average multiple (in most industries) for a company less than $25 million in value was between 5.5 and 7. A multiple is the multiplier of EBITDA (earnings before interest, taxes, depreciation and amortization) used to estimate enterprise value. For example, if a company had an EBITDA of $1.5 million and a multiple of 6.0, the enterprise value was $9 million. Multiples in this range were artificially high due, in large part, to the dot-com frenzy at the time.

As a general rule of thumb, multiples today (early 2008) are between 4 and 6. In 2002, the multiple for the same-size companies was in the 2 to 3 range. The only people selling in that range were desperate. Everybody else toughed it out. An illustration of average debt multiples for the past 15 years is provided on the following page.

The speculation on Internet (or dot-com) companies is a dramatic example of how outside forces can affect the climate for selling a company. The early dot-coms were fueled by innovative new ideas based on the instantaneous mass communication power of the Internet. As these companies began to show promise, investors started taking notice. Stock prices of these dot-coms were based on, what we now know to be, unrealistic expectations. Initial Public Offerings (IPOs) were commonplace, as visions of huge profits danced in investors' heads.

Sadly, the "Get Big Fast" strategy that guided many of the early dot-com businesses was inherently flawed. Many dot-com entrepreneurs believed they could create massive brand awareness first, and worry about generating profits later.

How quickly did the bubble burst? A quick look at Super Bowl advertisements gives us a clue. In 2000, 17 dot-com companies each paid more than $2 million for a 30-second spot. Just one year later, only three dot-coms bought advertising.

While there were some survivors of the dot-com disaster (Amazon and eBay), the vast majority failed. Some of the more celebrated flops (according to CNET.com) included Webvan.com, Pets.com, Kozmo.com, eToys.com, Go.com and the United Kingdom's boo.com.

From a historical perspective, technology-based booms are nothing new. Railroads (in the 1840s), cars and radios (in the 1920s), and transistor electronics (in the 1950s) all precipitated market booms. Each advance caused market shakeouts, and affected market cycle behavior.

Today's buyers and sellers must take note of such events and put them into proper perspective. Doing so can be difficult when around-the-clock media coverage quickly transforms an accounting scandal (once confined to the business pages) into a full-blown drama. Both buyers and sellers must work hard to separate the truth from the hype. Your investment banker should have enough experience in the marketplace to provide some necessary perspective.

Changes In The Global Economy. Although we are discussing buying and selling businesses in the U.S. marketplace, the international economy plays an ever-increasing role in the overall health of the U.S. economy. Today, the growing economic power of China affects the balance of the United States' markets as Japan did during the 1980s and 1990s.

In addition to a changing cast of players, entering the world of international trade has become easier. For many years, only the largest companies could afford to do business with or in China. Now, even $10 million (revenue) companies can use Chinese (low-cost) suppliers. Communication barriers have collapsed as the Internet allows for cheap, instantaneous communication. Cultural barriers now are surmountable as American companies make great strides in learning how to create and maintain successful international business relationships. Savvy U.S. companies are opening up plants in China to compete. As China becomes more sophisticated, its prices will rise. Already, provinces in China are starting to specialize in certain manufacturing processes and charging a premium for their expertise.

Cycles play a role here too. While an emerging market (such as China) may have a significant impact on the U.S. economy, that impact dissipates when its competitive advantage diminishes and other markets emerge. As other nations become international players, the competitive advantage of dealing with China diminishes. Once again, the market finds a balance.

Interest Rate Manipulation. The Federal Open Market Committee of the U.S. Federal Reserve System uses, among other tools, interest rates to stabilize prices, stimulate economic growth, and foster full employment. Its actions to influence the cost and availability of money and credit have a direct effect on the M&A market. During the booming economy of the late 1990s Federal Reserve Board of Governors Chairman, Alan Greenspan, raised the Federal Reserve funds rate as high as 6.5 percent. Rates held steady from May 2000 until January 2001, when Greenspan began cutting them as the dot-com bubble burst, stock prices fell and layoffs increased. Despite Chairman Greenspan's best efforts, the events of September 11, 2001, sent the M&A market into a free fall right along with the stock market.

Stock prices and the prices paid for privately held companies remained low during 2002 and 2003 and gradually started to climb in 2004. During this period, the Federal Reserve lowered the federal funds rate six times (through June 2003) to 1 percent, in an attempt to help corporations and the stock market recover. By 2006, stock prices and business purchase prices were back to their pre-September 11 levels.

FLUCTUATIONS IN THE M&A CYCLE

In Chapter 4, we discussed the impact that the M&A cycle has on sale prices. Specifically, we looked at multiples in transactions worth less than $100 million, (see page 43.) On the following chart, we look again at multiples for two reasons: (1) to reinforce the argument that the health of the M&A market has a huge impact on the value of your company; and 2) to illustrate the huge amount of bank-supplied cash that has poured into the marketplace.

The following chart illustrates that buyout activity reached all-time highs during 2007. Deal values as well as bank funding levels were driven higher as demand for acquisitions increased.

From 2002 to 2006, strategic acquirers have been fueled by an economy that has grown by 26 percent. Over the same period, Private Equity Groups raised a record $303.6 billion of acquisition-related capital. This combination has created significant demand for deals, thus driving up prices. With current interest rates still considered to be relatively low by historical standards, traditional corporate borrowers flush with cash from the economic growth, and with acquisition lending as a prime source of new business, banks loosened their credit policies to compete for buyout transactions. As a result, the multiple of bank debt to EBITDA banks are willing to lend for an acquisition rose from 2.5 times in 2002 to 5.9 times in the second quarter of 2007, a level that is almost twice the average over the last fifteen years.

AVERAGE DEBT MULTIPLES
AVERAGE DEBT MULTIPLES OF HIGHLY LEVERAGED LOANS

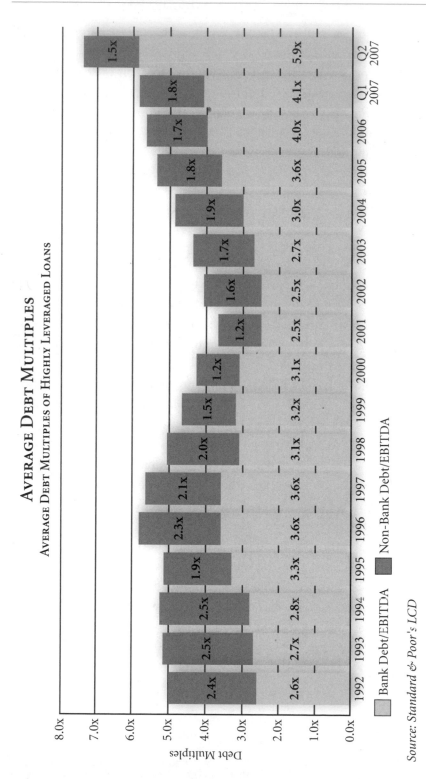

Source: Standard & Poor's LCD

Owners who have properly prepared their companies for sale, enjoy more flexibility in waiting out the market's down cycle. In my investment banking practice, I tell sellers that if they miss the peak of the current M&A cycle, they should be prepared to wait five years for the next market peak. As you can see from the charts in this chapter, historically, that is about the amount of time between peaks.

We also tell owners who choose to wait until the next peak that this waiting time is far from passive. They should get busy working with their Exit Planning Advisors to increase the intrinsic value of their companies. (See Chapters 6 and 7 on Value Drivers.) We encourage them to stay in touch because we can monitor changes in how the market values their industry, within their specific region and with their particular strengths.

Conclusion

Whether the current market is favorable or unfavorable, the goal of the Exit Planning Process is to leave your company to the successor you choose, at the time you choose, for the amount of money you want. Depending on market conditions, you may have to postpone (or move forward) your ideal departure date. Most owners are willing to compromise a bit on the timing element in order to put the cash they want and need in their pockets. Your investment banker can help you assess market conditions so you can reach your ultimate goal: closing the biggest deal of your life.

SECTION FOUR

USING PROMOTED VALUE

The sale process itself can increase the value of your company. Using experienced advisors can increase the value of your company. How? The type of sale process that we recommend is called a controlled auction. Several (or many) buyers bid simultaneously for the privilege of buying your company. Rather than paying what you (or some valuation specialist) think your business is worth, buyers competing against others pay what it is worth to them. We'll look at how this is done and the type of advisors skilled in controlled auctions in this section.

Sellers who use skilled advisors (skilled in conducting auctions and in understanding the emotions of buyers) to bring a number of qualified buyers to the table in a controlled auction process are able to identify the buyer for whom the business has a greater strategic value. In the past, it was difficult to quantify the value that a transaction advisor brings to the sale process; however, a recent study conducted by Mercer Capital found, "empirical evidence supporting the retention of a financial advisor when selling your business."

Finally, we begin the next chapter by discussing an alternative to a sale of the entire business—recapitalization.

THE IMPORTANCE OF A TRANSACTION ADVISOR
PRICING OVERVIEW

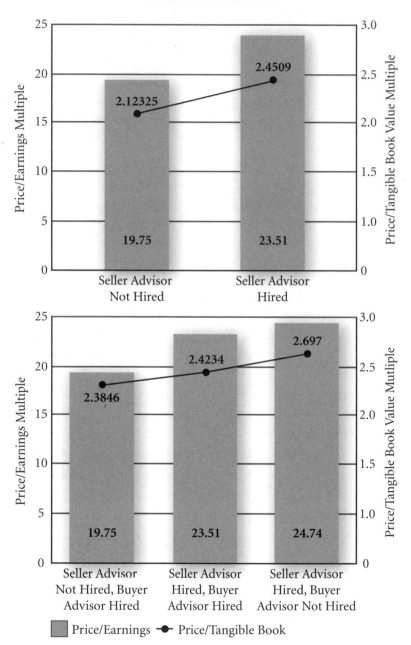

Source: Mercer Capital, www.mercercapital.com.

In this Mercer Capital study, the pricing multiples received by those sellers who retained a transaction advisor were compared to those who did not. Our (Mercer Capital) analysis revealed that the pricing multiples received by those sellers who retained a transaction advisor were significantly higher than those who took the For Sale By Owner (FSBO) approach, selling their businesses without hiring a transaction advisor. In conducting this analysis, we (Mercer Capital) reviewed transaction data in the banking industry, which is one of the few industries where this type of analysis is possible, particularly for smaller private companies.

Many of the owners whose stories you will read in the final chapter of this book chose to use an experienced transaction advisor and in almost every case, to engage in a controlled auction. Each one of these owners speaks eloquently about the uniformly favorable results, which anecdotally supports the results illustrated on the Mercer Capital graphs.

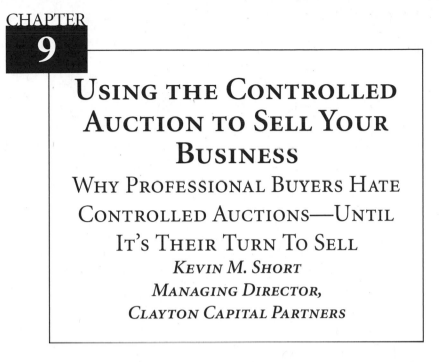

USING THE CONTROLLED AUCTION TO SELL YOUR BUSINESS

WHY PROFESSIONAL BUYERS HATE CONTROLLED AUCTIONS—UNTIL IT'S THEIR TURN TO SELL

KEVIN M. SHORT
MANAGING DIRECTOR, CLAYTON CAPITAL PARTNERS

In this chapter, Kevin Short explains how the controlled auction increases the sale price of your company. If you already know this, (and are familiar with the reasons you might use a recapitalization) you can skip this chapter until you need it as a reference source for your own sale. If you aren't convinced that a controlled auction is, by far, the best way to reach your Exit Objectives, don't miss this important chapter.

—John Brown

CHAPTER HIGHLIGHTS

O   The Auction Process
  Marketing To Find The Best Buyer
  Buyers: Who They Are And How To Find Them
  Entering The Market
    Confidentiality Agreements
    Sell, Sell, Sell
  Let The Auction Begin!
    Expression Of Interest
    Letter Of Intent
    Deal Structure
    Due Diligence
  Keeping Your Cool
    Minimize Sale Impact On Employees
    Focus On Business Profitability
    Maintain Objectivity
    Manage Your Emotions
  Negotiating The Land Mines
  The Buyer's Bag Of Tricks

Controlled Auction vs. Negotiated Sale

Most sales to third parties occur in one of two ways: a negotiated sale or a controlled auction. Each process has its own set of benefits and challenges, but controlled auctions generally (but not always) garner the best results for the seller. In a negotiated sale, a specific buyer has either already been identified or, as is more likely, a buyer has discovered your company and you decide not to seek additional suitors. If, on the other hand, you decide that other unknown buyers may offer more money, more opportunities, or better fit your company, the controlled auction methodology is more appropriate.

In most business sales, owners who seek multiple buyers receive substantially greater benefits (monetary and otherwise), than those who restrict the playing field to negotiating with one buyer. Nevertheless, in many situations a negotiated sale is the best choice.

RECAPITALIZATION

Before we return to our discussion of exactly how the controlled auction process works, we want to make a small, but important detour, to the subject of recapitalizations—another form of a third-party sale.

In Chapter 1, we described how you determine how, when, and for how much you will sell your company. The very premise of this book assumes that you wish to sell your company to a third party (not to key employees or children) for the maximum price.

In our discussion of recapitalization, we refine that objective just a bit by assuming that all of the above applies, but that you are not quite ready to leave your company. You may want to take your company to the next level, but are not prepared—either financially or emotionally—to do so. Or, you may want to stay active running your business, but want to take your chips off the table. In either case, a recapitalization may be the best strategy. Let's look first at what recapitalization is before we look at the reasons why this strategy may or may not be a good choice for you.

Meeting The Owner's Objectives.   Recapitalization is a variation on the sale to a third party. Like any sale to a third party, the company should be successful and on an upward earnings trend. Buyers look for the same Value Drivers (especially the presence of stable and skilled key managers) as they do in any other type of third-party sale. During the recapitalization process, owners can expect a similar controlled auction, and same high level of due diligence, as they would in any other type of third-party sale.

The buyer in a recapitalization is typically a Private Equity Group (PEG). PEGs look for companies with not less than $10 million in revenue, ($1 million to $2 million in EBITDA) although the typical deal size is EBITDA of greater than $5 million (or value of $30+ million). The deals we see at the low end of the range ($1 to $2 million of EBITDA) occur when PEGs compete to buy a good company.

If a company meets the PEG's size criteria, the PEG then looks to see if the company can provide a return on its investment of at least 20 percent per year. When the PEG sells the company (probably three to five years down the road), the PEG expects to have earned between 20 and

30 percent per year. While it owns the company, PEGs expect to invest about 2 percent per year in management.

Again, if your company is capable of achieving this type of growth, the PEG will want to assume a majority position of 70 to 80 percent, leaving you in control of 20 percent and making 10 percent available to members of the management team. In today's hot M&A market, however, PEGs are willing to assume minority positions (in the range of 30 to 50 percent). Keep in mind, however, that very few PEGs are interested in purchasing a minority position.

Let's look at a typical recapitalization scenario.

Arch Bottling Company (ABC), headquartered in St. Louis, Missouri, was founded in the late 1940s and had grown to become one of the Midwest's largest specialty soda producers. In 2002, with EBITDA at an all-time high of $2.5 million and forecasts projecting positive growth, the sole shareholder of ABC, Archie Bumstead, still wasn't achieving his personal wealth objectives.

With all of his net worth tied up in the business, Archie (age 45) wasn't ready to exit, but desired to take some of his chips off of the table in order to achieve liquidity. In an effort to do so, Archie engaged an investment banking firm to locate and attract a financial investor interested in participating in a recapitalization transaction.

Archie's investment bank identified a suitable investor (a St. Louis-based private equity firm). It then facilitated the transaction in which 75 percent of ABC was sold to the PEG for $14 million.

In this transaction, the PEG paid $7 million in cash directly to Archie allowing him to realize his liquidity objective. The transaction also allowed Archie to retain a 25 percent minority equity position and retain his role of Chief Executive Officer.

As this example illustrates, recapitalization was the appropriate strategy to enable the owner to:

- Convert part of his business interest to cash (and thereby obtain financial independence);

- Remain in charge of the company;

- Infuse the company with the funds necessary to grow; and

- Reap even more value on his remaining 25 percent interest.

Let's look now at the financial and personal reasons owners pursue the recapitalization sale strategy.

Financial Motives

While recapitalization is a great strategy for owners who want to reduce their financial exposure but remain active in the business, it also works well for those who want to (but cannot afford to) buy out a co-owner. Let's look again at a fictional example.

Jane Billingham and Reba Rothschild started a small decorating business in Jane's basement when their children started high school. Twelve years later, B&R Designs had three showrooms, employed 70 designers and represented nearly 50 manufacturers of various floor coverings, fabrics, furniture lines and lighting. Business could not have been better when Reba's husband was diagnosed with a rare form of cancer. Reba wanted out but with a business value of between $10 million and $12 million and EBITDA of $2 million, Jane simply could not afford to buy Reba out.

It was at this point that Jane and Reba met with an investment banker. Jane made it clear to the banker that she was not interested in selling. In fact, she'd just nailed down an exclusive contract with one of New York's hottest designers and had plans to expand the company into other markets.

After looking over B&R's financial statements and growth projections, he suggested to the two owners that he market their company to a Private Equity Group who would purchase between 70 to 80 percent of the company. Reba was immediately relieved but Jane was worried, "I'll be a minority shareholder?" The investment banker confirmed that indeed, Jane would own only 20 to 30 percent of the company, but that the cash infusion from the PEG would enable her to pursue her ambitious growth plans. He also told Jane that the PEG, as majority owner, would insist on renegotiating her compensation.

> *Given that Jane and Reba had not taken excess compensation or given themselves extravagant perks, the investment banker was confident that they could negotiate favorable terms.*

Recapitalization also can provide the infusion of capital necessary to expand your company into new territories, hire additional sales support or fund additional acquisitions. It also can inject board-level business expertise available only to the largest companies.

No matter your financial motives, keep in mind that the remaining owner (you) must be able and willing to work with a partner, either in a minority or majority position, who will take an active role in running the company. As you read, ask yourself the following question: Am I willing to share decision-making responsibilities with someone else?

Personal Motives

Reducing financial risk is just one of the reasons owners pursue a recapitalization. Some owners chose this path because they are not ready to relinquish day-to-day operating control of their companies.

Others want to exchange their illiquid stake in their companies for cash. Some want the liquidity for themselves so they can take advantage of other investment vehicles. Other owners want the cash so they can pass liquid assets to their children.

Owners who are willing to stay active in their companies, often see recapitalization as a way to recognize significant future equity returns. They realize that the infusion of capital and business expertise that comes with recapitalization offers them greater opportunity than did the company under their sole ownership.

Finally, recapitalization can reward key employees for their efforts in growing the company. How? When a PEG considers investing in a company, it looks closely at the ability of the management team. PEGs typically invest only in those companies whose management teams can be expected to stay and to propel the company to a new level of growth. In order to motivate the key managers, the PEG usually creates option plans that give key managers a piece of future company growth.

Taking On A Partner. During the controlled auction sale process, your advisors carefully investigate potential buyers to see if they are able to pay your sale price. Unless you have other objectives, (such as finding a buyer who fits the culture of your company) they will focus exclusively on the buyer's financial suitability. This is not so in a recapitalization because in this case, you are not leaving the company. In fact, you will be working closely with (and usually for) your new co-owner.

For that reason, when your investment banker is marketing your company to various PEGs, he or she will vet them, not only for financial strength, but also for:

- **Culture Fit**. Does this type of PEG share your business philosophy?

- **Owner Fit**. Is this a PEG that you can work with for more than a few months?

- **Industry Expertise**. Does this PEG have a track record in your industry or in industries like yours?

- **Growth Strategy**. How has this PEG behaved historically? Does it sell its acquisitions in less than or more than five years? What kind of return has it created in companies like yours?

As you consider transaction intermediaries to represent you in this transaction, you would do well to find one who has considerable experience in recapitalizations and in unearthing information about PEGs.

Disadvantages. Recapitalization is not a strategy for everyone. First, it is appropriate only for those who want to stay with their companies and can work with (or for) a new owner. The latter is enough for most owners to cross this idea off their lists.

For those of you who still have the fire in the belly to stay on and the flexibility to take input and direction from a majority owner, consider the following possibility: if your company is successful, everybody is happy. If unsuccessful, however, the PEG may fire you (depending on the terms of your employment agreement) or abandon you by selling their share to another PEG or to a competitor that you didn't like before it became your partner! Say hello to the new co-owner you did not choose.

The possibility does exist that, despite the PEG's capital infusion and business expertise, your company could fail to meet the PEG's revenue expectations. For that reason, as you negotiate recapitalization, you and your transaction intermediary need to evaluate:

- How you might retain control via leases.

- How you might retain control via classes of stock.

- Whether you have enough cash to absorb the loss of your retained interest.

Recapitalization is a complicated strategy so it requires both a skilled transaction intermediary and attorney. If you choose this strategy, make sure both of these advisors have significant experience in this area.

NEGOTIATED SALE

The negotiated sale generally occurs when one of the following conditions exists:

1. A specific buyer contacts you and is apparently qualified. While you did not solicit the buyer, you are willing to listen.

2. You identify a specific buyer to whom you want to sell the business. More accurately, a buyer has identified you as an acquisition target. That buyer seemingly offers a fair price and holds out the attraction of a compatible and mutually beneficial purchase. This is often the situation when an owner feels that there is only one likely buyer for the company, such as a key supplier or customer.

3. You need to sell the business quickly. Health, finances or total burnout may trigger a need to sell the business to the most convenient buyer. Under this scenario, using an investment banker is critical. As callous as it may seem, there are always people ready to take advantage of your misfortune. Gossip about impending divorce or poor health can bring bargain hunting buyers out of the woodwork. If you have an Exit Plan in place, the impact of unforeseen trouble can be minimized. Consider a good Exit Plan to be an insurance policy for your business.

4. You have decided to sell to your management team or a family member.

5. A buy/sell or franchise agreement gives one party a right to purchase—before the company is sold to other "outside" parties—and you feel compelled to sell your business pursuant to that agreement.

6. Your business isn't attractive to multiple buyers because it is too small to generate the interest of identifiable cash buyers. A negotiated sale with a single buyer may simply be evidence that a business does not have sufficient value to attract buy-out funds, as well as financial or strategic buyers willing to pay cash for a well-run business.

7. You are interested in a specific, non-financial Exit Objective that outweighs a desire to maximize financial gain. This last condition requires further explanation. A primary goal for some owners is to ensure that their businesses will continue along the same path, enjoying the same company culture and values, perhaps in the same community with the same employees. Restrictions such as these may limit the universe of interested buyers and it may be appropriate to locate and negotiate with a single interested buyer willing to accept the limitations dictated by your objectives.

In negotiated sales, the buyer and seller generally interact directly. The process usually begins when the suitor, an industry competitor or a company in your supply chain, approaches you. Each side brings its requirements to the table, and works to hammer out a deal. Buyers typically prefer this negotiated purchase to a competitive auction, because competing bids often force buyers to make concessions or to pay higher prices. In fact, we've seen motivated buyers willing to pay a premium to avoid an auction.

Owners often ask me some variation of the following question, "I've been approached by a buyer with a decent offer. Everything seems legit, Kevin, so why do I need you?" These owners generally believe that my only job is to find buyers. In response, I pose my own question, "Do you think that the guys running the PEGs and major U.S. corporations only use investment bankers to generate deal flow?" That answer is always negative. As buyers, the big players use their investment bankers' expertise to search for chinks in the financial armor, to drive down prices, to negotiate terms and most importantly, to increase the probability of closing the deal.

If the buyer looking at your company has an investment banker, you'd better be similarly armed. If that buyer does not have an investment banker, the banker you hire may not be able to promise to drive up the price you'll get from that buyer (although that is usually the result), but he or she can guarantee that the probability of closing the deal will improve from "questionable" to "near certainty."

Buyers like the leverage that they enjoy in a negotiated sale. Without the presence of competitors, a single buyer can demand concessions that competing buyers in controlled auctions simply cannot.

Do you remember Kevin's client, Harry Mueller, from Chapter 7? He has grown his business through numerous acquisitions over the past several years. In each of these acquisitions, we have identified the target acquisition, and conducted a negotiated sale with the seller. As a buyer, Harry understands that a negotiated sale gives him leverage that he simply would not enjoy as one buyer among several in a controlled auction.

Sellers, on the other hand, prefer the arms-length nature of the controlled auction because it levels the playing field. The seller uses the same type of expert advisors as does the buyer. Second, sellers quickly realize that in negotiating with one buyer, they are often negotiating directly with their future bosses. Because most sellers are required to stay with the company for some period after closing, a negotiated sale pits seller against buyer right up to closing when their roles suddenly change to employee and employer. This is not a prospect that most sellers relish.

CONTROLLED AUCTION

Without realizing it, most people have experienced a controlled auction. If you have bought or sold a home, you have an idea of how the auction process works. Buyers compete with each other without knowledge of other offers on the table. In a "hot" market, buyers can eventually bid more than the seller's asking price—more than the home's value—in order to get it.

Sellers consider factors other than price when examining offers. They consider the buyer's ability to secure financing. They look at the contingencies that might provide obstacles to certain buyers.

As a deal progresses, buyers want to know every detail about your home, determined to negotiate a lower price before the deal closes. Like selling a business, selling a home can be fraught with land mines, only on a smaller scale. Failed financing, unexpected findings in the home inspection report, contingencies or even finicky buyers surprise even prepared buyers and sellers. External forces, such as hurricanes and terrorist attacks, derail deals without warning. Thousands of real estate deals collapsed in the weeks after Hurricane Katrina and 9/11, and the market for mid-sized businesses followed suit.

Of course, selling your business is far more complicated than a home sale. In a home sale, there are a limited number of factors that can change during the course of the sale. In the sale of a company, the number and variety of factors that can derail the deal increase exponentially. To navigate these, you or, better yet, your transaction advisor, must know how to manage the disclosure of information. It's a bit like dating: telling your life story on the first date seriously jeopardizes the likelihood of a trip down the aisle! Instinctively, you reveal information about the problematic ex-wife, or that huge college debt as the relationship grows. Your intended is in a better position to accept the skeletons rattling around in your closet *after* making an emotional investment. Deals are the same way. Information must be presented at the correct time and in the appropriate way. Too much information too early in the process can scare off a buyer. Too little information can result in a lawsuit.

Real estate and business sales differ in two other important ways. First, rarely are home owners as emotionally attached to their homes as are owners who have spent their entire adult lives building their businesses. Most owners have poured their time, effort, cash and often, egos into their companies. For that reason, emotions can become quite intense in the business transaction.

Second, in a business transaction, the number of possible mistakes and misunderstandings increases exponentially. In a real estate sale, the asset itself does not change. Throughout the sale, there are still four walls, one roof and the two-car garage. While the inspection can, and often does, bring up numerous opportunities for negotiation, there is no argument about square footage. A business, however, is a living entity. People, inventory, markets and customer needs can change slightly or significantly during the sale process.

One of these variables is working capital. The working capital of a business is defined as current assets (typically cash, accounts receivable and inventory) less current liabilities (typically accounts payable, accruals, taxes and wages, and salaries payable). Working capital goes up and down each day as a result of business transactions. How can one purchase working capital when its value changes every day?

Buyers state what they assume to be the amount of working capital in their Letters of Intent. On the day of closing, the buyer conducts a physical inventory and makes a valuation of the components of working capital. If this day-of-closing valuation varies from the value stated in the Letter of Intent, (and it always does) a corresponding adjustment will be made to the sale price.

This adjustment can be quite large. Its size not only depends on the organic changes in the business, but it also depends on the accounting protocol used to calculate it. As you may have guessed, choosing the protocol is another negotiating point for your investment banker.

Inventory and other assets also can become the object of conflict. As components of the purchase price, they are valued twice; once at the time of the Letter of Intent and again just prior to closing. If there is a variation in those two valuations, the buyer will want to adjust the purchase price. Here again, the investment banker's most effective tool to defend against any purchase price reduction is the presence of other buyers waiting in the wings.

Even though seller and buyer do not interact directly, (as in a negotiated sale) a seller has more control in an auction than in a negotiated transaction because bids are solicited through a process the seller's team creates and controls. The process gives the seller more control over important factors such as timing, the extent of due diligence, the first draft of the definitive agreement and the ability to compare multiple competitive bids and choose an ultimate winner.

The auction process shifts deal risk from the seller to the buyer. The chance of a transaction failing is less likely in an auction process. For example, a bidder assumes the risk of financing in an auction process whereas that same bidder, in a negotiated transaction, is more likely to insist on a financing condition. At the end of the day, a deal that results from an auction process should yield a higher price, more seller-friendly agreements, and less risk for the seller.

Another advantage of an auction is that it gives the seller more options. Through the investment banker's networks, sellers reach buyers they might not have even considered. For example, owners often don't think about international buyers or Private Equity Groups. Buyers from "adjacent" industries are becoming more common. (For more information about these buyers, see "Buyers: Who They Are And How To Find Them" later in this chapter.) In about half the deals we see, it is virtually impossible to predict who will ultimately turn out to be the successful bidder. It is easier for sellers to find the right fit when they can choose from among several buyers, as well as several deal structures.

In summary, the controlled auction promotes value by offering the seller the following advantages:

1. Competition among buyers motivates them to pay more than they would without competition.

2. A buyer considering several offers can pick the one that offers the least risk and can best meet the seller's objectives (financial and otherwise).

3. The process allows the seller to release information in a controlled manner.

4. Competition among buyers gives the seller negotiating strength on nearly every deal point (purchase price, timing, the extent of due diligence, etc.).

5. All the seller's eggs are not in one basket. Several buyers means there is less risk to the seller of the deal not closing.

6. The investment banker's marketing activities reach buyers the seller may never have considered.

Of course, controlled auctions do present their own set of challenges. First, controlling confidentiality when multiple bidders are involved is difficult, but far from impossible. Second, because auctions inherently tend to favor the seller, some sophisticated buyers may be reluctant to participate. If this is the case, the auction could inadvertently exclude the best buyer. An experienced investment banker knows how to keep these buyers at the table.

Finally, successful controlled auctions require skilled investment bankers, and skilled investment bankers cost money. Owners who desire to sell their companies (for all of the reasons discussed in this chapter) using the controlled auction, often wonder why their lawyers or accountants cannot conduct the auction. They wonder what value the investment banker brings to the table. As an investment banker, I hope you will finish this chapter convinced of the value the experienced investment banker brings. But if you prefer an unbiased opinion, perhaps the experience of one of my clients (whose name and company details have been changed) is the best place to start.

INVESTMENT BANKERS: ARE THEY WORTH WHAT YOU'LL PAY?

We represented Big Time Enterprises (BTE) in its sale to Quick Supply Company. BTE is a rapidly growing full-line distributor of gaming supplies and equipment.

The owner of BTE, Jibben Nair, had experienced health issues and decided it was time to sell his company. Further, he had been approached directly by a number of industry participants. Nair told us that several years earlier he had attempted to sell the company, without an advisor, but the deal fell apart.

When Nair approached us, he had, in hand, a written offer from yet another suitor. As in his previous sale attempt, Nair wanted the highest value and best terms. This time, however, he wanted our expertise and experience not only to reduce risk, but also to improve the likelihood of successfully completing the transaction.

My firm's controlled auction process produced a number of motivated, high-quality buyers (both strategic and financial). It also produced a final purchase price more than 80 percent higher than the offer on the table when Nair engaged us. Not only did the process drive the price higher, the terms of the new all-cash transaction were far more favorable than Nair's original offer, which had required seller financing and contingent payments based on future company performance. Furthermore, to Nair's great relief, we were able to maintain confidentiality throughout the process by carefully qualifying potential buyers and through deliberate control of the dissemination of information to interested parties.

During a post-closing conversation, I asked Nair if the controlled auction process had been worth it. He admitted that he had thought hiring an investment banker would be too expensive. "At the end of the day," Nair confided, "I couldn't afford not to."

To summarize then, the controlled auction requires finesse in managing complexities, revealing information and keeping buyers at the table. It also requires patience and a dispassionate advisor to keep emotions in check and the deal on track. We tell owners at the outset that attracting the offer is the easy part: the real work begins as the deal inches toward closing. Owners don't believe us until they encounter the complexities of the controlled auction process. At that point, they begin to appreciate the value of using a seasoned dealmaker.

If you decide that the controlled auction offers you the best opportunity to reach your Exit Objectives, we suggest that you retain a skilled investment banker, a transaction attorney and an accountant who has worked in the deal arena. To be successful, an auction is a team effort. The investment banker assumes the central role on that team.

THE AUCTION PROCESS
MARKETING TO FIND THE BEST BUYER

When selling your business, your goal is not to find *one* buyer; rather, it is to find the *best* buyer. In failing to make this distinction, too many business owners sell for far less than their company is worth because they accept the first offer they receive. You are looking for the buyer that meets the personal and financial goals you established during the earliest part of The Exit Planning Process. Finding the best buyer takes an amount of research, persistence and skill that few owners possess. It is the investment banker who knows where to look for buyers, how to qualify them and how to keep them at the table until closing.

When owners first meet with an investment banker they often bring a list of potential target buyers. They are certain they know who will be *the* buyer. Rarely do we end up selling to any party on that list. To find the best buyer, your team must think creatively. For example, part of the investment banker's job is to find ways to position the company so that it is desirable to less-obvious buyers.

Some investment banking firms look at obvious targets and narrow the focus of their search to 15 or 20 companies. While that is one way to approach the situation, it can exhaust the list of potential buyers very quickly. Instead, we suggest that your investment banker take a much broader approach that invests hundreds of hours of research into, on average, 500 companies. We are convinced that considering all options, not just the obvious or seller-suggested ones, is the most successful path to finding the *best* buyer.

Casting a wide net is something sellers cannot do on their own. Sometimes, personal experience and biases can prevent sellers from considering the best possible buyers. Consider the case of a fictional company we'll call Midwest Metals.

In the Eye of the Beholder

Abe Tanaka, the owner of Midwest Metals, wanted my firm to sell his business. Tanaka had done his homework, and presented us with a detailed list of companies he thought might be good candidates for an acquisition. One of the most obvious choices, however, a large steel company ("All Steel") was glaringly absent from the list. We asked Tanaka about this oversight. Tanaka, a savvy Japanese businessman, believed All Steel was simply not trustworthy. We took his comments at face value and began our negotiations with other companies.

The vehemence of Tanaka's feelings impressed me, but I wondered about the source. Eventually, I asked him why he felt so strongly about All Steel. Apparently, Tanaka and the president of All Steel had played golf several years before. Throughout the entire game, the president consistently picked up his ball to improve his lie. Note to non-golfing readers: picking up the ball could be interpreted as cheating. To Tanaka (and to most other Japanese golfers) improving a lie borders on criminal behavior. Consequently, Tanaka felt the company president was not honorable. Furthermore, he had heard that All Steel bought companies with stock and not cash. For business reasons, Tanaka was only interested in a cash deal.

By pure chance, I learned that a friend of mine was a member of the same country club as the president of All Steel. Curiosity got the best of me, and I asked my friend to arrange a foursome. At the first tee, the president of All Steel turned to us and said "I think it was Mark Twain who said, 'Golf is a good walk spoiled.' Since none of us is playing for money or glory, would anyone mind if I improve my lie?" Of course, none of us did. At that moment I realized Tanaka had probably missed a similar announcement during his round of golf.

As the game progressed, I casually asked about other companies All Steel had purchased. I learned that All Steel had indeed purchased other companies for stock in the past, but had recently changed its policy to make all acquisitions with cash.

> *Through a series of wrong assumptions, my client had eliminated the best and most logical buyer from consideration. In the end, we closed the deal—with All Steel—at two times more than the other offers we had obtained.*

Having said this, it is most important that you compile your own list of possible buyers. Think of those candidates outside of your own industry, as well as the more obvious candidates such as those players in your supply chain.

BUYERS: WHO THEY ARE AND HOW TO FIND THEM

As we saw in the case of Midwest Metals, the best buyer can be the least expected buyer. So, what types of buyers make good buyers? In general, we target four major types of buyers in our initial research.

- **Private Equity Groups (PEGs)**. These groups have grown tremendously, from about 1,000 groups ten years ago to an estimated 7,000 in the United States today. PEGs make good buyers because they have access to large amounts of cash and are highly motivated. Because investors believe PEGs to be solid alternatives to fixed-income securities, corporate bonds or bank instruments, there is a tremendous amount of money in them. Some sources put the amount raised by PEGs in the US during 2006 at $215.4 billion (Dow Jones Equity Analyst). Capital investors want to see action and results so PEGs are under constant pressure to buy companies. From a seller's perspective, however, the downside to PEGs is their experience: they are seasoned negotiators and are familiar with all of the tricks of the trade. They are professionals who buy and sell companies to survive.

- **Industry Players**. These are businesses that do the same thing you do, but don't directly compete with you. For example, the owners of an advertising agency in Los Angeles may be seeking to expand to Chicago by buying an agency there. Industry players can be very good buyers because they are sometimes willing to pay a premium for synergies such as geographic coverage, new customers or overhead elimination.

- **Adjacencies**. Adjacencies are businesses that are synergistic to, or complement, your business. For example, a company that sells plumbing supplies may consider buying a business that sells electrical supplies in order to expand its product offerings and customer base. The two companies aren't in the same business, but they share a common customer base, making an acquisition logical. Adjacencies can be attractive prospects because they aren't as familiar with your particular industry.

- **Competitors**. A competing business often seems like an obvious buyer candidate because a competitor can likely increase its market share and decrease its competition by buying your company. However, approach competitors with caution. They know all of the "dirt" on your industry and can be dangerous when armed with what they learn about your company during due diligence.

Do you remember the question about the value of an investment banker? Keep that in the back of your mind as we talk about the challenge of researching potential buyers. Unlike large, publicly traded companies, there is limited information published about small- to mid-sized companies. This means your investment banking team must be prepared to dig.

Here are some additional ways that investment bankers find buyers.

- **Experienced Buyers**. To find buyers who will bring strong deals to the table, we look first at experienced buyers in the market. We research who has already been buying in the industry, what they paid and the terms they negotiated. Those companies are always strong candidates, because they are in a growth mode. Unearthing non-disclosed information about privately held companies takes creativity, tenacity and more than a passing understanding of the industry.

- **Trade Associations**. Trade associations also are valuable sources of buyers. The executive directors of these associations have volumes of information about their members on their Web sites, making the search for industry players simple. They often have personal relationships with their members and can make introductions to potential buyers for you.

- **Media And Internet Searches**. While seemingly obvious, doing basic research is often overlooked. Articles in industry trade journals can be a gold mine of information, as can the Internet. For example, we always use a Google search to find out information on company executives. We also piece together financial information from a complex set of subscription databases. Capital IQ and Factset are just two. We mention them only to demonstrate that you and your advisors have likely never heard of them. Using these databases correctly can mean millions of dollars to you. These databases can be challenging to interpret correctly, and generally require the expertise of a trained professional. Access to databases can be prohibitively expensive to the seller trying to negotiate a deal alone.

- **Networking**. As with most business situations, networking remains an invaluable tool. Find someone in a potential buyer's company who can introduce you to the CEO. Schedule a golf game with key executives, or attend industry events. The old adage that "It's all about who you know" is never truer than when searching for a potential buyer.

ENTERING THE MARKET

After creating a list of potential buyers, it's time to take your company to market. Your skilled investment banker will begin by sending letters or e-mails to a large and well-researched list of prospects. This is promptly followed by a call to key prospects to spark (and gauge) their interest.

It is important to use a third party to make the initial approach to all buyers. No matter how you package it, there is nothing discreet about you approaching someone to buy your company. Regardless of what you say or how you say it, your hat is in your hand. It is always better to have a third party make the approaches for you.

Your investment banker can make "blind" approaches to gauge a prospective buyer's appetite for acquisitions. You maintain your confidentiality until the prospective buyer expresses interest. Also, the investment banker acts as a buffer between you and the potential acquirers, allowing you to maintain some degree of autonomy and leverage. Lastly, the process of making approaches and interacting with an array of suitors can become very time-consuming. Your efforts are better spent running your business.

Confidentiality Agreements. Anyone expressing interest in your company will sign a confidentiality agreement, or non-disclosure agreement (NDA). In these agreements, prospective buyers agree not to disclose either: (a) that your company is for sale, or (b) any of the data on your company that will be provided. Always insist that any potential acquirer executes a confidentiality agreement before you divulge the name of, or any other information about, your company.

You should be aware that confidentiality agreements are difficult to enforce. The onus is on you, the seller, to prove a breach of the agreement, and then to prove damages. It is generally very difficult to trace the exact source of any leak, let alone to prove damages.

A confidentiality agreement does, however, achieve a more limited goal: it sends a clear signal to any potential suitor that you consider the information that you are providing to be confidential, and that you expect it to be treated as such. Generally, those who are experienced in mergers and acquisitions respect the confidential nature of any data provided to them. Confidentiality problems generally stem from smaller, less sophisticated groups with little experience in mergers and acquisitions.

Sell, Sell, Sell. After a NDA is signed, the potential buyer will be interested in learning more about your company. It is important to "sell" the information you're giving out. For example, if four members of your top management team have Harvard MBA degrees, make sure to point that out. If you've won any awards, put that information front and center. If you have a patent on the best technology in the industry, let that be known. Be sincere and honest, but put your best foot forward at all times.

By this point, most investment bankers will have created the "Book," a Bible of information about your company. Designed to spark interest and excitement among buyers, this book will contain key information about the company being sold.

Like most investment bankers, we advocate the creation of a book, but tend to shy away from sharing the entire book at once. Instead, we like to dole out information in small doses. This allows better control of the process and holds the door open for further conversation with the prospect. An added benefit of proceeding in this way is that it helps protect the security of clients during the process, by not giving away confidential information before it is necessary.

LET THE AUCTION BEGIN!

Once your investment banker has narrowed down the list of potential buyers to four to six interested suitors, the controlled auction is set to begin. This remaining group of buyers is given a date by which to submit their Expression of Interest (EOI). Expect the buyers to have questions right up to the EOI due date.

Expression of Interest (EOI). Prospective buyers submit their EOIs to your investment banking team. The EOI document should cover major points of a prospective buyer's offer or intent. For example, a prospective buyer may offer $20 million, half cash/half stock and want the CEO to stay for five years. Your investment banking team will use the EOIs to qualify and to eliminate prospective buyers.

After the EOIs have been collected and analyzed, the investment banker will go back to each party and attempt to solicit an offer that better matches your Exit Objectives. Clarifying and improving terms can last a week or so and involves several discussions. Based on these discussions, the owner decides which prospective buyer to invite to the Letter of Intent stage.

Letter of Intent (LOI). A LOI communicates the intent of the buyer to negotiate a sale. The LOI is not legally binding, but it begins to provide deal-specific information such as:

- Working capital adjustments.

- Representations/warranties.

- Financing sources.

- Guarantees—personal guarantees from the buyer that the money will be paid.

- Hurdle dates that buyers must meet to avoid termination of the LOI:
  - Due Diligence Completion

- Legal Document Draft
- Legal Document Completion
- Financing Commitments
- Board Approval
- Audit Completion

Only in rare cases in which the seller has extreme leverage over the buyer, is it possible to skip the LOI. In the LOI, about 95 percent of buyers ask for an exclusivity period or "stop-shop" agreement (lasting between 60 and 120 days) in which the seller agrees to cease discussions with any current or future potential buyers.

We often spend considerable effort negotiating the amount of time the seller is asked to take the company off the market. That effort pays off most of the time. Just as the leverage created by a number of suitors works to the seller's advantage in other issues, so it applies here. Our best argument in convincing a buyer to forgo the stop-shop is to concentrate on the warranties and representations section of the purchase contract. If the buyer is concerned about the company's financial reports, for example, it could (and we'd argue should) require the seller to warrant that those numbers are correct. If they are found to be incorrect, the seller is held liable. Using the warranties and representations approach serves both the interests of buyer and seller. The buyer ultimately gets the assurance and redress it needs should something be misrepresented. The seller keeps his/her company on the market and can continue to negotiate with others should this buyer walk away.

Let us insert one warning here to sellers who might think that re-entering the marketplace is not a big deal. If you agree to a stop-shop agreement in the LOI and the buyer pulls out, you must re-enter the market. At that point, you will likely be viewed by potential buyers as "tainted goods." They will wonder why the other buyer disappeared. They will be so curious that they will dissect each and every piece of information you disclose. They will ask for everything that the first buyer did and you will suddenly find yourself in the same position as the husband who is asked, "When did you stop beating your wife?" No matter the answer, the seller loses. Turn over everything and this buyer will find something. Refuse to turn over everything and the seller ends up liable for any omissions. Inevitably the price offered by the second buyer will be lower and the deal will include escrow, a promissory note or both.

Note that an LOI is just the *beginning* of the negotiation process. A good investment banker should guide you through all the inevitable retrading by negotiating the numerous elements of a deal during the LOI period. Your investment banker knows where potential land mines are and settles them up-front, before due diligence begins. This is where the experience of your advisors really counts.

We recommend that sellers insert a "no retrading during due diligence" clause into the LOI. This clause says that if the buyer verbally, or in writing, attempts to change the terms of the deal during the due diligence process, the stop-shop provision is immediately lifted.

Deal Structure. Deals may be structured in many ways, but most contain a combination of cash, stock, promissory notes and earn outs. Deal structure determines not only the "how much" but also the what, when and how parts of the deal.

- How much will the seller pay in taxes?

- What is the buyer purchasing: assets or stock?

- When is the buyer paying: at closing or over time?

- How is the buyer paying: in cash, in stock, or as a promissory note?

We'd also argue that it is the 'what else' part of the deal. What else is the buyer willing to do: assume the seller's line of credit, entice current employees to stay on, employ the owner as a consultant? As you can see, there are endless varieties of deal structures and there is certainly more to a deal than the purchase price.

> This is where the Deal Team—especially the investment banker—earns its money not just in finding a buyer, but in structuring the deal on terms most favorable to you.
>
> —John Brown

Due Diligence. After the deal structure is hammered out, due diligence begins. Most owners are shocked by the depth and breadth of the due diligence process. This is the process of "full and fair" disclosure that enables a buyer to verify all provided data and review *all* information about the company. "All" includes anything that would interest the buyer at any level. This review generally occurs after the deal has been negotiated, but before closing. Most business owners are highly independent people who find this disclosure process extremely uncomfortable.

Although the specific targets of due diligence vary depending on the nature of the business being acquired, the investigative process always has the same goals.

First, the buyer is looking for malfeasance or undisclosed material risks. Simply put, he or she is looking for the skeletons in the closet. Chances are your buyer has hired someone who is very good at finding those skeletons. Some of the areas that are targeted during the process are:

- Fraud on the part of the owner or manager;

- Misrepresentation made by the sellers, such as improperly recognized revenues or expenses; and

- Omitted information, such as unpaid taxes, pending or threatened litigation, or obsolescent business equipment, processes, products or services.

Second, the buyer is looking for information that would affect the value of the company and the advisability of purchasing it. Up until the point that due diligence begins, your buyer has had limited access to company information. The buyer has formed an opinion of you and your company based on the details you've provided thus far. Once due diligence begins, however, the buyer may discover things about your company that can quickly distort those rose-colored first impressions.

Third, if the buyer has yet to find any malfeasance, undisclosed risk or information that would greatly affect its value, the hunt is on for anything that could be used during negotiations to lower price or improve its terms. This ulterior motive—forcing you to lower your price—permeates the entire due diligence process.

Before you assume that the buyer has only less-than-honorable motives, remember that the buyer is also looking to pinpoint areas of your company where he or she can make immediate improvements. Second, the buyers are examining information with an eye on how they can integrate your existing systems and processes with theirs post-closing.

Throughout the due diligence process, the buyer will be asking numerous questions. Your goal is to answer every one in a way that meets certain criteria. Before you present any information to the buyer, ask yourself the following questions:

1. Is this answer completely factual and legal? Due diligence results may eventually become the foundation for post-closing adjustments or lawsuits, so make sure nothing comes back to haunt you.

2. Could the way I am answering this question greatly affect the perceived value of the business? For example, never answer a question with the words "Yes, that is a problem." Be prepared to explain why your non-traditional accounting methods work better in your particular industry or why your new ad campaign works better than direct mail. Locate your perceived weaknesses and be prepared to defend them in advance.

3. Can this information help the new owners make immediate improvements to the business? On the one hand, this information is music to a buyer's ears. You will want to present it with some fanfare. On the other hand, ask yourself if the information will make the buyer question your management ability. Will the buyer leave this conversation scratching his head and wondering why, if this improvement was so obvious, you didn't make it yourself?

4. Does this information help or hinder the post-closing integration of your systems with the buyer's? As the buyer collects information, he or she is constantly evaluating how smoothly and efficiently the business will transfer from your leadership to its own.

Keeping these points in mind during due diligence, improves your chances for closing your deal and enjoying your post-closing life dramatically.

KEEPING YOUR COOL

The sale process is many things: exciting, fulfilling, frustrating and unpredictable, to name just a few. What it cannot be is distracting. During this process, your focus must be on maintaining business profitability and on minimizing employee impact. While you focus intensely on these two issues, you must maintain the mental objectivity to walk away from the deal at any time. Let's look at each of these owner behaviors.

Minimize Sale Impact On Employees. We suggest that you inform only those employees who need to know of your sale plans. If you announce your plans to sell before a deal is at hand, you will create tremendous insecurity and disruption in your workforce and among your customers and suppliers.

Once a deal is announced, the employees will know the identity of the acquirer. Knowing exactly who will take over goes a long way in making employees more secure and comfortable about their futures. It is the period between the decision to sell and the announcement of a deal, when the future is uncertain and the identity of the buyer unknown, that employees focus exclusively on their own security. In Chapter 6, we discussed the Stay Bonus Plan, which will help your employees feel more secure during this transfer.

If a sale is conducted properly, you should be able to go through the process without employees discovering your plans. Conduct plant tours very carefully; perhaps after hours or by introducing a prospective buyer as a prospective customer/supplier. Hold meetings and phone conversations off-site. Some sellers set up separate e-mail addresses and have all written correspondence sent to their homes. By taking reasonable precautions, the only way that your employees will have suspicions is if you start to act suspiciously.

Focus On Business Profitability. We cannot stress enough how important it is that you continue to operate your company as if no sale were pending. Why? Sales fall through. Given the possibility that you may own your company longer than you anticipated, it makes sense for you to keep it running as profitably as possible.

Too many owners take their eyes off running their companies during the sale process. This is a grave mistake. You need to keep your business operating at peak performance throughout the process to demonstrate its worth to suitors. Nothing jeopardizes your chances of maximizing value better than showing disappointing operating results in the middle of negotiations. Remember, interest and value are often based primarily on *perception.* If your profits or prospects drop, so, too, will your company's value and your negotiating strength.

In addition to resisting the temptation to focus on the sale, you must also resist the temptation to sacrifice the future for the present. In an effort to show attractive earnings, many owners curtail necessary spending on such things as advertising and development, or raise prices to show immediate margin increases. This kind of "short-term" thinking will likely backfire. Again, if you do not sell, you will have to live with the long-term consequences of such moves. Secondly, you should always assume that buyers are at least as canny as you are; they will probably eventually uncover such financial maneuvering. When they do, you will certainly lose credibility and you may also lose a deal.

Maintain Objectivity. Owners often become so emotionally invested in one buyer that they cannot walk away. Your willingness to do exactly that—walk away—is one of the most powerful negotiating tools you have available to you as a seller. You must maintain a frame of mind that allows—even encourages— you to walk from the table if your Exit Objectives are not being met by the negotiations. (For an example of one owner who used this technique to his advantage, read about Regis Hillow in Chapter 12.)

Manage Your Emotions. Most deals fall apart at least ten times before they close. That's why it's essential to have an advisor who can manage emotions—his or hers, yours and those of the buyer. Managing emotion is often the difference between closing the deal and not closing the deal. We hope this story helps owners understand how important it is to be able to manage the emotional rollercoaster of a sale.

NITPICKED NEARLY TO DEATH

In one recent deal, the buyer asked for small concessions at every stage of the process. While none of these concessions was a deal-breaker, the requests soon began to wear on everyone involved. After careful consideration, (and sometimes considerable mental anguish) our client repeatedly refused each request. But with each new request, the angst grew. Finally, on the eve of closing, the buyer made a very minor last minute request. Emotionally drained, our client blew up and wanted to back out of the deal on the spot.

After retreating to a more relaxed setting, I asked why he was so upset. He replied, "I've given in time and time again. Now they want us to pay the Federal Express charges! That's it! I just won't do it." It was only when I pointed out that he had not given in on one single concession that he began to calm down. I helped him realize that he was reacting to the strain and stress of the buyer's repeated requests. As requests multiplied, the stress intensified. In reality, the buyer had been very reasonable and had stayed in the deal despite the fact that his requests were repeatedly denied. This owner's fatigue stemmed from the emotion of the exchange, not the quality of the deal. Deals take time to complete, and the process wears on everyone. We see it all the time.

NEGOTIATING THE LAND MINES

Challenges inevitably arise in the sale process. Knowing what those challenges (or land mines) are and how to defuse them keeps the deal headed toward closing (and earns your investment banker his or her fee!).

Owners often anticipate that price will be the "hottest" issue. It can be, but we look at many factors when evaluating the deal landscape. Before listing the issues most likely to explode during the sale process, let us point out that "land mines" give leverage to the buyer in two ways. First, when a land mine explodes, the process slows while the parties assess the damage and figure out how to move beyond it. Time, for reasons outlined below, is the ally of the buyer, not the seller. The second effect of land mines is the damage that they cause.

In our experience, those land mines that have both the power to derail a deal and that invariably crop up are:

- Stop shop. Stop-shop agreements temporarily prevent the seller from negotiating with another buyer while a top prospect works on the final offer. Stop-shop agreements should be carefully structured for two reasons. First, they take the company off the market for a given period of time or until the deal successfully closes. Second, if the deal does fall apart, it is not easy for sellers to pick up where they left off. Potential buyers tend to "cool off" during this period and begin to believe your company is tainted. They realize that your deal failed to close during the stop-shop period, and begin to wonder why. The seeds of doubt are planted.

- Due diligence. There are two areas of due diligence that always create challenges: working capital and audits.
  - As we mentioned earlier when discussing how a business is not a fixed asset, working capital is an area of contention at the end of the deal and post-closing. It is a tricky figure because it tries to assign a value to some component of the business—inventory, accounts receivable, etc.—at the time the deal is signed. In the normal course of business, value constantly changes and change can be contentious.
  - Audits also can wreak havoc on a deal for two reasons. First, if not properly prepared for, they can add two to four months to the length of the deal. Secondly, audits provide buyers with a host of reasons to lower the price. We generally try to avoid audits altogether by negotiating them out of the deal before due diligence ever starts. Our success rate in doing so is usually directly related to the number of buyers at the table. More suitors means more negotiating leverage for the seller.

To avoid, or at least minimize, these roadblocks, we suggest that you and your advisors engage in the legal and financial pre-sale due diligence described in Chapter 8. (To see a list of items included in pre-sale due diligence, please visit www.BEIBooks.com.)

- Speed. Buyers want to go slow in a deal—checking and re-checking each detail and looking for ways to negotiate a lower price. Sellers, never sure that the deal will close, and always sure that confidentiality is about to crumble, prefer a less leisurely pace. The longer the deal lingers in limbo, the greater chance that the news will leak out to employees, customers and competitors. As the seller's advocate, we attempt to lock buyers into a strict schedule of hurdle dates to help the deal move swiftly toward a successful closing. (Hurdle dates are set by the seller and require a buyer to perform certain tasks in order to assure the seller that this buyer is progressing toward closing.)

- Legal documents. Perhaps the most problematic of all areas are the legal documents necessary to consummate the deal. Buyers typically have a small army of lawyers skilled in the art of hiding land mines in documents. If you are negotiating with a publicly held buyer, understand that they must adhere to extremely stringent legal requirements. If we suspect the legal battles will become overwhelmingly problematic, we sometimes will turn our efforts to another buyer.

- Financing. One of the purposes of the LOI is to identify the buyers who actually have or will be able to obtain the financial resources needed to close the deal. Buyers love financing contingencies because they offer a safe exit from the deal at any time.

- Boards of directors. Most everyone has bought a car from the salesman who periodically ducks out of the negotiations to meet with the mysterious and always invisible "sales manager." Prospective buyers may play the same card, ducking out to "get board approval." As on the showroom floor, this ploy is usually a stalling tactic. Don't fall for it.

The Buyer's Bag Of Tricks

In today's market, almost all buyers are professionals and you'll need to have a clear picture of what you are up against when you decide to sell your company. Your buyer may be a principal with a private equity firm, and negotiate for a living. Or, your buyer may be the "Director of New Business Development" for the corporation who is buying your company. In reality, he or she is a sophisticated shark, just waiting for you to make a mistake. Or, you may encounter a savvy investment banker who is just as smart as the one you've hired. Under any scenario, you need to proceed with extreme caution—and with the best possible transaction advisors.

Here is how one company lost half of its lunch to a smart investment banker.

CANNIBALIZING HANNIBAL

Hannibal McTavish was the owner of an extremely popular local restaurant, a well-established tourist destination because of its unique dining experience. Hannibal was confident he could sell his restaurant on his own, despite the fact that the buyer was represented by an experienced investment banker.

The investment banker offered Hannibal four times EBITDA (an attractive multiple in the restaurant business) and agreed to adhere to GAAP (Generally Accepted Accounting Procedures) standards throughout the deal. Confident he knew his books better than anyone else, Hannibal quickly agreed to the deal. Little did he know that the investment banker had already studied the books, and had identified numerous problems that he planned to bring up during due diligence.

Sure enough, when the deal closed, Hannibal received only half of his original asking price due to multiple price reductions to accommodate for "unforeseen" problems.

Here's another trick that we've seen buyers play on sellers, with equally troubling consequences.

IGNITING A FIRE SALE

While enjoying a celebratory drink at his country club bar, Skip Ingenue, the owner of Innocent Manufacturing, received a disturbing phone call from the investment banker of the company that was just about to purchase Innocent. Although the deal had gone smoothly and was now only two weeks from closing, the buyers had a change of heart. "Skip, I'm so sorry but the deal is off," announced the buyer's investment banker. Skip learned from his lawyer that an overlooked loophole in the final agreements enabled the buyer to legally walk away from the deal.

The next day when Skip confessed to his executive team and key customers that the deal was off, chaos erupted. Within weeks, the key management team had left the company, and several key customers were investigating other more business-savvy suppliers. Within a month, Innocent Manufacturing was in real trouble. It was at this point that the original buyer reappeared on the scene. Again, the investment banker called Skip, "My client has changed his mind. I'd like to make another offer—adjusted, of course, to take Innocent's current troubles into account. Our offer is half of our first. Take it or leave it."

Clearly, buyers can do more harm than sellers. They are in a better position to set traps, especially for unsuspecting owners who have never engaged in the sale of a company. For that reason, we strongly recommend that you:

1. Pursue a process that limits the impact of any particular buyer. The controlled auction process brings several buyers to the table making each one less willing to jeopardize his or her position. Multiple buyers reduce the seller's risk.

2. Level the playing field by retaining an advisory team that is at least as skilled as your buyer's team. Keep in mind that your buyer will almost always be larger (and better resourced) than you.

Assembling the best team possible prior to the sale can make or break the deal. To properly navigate through the sale process, you'll need your deal attorneys, CPA firm and an investment banker to quarterback the transaction team. Armed with the right advisors, a controlled auction gives you the best shot at: 1) the best price; 2) the best terms, and last, but certainly not least, 3) the best chance for a successful closing.

10

GETTING WHAT YOU WANT IN THE DOCUMENTS

THE CONFIDENTIALITY AGREEMENT, LETTER OF INTENT AND TERM SHEET

CHAPTER HIGHLIGHTS

○ Executing The Confidentiality Agreement

○ Letter Of Intent

○ Term Sheet Considerations

You may want to skim this chapter until you begin the sale process. For now, you might read only the descriptions of the documents so you have a better understanding of what's included in each. Once your deal process begins, we suggest that you use this chapter as a guide.

EXECUTING THE CONFIDENTIALITY AGREEMENT

Every business sale involves a Confidentiality Agreement. Every seller should have one and every potential buyer expects to sign one. But every Confidentiality Agreement is not the same. (That said, you can review a "standard form" on our Web site www.BEIBooks.com.)

A Confidentiality Agreement is a legal document subject to negotiation. In addition, specific or peculiar circumstances may require your transaction attorney to amend confidentiality language to give you and your company proper protection. The primary purpose of a Confidentiality Agreement is quite simply to protect your business from unauthorized disclosure or use of confidential information by potential buyers (including the fact that a potential transaction is contemplated). This may include, for example, standard non-disclosure provisions, but also a prohibition from using, in any way, your company's trade secrets and intellectual property that are disclosed to potential buyers. Before you sign a Confidentiality Agreement, have your attorney review it. Better yet, your attorney should draft the Confidentiality Agreement that you will require potential buyers to sign.

Letter Of Intent

A Letter of Intent (LOI) *should* be a non-binding agreement that describes the business terms of the contemplated transaction and begins to set forth certain contingencies to closing. These contingencies can be financial in nature, such as the ability of the buyer to obtain financing, and legal, such as the satisfactory completion of due diligence or approval by all necessary parties, and so on. In short, the LOI outlines the terms of the deal.

Stepping back for just a moment: when you assembled your Deal Team, you should have communicated, quite clearly, your requirements for any sale transaction. We ask our owners to put in writing their sale objectives. Remember fictional owner Jibben Nair from Chapter 9? He provided his Deal Team with the following memo.

Memorandum

To: Transaction Team Members
From: Jibben Nair

Given: I don't have to sell my business today so I will sell only if I can get everything I want. I want the following:

1. *Financial Security. For my family that means $10 million cash, after-tax.*

2.   *I am not willing to be an employee of a new owner. I am willing to stay on for a limited time (no more than 90 days) to allow for a smooth transition.*

3.   *I am not interested in any form of payment other than cash at closing. I don't want to carry a promissory note; I will not be subject to earn-outs and I will not accept the stock of the acquiring company.*

4.   *I want to provide my five key employees with some benefit as a result of the sale. I'm not exactly certain what that means—perhaps a guarantee of future employment with the new owner, as well as some type of cash bonus? (I'd be comfortable with a bonus of up to $150,000 each.)*

5.   *I want the buyer to enter into long-term leases with me for the properties I own (used in the business) or to buy them from me for fair market value at closing. I would consider financing this part of the sale using the properties as security.*

6.   *I am willing to enter into any kind of covenant not to compete that the buyer desires.*

7.   *I am willing to sell to any buyer except the following three companies that I believe are less than completely reputable (X, Y and Z). I don't want my employees to be forced to work for companies they don't respect.*

Your Deal Team advisors will use your objectives to qualify potential buyers. At the LOI stage of the deal, your Team will use your instructions to evaluate a buyer's LOI terms such as earn outs and carry backs.

The LOI should be non-binding and it is your attorney's job to ensure that it is generally non-binding except for one item the buyer will likely insist upon: your agreement to take the business off the market for a limited time period—usually 90 to 120 days (perhaps more)—while the buyer conducts final due diligence, negotiates the terms of the definitive purchase agreement and obtains any necessary financing. (Kevin discussed this "stop-shop" provision at some length in Chapter 9.)

Removing your company from the market may not sound like a big problem, but it carries with it serious ramifications. Once off the market, getting back on is problematic.

The controlled auction process is like a steam locomotive. It builds up a big head of steam, carried along by the buyer's enthusiasm and your thorough preparation. Suddenly, the train reaches a station as you sign your buyer's Letter of Intent. (But remember, there is still a lot of rail to ride before you arrive at the bank.) If the buyer you choose proves to be unsuitable or unqualified, the steam engine needs time and fuel to regain its cruising speed. Further, unless your investment banker has maintained the relationships, it may be difficult to go back to the once-interested, then-spurned would-be buyers. New buyers will need to be found and, if the investment banker did his or her job well, the best target buyers were part of the original auction. Your entire sale process is temporarily derailed. Getting back to this point—signing an LOI with a new buyer—may take months.

In a negotiated sale, the consequence of removing your company from the market can be even more serious. In that case, you never started with a pool of buyers. This is a major disadvantage of the negotiated sale and it is precisely why the buyer—rather than you—has the leverage in a negotiated sale transaction.

Consequently, as non-binding as the LOI may technically be, the consequences are dire if the buyer walks away (which the buyer can do). If the buyer proceeds, the LOI contains the major deal points upon which the entire transaction rests. Your investment banker, transaction attorney and CPA negotiate these deal points with great intensity, as well as with your continual involvement and assent. Typically, these deal points are set forth on a "Term Sheet," are attached to the LOI and include: deal structure (asset purchase, stock purchase or merger), purchase price, payment of purchase price, escrow/holdback information, non-compete, etc.

Caveat: Do not be lulled into thinking that this "non-binding" Letter of Intent is anything less than one of the most important and consequential documents you will sign in your entire business life.

Because the terms outlined in the Letter of Intent define the transaction, we will examine each term of the letter Jibben Nair (from Chapter 9) received from his prospective buyer.

LETTER OF INTENT

PRIVATE & CONFIDENTAL

Jibben Nair
Big Time Enterprises, Inc.
Evansville, Indiana

December 1, 2007

Re: Non-Binding Letter of Intent

Dear Mr. Nair:

This non-binding letter ("Letter") sets forth the mutual understanding between Quick Supply Company, an Illinois corporation ("Buyer") and Big Time Enterprises, Inc., an Indiana corporation (Seller"), with respect to a proposed acquisition of the business of the Seller in accordance with the terms and conditions of the non-binding Term Sheet attached hereto as *Exhibit A* (the "Proposed Acquisition"). This Letter will establish a general basis of negotiations which, if negotiations are successful, will result in terms and conditions set forth in the Definitive Agreements (as defined below). Neither Buyer nor Seller considers this Letter to be legally binding or enforceable against either party, except as otherwise specifically provided in the section entitled *Binding Provisions.*

NONBINDING PROVISION

Basic Terms of the Proposed Acquisition.   The parties hereto will collectively and promptly proceed with the negotiation, preparation and execution of a definitive acquisition agreement (together with all related agreements, documents and instruments, the "Definitive Agreements") containing among other things, the terms and conditions set forth in the non-binding Term Sheet attached hereto as *Exhibit A*. Buyer's counsel will be responsible for the drafting of the Definitive Agreements.

BINDING PROVISIONS

Access to Information.   From the date hereof, Seller shall afford the Buyer, its attorneys, accountants and other representatives and agents full access to all of the facilities, management, and outside advisors, and to all books and records, accountant's work papers, if available, documents, financial information and data pertaining to Seller's business, its operations, assets and liabilities (the "due diligence"). In addition, Seller shall fully cooperate with Buyer in the discovery and identification of due diligence. Buyer shall have the full opportunity to conduct its due diligence review of Seller's business, operations, assets, liabilities, books and records and obtain all information requested by Buyer as to the business of Seller and the principals of Seller. The Proposed Acquisition is conditioned on the satisfactory completion of due diligence by Buyer and through its representatives and agents, at Buyer's sole and absolute discretion.

Confidentiality Agreement. Buyer and Seller each acknowledge the existence of that certain Confidentiality/Non-Disclosure Agreement dated November 15, 2007, by and between Seller and Buyer and continue to be bound by its terms and conditions.

Operations. Seller shall operate its business and maintain all its assets during the period from the date hereof until the closing date of the Proposed Acquisition in the same manner in which it has been operated and maintained in the past. Seller shall take no action during the period from the date hereof until the closing date of the Proposed Acquisition that would change the nature of Seller's business or Seller's relationships with its customers, employees, vendors and suppliers.

Third-Party Dealings. Except as provided in the section entitled *Announcements* below, Seller shall not disclose to any third party, except its professional advisors, the terms and conditions of this Proposed Acquisition or that Seller is in communication with Buyer regarding a Proposed Acquisition. Through the Termination Date (defined below) Seller shall not solicit or entertain offers from, negotiate with or in any manner encourage, discuss, accept, or consider any proposal of any other person relating to the acquisition of the Seller's assets, business or shares of stock, in whole or in part, whether directly or indirectly, through purchase, merger, consolidation or otherwise.

Fees and Expenses.   Each party shall be responsible for the payment of all fees, costs and expenses incurred by it in connection with the transaction contemplated hereby and shall not be liable to the other for the payment of such fees, costs and expenses, including without limitation, brokerage or finders' fees incurred by the other party.

Announcements.   Unless required by law or by regulation of the Securities and Exchange Commission, prior to the execution of the Definitive Agreements no party to this Letter shall disclose or issue any statement or communication to the public or any third party, except its professional advisors, regarding this Proposed Acquisition without the prior written consent of the parties hereto.

Termination.   This Letter shall automatically terminate on the earlier of (i) March 15, 2008, or (ii) the execution of the Definitive Agreements. Upon any termination of this Letter, the parties shall have no further obligations hereunder, except the obligations set forth in the Binding Provisions of this Letter and in the Confidentiality Agreement, each of which shall survive any termination of this Letter.

Controlling Law/Assignment.   This Letter and the Definitive Agreements shall be construed in accordance with the laws of the State of Illinois. This Letter and the obligations hereunder may not be assigned by Seller to any person or entity.

Counterparts/Facsimile Signatures.   This Letter may be executed in two or more counterparts, each of which shall be deemed to be an original, but all of which taken together shall constitute one and the same document. This Letter may also be executed by facsimile signature that will be accepted by the parties as an original signature. This Letter shall only be effective upon the signature of all parties.

With the exception of Binding Provisions, this Letter with the non-binding Term Sheet attached hereto as ***Exhibit A*** does not constitute a binding agreement between the parties. This Letter is written solely as a summary of terms upon which the parties would consider the Proposed Acquisition and is intended to serve merely as a guide to the preparation of the Definitive Agreements. It is expressly understood and agreed that

(a) ***Exhibit A*** to this Letter is not considered to be a part of the Binding Provisions; (b) no liability or binding obligation is intended to be created between or among any of the parties to this Letter, except with respect to the Binding Provisions; and (c) other than with respect to the Binding Provisions, any legal rights and obligations between or among any of the parties to this Letter will come into existence only upon the parties' execution and delivery of the written Definitive Agreements, and then only in accordance with the terms and conditions of such Definitive Agreements.

If you are willing to proceed on the basis as outlined above, please sign and return one copy of this letter to Buyer no later than 5:00 p.m. Central Standard Time the 15th day of December, 2007. This Letter will be null and void if not executed by all parties and delivered to Buyer before such time.

Yours very truly,

Quick Supply Company

ACCEPTED AND AGREED TO this _____ day of
_____, 2007.
BIG TIME ENTERPRISES, INC.,
an Indiana corporation
By: Jibben Nair, President

* * * *

The Exhibit that Jibben's buyer included with the Letter of Intent was the non-binding Term Sheet that follows. An outline of various Term Sheet points and considerations can be found at www.BEIBooks.com.

EXHIBIT A

QUICK SUPPLY COMPANY
Asset Acquisition—Big Time Enterprises, Inc.
Term Sheet

QUICK SUPPLY COMPANY (the "Purchaser"), is please to submit this non-binding "Term Sheet" to summarize the main terms on which

Purchaser would be willing to acquire certain assets of BIG TIME ENTERPRISES, INC., and its retail stores known as BIG TIME (the "Seller"). The parties wish to begin negotiating the definitive written asset purchase agreement for the potential Acquisition ("Definitive Purchase Agreement"). Purchaser's counsel is to prepare the initial draft of the Definitive Purchase Agreement. The terms of the Acquisition to be included in the final Definitive Purchase Agreement to be executed by the parties are to include, among other terms, the following:

Buyer: QUICK SUPPLY COMPANY, INC. or its designees or assigns ("Purchaser").

Structure: The purchase will be structured as an asset purchase of all of Seller's retail inventory and co-op advertising receivables, as well as the trade and lay-away receivables, furniture, fixtures and equipment, and leasehold improvement of six (6) retail stores as listed on Exhibit 1 ("the Acquired Stores"). (*Not included here.*) The assets will be transferred by Seller free of all liens, liabilities and encumbrances.

Excluded Assets: All cash accounts owned by Seller, all other trade receivables and short check receivables.

Liabilities Assumed: Purchaser will assume the store operating leases for the stores listed on Attachment 2, (*Again, not included here.*) except for any unpaid rent, percentage rent or allocated common charges that accrue through the date of Closing. Purchaser also will assume outstanding inventory purchase order obligations as of the Closing date.

Purchase Price: $13,000,000 which includes the net tangible book value of assets acquired, excluding the value of the leasehold improvements. The Purchaser agrees that it will acquire at Closing, a minimum of $6,000,000 of inventory, net of all obsolescence reserves, at Closing. To determine the inventory value, Seller shall provide to Purchaser an analysis of its inventory sorted by department, class and style. This report shall be provided to Purchaser no later than the week of April 30, 2008. Purchaser and Seller shall jointly analyze the report to determine the extent to which inventory markdowns and obsolescence reserves are needed.

Immediately after reviewing the inventory analysis, Purchaser and Seller shall jointly determine a formula for computing the inventory obsolescence, but such formula shall not allow for an obsolescence reserve exceeding 10 percent of Seller's aggregate book value, as stated in accordance with its past practices. The agreed formula shall be applied to the inventory at Closing.

The inventory will be subject to a physical count on the day of Closing, with a determination of cost to be made no later than 30 days after Closing by an independent CPA firm to be mutually agreed upon by the parties. The cost of the physical inventory and the cost to pack and ship the inventory from closed stores to the Acquired Stores will be shared equally by the parties.

Consideration: $3,000,000 of the Purchase Price will be payable via a note. The note will accrue interest at an annual percentage rate of 9 percent and will be paid as follows: quarterly interest payments until maturity with three annual principal payments of $1,000,000 each on November 1, 2008, 2009 and 2010. To the extent permitted by Purchaser's senior lender, the note will be secured by a second security interest on all Purchaser's inventory and fixtures. If a second security interest cannot be obtained, then the interest rate shall be increased to 10 percent per annum. The Purchaser shall have the right to offset against the note any Purchase Price adjustments, as well as any indemnification claims to the extent such claims are consistent with the indemnification provisions as provided in the Definitive Purchase Agreement.

The remainder of the Purchase Price will be payable in cash at Closing via wire transfer.

Facility Leases: Purchaser will assume the store operating leases for the Acquired Stores as listed on Attachment 2. Purchaser and Seller mutually agree to use all reasonable efforts to assign the leases to the Purchaser and to remove Seller from its obligations under the store operating leases for the Acquired Stores. The Purchaser's ability to change the terms of any lease shall not be a condition of the Closing.

Seller will use its best efforts to terminate leases of all stores not sold by the Closing date and not included in the Acquired Stores.

If Seller is unable to close or sell such other stores prior to Closing under commercially reasonable terms, then Purchaser agrees that it will operate such stores under a management agreement until they can be sold or the leases terminated.

Employees: Purchaser agrees that it will interview all exempt employees of the Acquired Stores, and will offer employment to those exempt employees that meet Purchaser's standards of employment. Purchaser agrees that it will retain non-exempt employees according to Purchaser's conditions of employment. Seller shall notify its employees, as per WARN Act statutes, that Purchaser may engage in employment losses to include: termination other than discharge for cause, a voluntary departure, or a retirement; layoffs exceeding six months; or a reduction in hours of work more than 50 percent during each month of a six-month period. Seller shall be responsible for all liabilities that may occur under the WARN Act after the effective date of the sale with respect to the Acquired Stores. Seller will retain responsibility for all earned and accrued employee benefits through the date of Closing, including but not limited to: vacation; profit sharing and pension plans; health plan claims (asserted or unasserted); claims (of any kind) or benefits (of any kind) that may have accrued prior to the effective date of sale; or any other employee benefit plans that the Seller may have in effect as of the date of Closing.

Non-Compete: The Seller shall enter into an agreement with Purchaser prohibiting Seller's right, for a period of one year following Closing, to open new competing retail stores in any state in which Purchaser operates retail stores. For a period of one year after Closing, Seller also shall agree not to actively solicit any retail store employees whom Purchaser has interviewed and extended offer of employment to.

Confidentiality: The parties agree that the Confidentiality Agreement dated November 15, 2007, will continue to be in full force and effect.

Due Diligence: Purchaser's intention to consummate the proposed purchase is based upon certain assumptions about Seller's business. From the date of this letter to the Closing of the transaction, Purchaser may, through its agents, accountants, attorneys and others, make such investigations of the Acquired Stores, at such times as designated by Seller, so as not to unreasonably disrupt Seller's business, that Purchaser may deem necessary or advisable, and the Seller will reasonably make available to such persons complete and accurate copies of the books, records, data and other information pertaining to the "four wall" data for the Acquired Store as Purchaser or its agents may request. Notwithstanding the foregoing, Purchaser shall not contact any of the Seller's employees without the express written consent of Seller. Seller shall not be restricted from contacting customers in the ordinary course of its business.

Exclusivity: In recognition of the considerable time and expense that Purchaser will invest in performing its due diligence and pursing this transaction, Seller agrees that, from the date this Term Sheet is executed through the earlier of (i) May 30, 2008, (ii) the date the Purchaser discontinues (if any) actively negotiating to finally close the Acquisition, or (iii) as provided in Purchaser's or Seller's Contingencies below, neither Seller nor any of its representatives will solicit or accept any offers to purchase the assets of the Acquired Stores.

Conduct of Business From the date hereof and until either the Closing or termination of this Term Sheet, Seller will, with respect to the Acquired Stores, conduct its business in the ordinary course without substantial change; take such actions as are reasonably necessary to preserve the Sellers' existing relationships with respect to the Acquired Stores with customers, employees and suppliers, and not to make any changes that would have a material adverse impact on the Acquired Stores.

Purchaser's Contingencies: The Closing of the Acquisition by Purchaser will be contingent upon its ability to secure senior debt financing from its existing lender (Bank Two). The exclusivity period shall be terminated if Purchaser has not supplied to Seller, on or before April 30, 2008, a written Term Sheet proposal from Bank Two evidencing its willingness to provide financing for the acquisition, subject to Bank Two's due diligence, documentation and necessary approvals.

Seller's Contingencies: The Closing of the Acquisition by Seller will be conditioned on the consent of its bank to fully release its security interest in the assets as collateral under Seller's line of credit, and to allow Seller to sell such assets outside the ordinary course of business.

Closing: Closing shall occur on or before June 15, 2008 ("Closing").

∗ ∗ ∗ ∗

In most circumstances the business terms of a merger or acquisition are summarized in a Term Sheet. These items become an Exhibit to the Letter of Intent, and ultimately lead to the definitive purchase agreement. The Term Sheet is a broad overview of a contemplated transaction, but is usually not a binding document. It also does not reflect all elements of a transaction, but serves as a touchstone for what the parties hope to accomplish. It is important to carefully consider the Term Sheet before signing it, because while not binding, it will continuously be referred to by all parties as they negotiate a transaction. Let's look at each Term Sheet element.

TERM SHEET CONSIDERATIONS

TRANSACTION STRUCTURE

The Term Sheet's first objective is to generally outline what it is that the buyer is agreeing to purchase. There are two basic structures for an acquisition: a stock purchase or an asset purchase. Because a merger always involves the exchange of stock for stock, it is, by definition, a stock transaction.

In a *stock purchase*, the buyer generally agrees to purchase the equity of a company for a defined price and to assume all of the seller's liabilities (such as bank debt and capital lease obligations). In this situation, the buyer assumes the risk of any undisclosed liabilities. The biggest advantage of a stock purchase from the seller's standpoint is that it generally yields the most favorable tax results.

From the buyer's perspective, however, there are three significant disadvantages; namely the loss of tax deductions that could otherwise be achieved via an asset purchase, the assumption of unknown contingent liabilities, and (but not always) the acquisition of corporate assets that it does not want (such as real estate, non-related business assets, etc.). For these reasons, buyers prefer to purchase assets and not stock. Stock transactions most commonly occur when both the buyer and seller are C Corporations, and when the buyer is a public company (because public companies are less tax sensitive).

Far more common in the sale of private companies is the *purchase of assets*. In an asset sale, the buyer can take a tax deduction for a significant portion of the price it pays for the company thereby reducing its after-tax purchase price by 40 percent or more. The buyer enjoys the further advantage of limiting its exposure to liabilities, both disclosed and undisclosed. In an asset purchase, the buyer explicitly states the liabilities that it will assume and restricts its assumption of potential unknown liabilities. In an asset sale, the buyer and seller negotiate how the purchase price is to be allocated to the various assets, and that allocation has a significant tax impact on the seller. (This is yet another reason it is so important to get tax advice before agreeing to the Term Sheet!)

As discussed in Chapter 5, if the seller is a C Corporation, an asset sale results in two tax events: the corporation is taxed on the receipt of the sale proceeds and the shareholders are taxed when they receive their distribution of the proceeds. The total tax bill may be as much as 55 percent of the sale price. C Corporations generally find the after-tax results of an asset sale to be unrewarding; thus the limited market for sales of assets.

Mergers are typically stock swaps, and, if properly structured, defer the taxes that would otherwise be paid in a stock or asset sale. Mergers can be complex because both parties in the transaction must conduct due diligence, be concerned about the value being exchanged, negotiate for managerial control and provide for a future exit for the shareholders. In addition, seller and buyer must determine post-merger corporate governance, and, perhaps most importantly, determine who is ultimately "in charge."

There is seldom a true merger of equals although sometimes it is not clear at the outset who is acquiring whom. That said, mergers can be excellent vehicles for building a company, or even exiting a business. Mergers carry distinct tax advantages and can tip an equation so that one plus one does, indeed, exceed two.

Another structure that is used to transfer ownership is a *tax-free reorganization*. In this transaction, a new company is created and the existing company merges into it. This structure allows for the deferral of taxes on all or a portion of the proceeds, while still allowing for a partial change in ownership. Again, consult your tax advisor before agreeing to this type of structure.

The last structure that transactions may take is a section 338(h)(10) election. The name refers to a section of the tax code that allows a corporation to structure an acquisition as a stock purchase, while treating the transaction as if it were an asset purchase, for federal income tax purposes. This structure also can avoid state and local property transfer taxes that might otherwise be paid if the assets were purchased. This structure has the advantages of both a stock and an asset purchase while eliminating some of the disadvantages of each. This transaction works very well if the seller is an S Corporation or partnership (because there is only one level of taxation), but not so well for C Corporations (two levels of taxation).

Purchase Price or Purchase Price Calculation

The second section of the Term Sheet defines the price to be paid for the assets or stock, and details how that price will be computed. More often than not the final purchase price is not known when the Term Sheet is signed. Instead, the parties agree on a formula that will be used to determine the price. These formulas are either tied to the seller's asset value, its expected earnings or a combination of the two. It is critical to understand the purchase price calculation contained in a Term Sheet because once agreed to, this item is the most difficult item to renegotiate.

Purchase Price Adjustments

Most transactions include a description of the buyer's expectations for earnings, working capital and net worth at the time the deal closes.

If these expectations are not met, the Term Sheet describes how the purchase price will be adjusted. These adjustments can be positive or negative to the seller, and in most cases should go both ways. If a seller exceeds a buyer's expectations he or she is rewarded, and if the seller falls short, he or she is penalized. More hours are typically spent negotiating purchase price adjustment criteria, than are spent negotiating the purchase price itself.

PAYMENT OF PURCHASE PRICE

The purchase price may be paid:

- 100 percent cash;

- 100 percent stock of the buyer;

- partial cash/partial note paid over time; or

- some combination of these.

The proceeds also may include payments that are contingent upon the future performance of the business, which may be paid in the form of a royalty, licensing fee, or earn-out. Sometimes a portion of the purchase price is paid in the form of above-market payments for property or equipment that continue to be owned by the seller and leased to the buyer. Consideration also may take the form of consulting agreements, payments for agreements not to compete, or payments for anything else that the buyer and seller agree to.

When evaluating a potential transaction, it is important to understand the risk associated with the currency that one receives. If you intend to receive stock, you must understand the value, liquidity and taxability of the shares that you will receive. This means that you and your advisors must perform due diligence on the buyer, and the current and potential future value of the stock. If the consideration includes a seller note, you and your advisor must probe the security of the note, as well as any restrictions that might limit your right to receive payments. If you plan to accept contingent payments (also known as earn-outs) you and your advisors need to assess the probability that you will receive such payments, and negotiate provisions to minimize the risk that such payments will not be received. If, as part of the consideration, you are willing to retain a portion of the ownership of your company, protect yourself by including minority shareholder safeguards.

EARN-OUT

In the sale of privately held companies, it is not uncommon for a portion of the purchase price to be structured as an earn-out. This is often the case when the acquired company has grown rapidly and its seller wants the value of expected continued earnings growth included in the sale price. Buyers generally prefer to value a company based on historical performance rather than future earnings. This gap between the seller's expectations of future growth and the buyer's reluctance to pay for an uncertainty (which we refer to as an "expectation gap") is often bridged by an earn-out. In an earn-out, the seller receives more for the company only if the growth in earnings materializes. If growth falls short, the buyer doesn't pay.

Earn-outs can be very complex, and the wording of the earn-out language needs to be very specific in order to avoid future disputes. To a seller, the benefit of an earn-out is that it receives more for the business than it may be worth on the sale date. On the other hand, if the seller does not control management of the company post-sale, and the buyer makes decisions that reduce the future earnings, the earn-out is unachievable. Earn-outs work well when a seller is willing to continue to manage the business during the period that the earn-out remains in effect, and when the business really possesses growth potential—potential that is enhanced by the synergies that the buyer brings to the company.

Kevin Short reports that, "In the last several years (during the peak of the M&A market) we haven't seen many earn-outs. We only see them when, in order to close the deal, we need to provide the buyer with some protection that what the seller says will happen, will indeed happen. For example, if a seller signs $12 million worth of contracts that will play out after the closing, the buyer does not want to pay for that future value at closing. Instead, the parties negotiate what portion of the $12 million will be held as an earn-out. Basically, earn-outs are financing vehicles that protect buyers in soft markets from risk."

ESCROW/HOLDBACK

Sales to third parties always include certain representations and war-ranties that the seller will make to the buyer, and vice versa, regarding the condition and operations of the business. These representations are sometimes referenced in the Term Sheet, but are not negotiated at this time. Specific representations and warranties are negotiated as part of the definitive purchase agreement. One item that is often negotiated in the Term Sheet is how much of the purchase price will be placed in escrow or held back by the buyer to ensure the performance on any breach of a representation or warranty. Typical terms for the escrow or holdback are 10 percent of the purchase price, to be released within one to two years after the transaction is completed. Active negotiation on the part of your advisors may reduce the amount and length of holdbacks or escrow.

ASSUMED LIABILITIES/NON-ASSUMED LIABILITIES

When the transaction is a purchase of assets, the Term Sheet typically describes the seller's liabilities that the buyer is willing to assume, either as part of the purchase price or in addition to the purchase price. Gener-ally, assumed liabilities include accounts payable and specifically identi-fied accrued liabilities such as accrued payroll, employee vacation accru-als, and liabilities associated with the normal operations of the business, such as assumption of building and equipment operating leases. Specifi-cally excluded liabilities include unpaid taxes, product warranties, and any unrecorded, unknown or contingent liability.

NON-REFUNDABLE DEPOSIT AND BREAK-UP FEE

Since the late 1980s, it is quite rare for a buyer to agree to pay a deposit when the Term Sheet is signed or for a buyer to agree to pay the seller a fee if the deal is not completed. Similarly, it is not customary for the sell-er to agree to pay a break-up fee to reimburse the buyer for the buyer's costs of pursuing an uncompleted transaction. Non-refundable depos-its are sometimes placed in escrow when the seller has serious doubts about the buyer's financial ability to complete a transaction, while the buyer is confident that it can, in fact, close. These escrow agreements specifically state when and if the non-refundable deposit can be paid to the seller.

We see break-up fees in the sale of public companies when the buyer wants protection from the seller accepting a better offer after the buyer has completed its due diligence, signed a definitive agreement, and publicly announced the transaction for its shareholders to consider. Because public companies have a fiduciary duty to maximize value for their public shareholders they may be forced to accept a competing bid that is submitted after they have already agreed to a transaction with another buyer. For this reason, a break-up fee is used to compensate the first buyer for its costs in initiating a process started that ultimately resulted in a sale to a higher bidder.

Break-up fees are used also in sales of private companies when, after the definitive agreement is signed and the buyer's due diligence is complete, the transaction fails to close because one of the parties changes its mind. It costs a lot of money to pursue an acquisition so it is not surprising that companies want compensation if they believe the other party didn't act in good faith to close the contemplated transaction.

Permitted Distributions and Operating Restrictions

After the Term Sheet is signed, but before closing, the seller maintains control of the company. This period of time can range from a few weeks to several months. During this period of time, the buyer wants to make sure that the seller does not significantly change the business or remove any of the assets that the buyer intends to purchase. Therefore, Term Sheets describe how earnings and assets will be distributed, as well as how the company will be operated until closing.

Transition Consulting Agreements and Employment Agreements

More often than not, buyers want the key managers/owners to remain with the business for a period of time after the transaction closes. The length, nature, and terms of the associated employment or consulting agreements are often noted in the Term Sheet, but not fully negotiated until other major elements of the transaction (such as due diligence, financing and negotiation of definitive agreement) are complete.

COVENANT NOT TO COMPETE

Covenants not to compete are a part of almost every transaction, because the buyer or merger partner wants to protect the value of the business that they are buying. It would hardly be prudent to pay a seller a large sum of money and then allow the seller to set up a competing business in the same market. Therefore, at the Term Sheet stage, covenants not to compete will be identified as a condition to closing the transaction, the details of which will be negotiated in a separate agreement. Covenants not to compete are quite specific in terms of geographic scope, length of time, and nature of the business restriction.

REAL PROPERTY LEASE AGREEMENT

Most businesses involve some use of real estate, either owned by the company, the company's owner outside of the company, or by a third party. The Term Sheet spells out the intention of the parties, for example, to purchase the real estate as part of the transaction, lease it from the owner, lease it with an option to purchase, terminate the existing lease with the third-party landlord, or continue the existing lease.

FINANCE CONTINGENCY

The Term Sheet should specifically state whether or not the buyer will arrange outside financing to complete the transaction. If there is no contingency, the buyer should be precluded from later using its inability to obtain financing as a reason for not closing the transaction. If there is a financing contingency, the Term Sheet describes how long the buyer has to arrange for such financing. If the transaction involves the exchange of public shares, then the transaction may be contingent upon the value of the shares being within a certain specified range at the time of the closing. If the value is not within that range, the Term Sheet details whether the transaction will undergo a repricing or will terminate.

OTHER CONTINGENCIES

When the Term Sheet is signed neither buyer nor seller have done much due diligence on each other, thus both want the transaction to be contingent upon completion and a satisfactory due diligence investigation. This contingency exists in almost every transaction.

Other contingencies may include the satisfactory negotiation of a definitive agreement, employment agreements with key people, the retention of key suppliers and customers, the execution of real estate leases and non-compete agreements. Contingencies also can include any other item that either of the parties wants to see happen or is concerned about prior to closing.

EXCLUSIVITY PERIOD/STOP SHOP

Because it takes time to complete due diligence, arrange financing and negotiate the definitive agreements, buyers require sellers to give them some period of time to complete these activities, without having to worry about the seller running off with some other buyer. The exclusivity period is typically 60 to 120 days. The shorter the time period, the better from the seller's perspective. Conversely, buyers prefer longer periods of exclusivity. (Again, please see Kevin Short's discussion of stop-shop agreements in Chapter 9.)

ANTICIPATED CLOSING DATE

The Term Sheet specifies the date that the transaction is expected to close. It is important to draw a line in the sand, otherwise the lawyers, accountants, and numerous other outside advisors won't appreciate the parties' time sensitivity regarding closing. Sometimes one party is willing to change a closing date if it believes that the other party is working diligently toward getting the deal done. Sometimes closing dates can become drop dead dates and it is important to understand that if one of the parties is very focused on a closing date, it can be fatal to miss it.

SELLER'S ROLE

We've all seen television commercials for automobiles that caution us not to attempt some driving reenactment maneuver ourselves—that "professional stunt drivers" are being used. Well, the same holds true for parts of the sale process. Your advisors will take charge and consult you as necessary during their negotiations for three reasons. First, you are likely to have little experience in the complexities of negotiating the structure and the sale of a multi-million dollar business.

Second, you will likely need to interact with the buyer (your soon-to-be new boss) after the sale of your company in an employee capacity of some sort—or at least in a capacity other than negotiator. So, it is important to stay in the background to avoid the strained relationship that often develops during intense negotiation. Let your lawyers and other advisors be your advocates—they don't mind if they develop strained relationships. They are used to it.

Third, you are probably too close to the sale process as it is. It is vital you keep your eye on the business—not on the sale process. If the revenues of your company dip during extended negotiations, the entire deal may be placed in jeopardy. This does not mean you should be detached. And you won't be. The negotiation of the terms of the Letter of Intent and Term Sheet are the very essence of your Exit Plan. Your advisors will be in continual contact with you to explain and brainstorm each offer, counter-offer and suggestion from the buyer. Even though the Letter of Intent is non-binding, it should reflect your Exit Objectives.

Finally, owners always ask, "How long does the sale process take?" Kevin tells his clients to expect six to twelve months to elapse between the time he markets the company and the closing. The owners in Chapter 12 all report about the same time frame.

The more you know about the sale process, the more helpful you will be to your advisory team, and the more nimble you'll be in handling buyer questions and concerns. Ultimately, you will be the winner.

11

TO CLOSING AND BEYOND!

AVOIDING POST-CLOSING
PAYBACKS AND MORE

CHAPTER HIGHLIGHTS

- Buyer's Final Due Diligence

- Negotiating Financial Contingency

- Creating The Definitive Purchase Agreement
  Representations And Warranties

- Maintaining Momentum

- Maintaining Confidentiality

- Closing The Deal And Beyond

Whether you have embarked upon a controlled auction or negotiated sale process, the time has come to "do the deal." You have completed the planning and marketing phases. The outlines of the deal have been established through the negotiation of the Letter of Intent and Term Sheet. The Confidentiality Agreement is cloaking the transaction and protecting the information you have disclosed about your company. So, what work remains?

1. Buyer's performance of final due diligence;

2. Negotiating financing contingencies; and

3. Negotiating the definitive purchase agreement and other transaction documents.

While all this is happening, you and your advisors must maintain both momentum and confidentiality.

BUYER'S FINAL DUE DILIGENCE

During the final phase of due diligence, the prospective buyer will make an on-site visit (if not done earlier) and may wish to meet with your customers and employees. The buyer also unleashes its lawyers, accountants and investment bankers on all of the material your transaction advisors gathered earlier in the process. Your transaction attorney should control disclosure of documents and information. This is the point at which your customers or your employees may (but not necessarily) learn of your desire to sell your business. Not until you have signed a Letter of Intent with a qualified buyer is it likely that some of your employees will discover that you intend to sell your company. Even then, most buyers wish to meet only a few select key employees.

If these employees react adversely, threatening to quit or refusing to cooperate, the deal may unravel.

Curly Jones, the long-time CFO of 820 Industries, had long dreamed of succeeding owner and founder, Seth Aubrey. In Curly's opinion, he was more capable and more devoted to the company and much of 820 Industries' financial success was due to his diligent efforts. Imagine his surprise when Seth confided to him that he intended to sell the company to an outside party and had hired an investment banking firm. A qualified buyer had signed a Letter of Intent and its deal team was visiting the plant to interview management, including Curly.

Curly was shocked by the lack of forewarning and that he'd been left out of the loop. He was determined not to let the opportunity to buy the company slip away. So, during his interview with the buyer's representatives, Curly described, in great detail, his perception of the company's challenges and issues. Curly chose to discuss those challenges and issues that would kill any acquisition plans a would-be buyer might have. In short, Curly torpedoed the deal.

Curly's actions went undiscovered until the second would-be buyer experienced the same treatment during a management interview.

> *This time, however, Seth discovered Curly's disloyalty and outright fabrications. Seth dismissed Curly and managed to save the deal. Curly's actions cost Seth the more lucrative first deal and added six months to the sale process.*

If you turn back to our discussion of short-term incentive plans in Chapter 6, the section related to the stay bonus describes exactly what Seth could have done to encourage Curly to be on the same page as Seth. Under this plan, if Seth sells his business, Curly receives an out-sized and substantial cash benefit.

The buyer now has poured through your financial and legal documentation, your contracts and your internal procedures. It has examined everything and has spoken with your employees. Every nook and every cranny—both above and under the ground—have been probed. (Environmental issues are the most common underground items.) Your facility has been inspected, viewed and reviewed (making your efforts to improve facility appearance back in Chapter 6 worthwhile). One more area may remain: your customers.

Don't be surprised if a buyer wants to meet your key customers. If your company depends on a small number of customers, count on it. That's why expanding and diversifying your customer base is so important. If your customer base is diverse, buyers feel less of a need to initiate these meetings.

NEGOTIATING FINANCIAL CONTINGENCY

Many buyers agree to purchase your company subject to obtaining purchase financing. Your transaction advisors will review their proposal to do so and will analyze the buyer's ability to complete their proposal successfully given:

- Its financial strength.

- The structure of the proposed financing.

- The current "metrics" of the financial marketplace.

Your investment banker must determine the likelihood of the buyer obtaining its financing before allowing you to sign the LOI and thereby taking your company out of play.

Once you take your company off the auction block, it is difficult to return. Signing an LOI does just that. If possible, do not sign an LOI without sufficient assurance that the major contingency—buyer financing—can and will be satisfied.

Your investment banker will maintain constant contact with the buyer to continually monitor the success (or failure) of the buyer's efforts.

Creating the Definitive Purchase Agreement

This is the process of converting the three-page Letter of Intent into a 60-page, binding purchase agreement (plus attachments). Normal individuals are incapable of transforming a simple agreement into a complex document with dense and obscure language. You need transaction lawyers for that. The reason for all of the complex detail is simple: while the Letter of Intent is nothing more than a statement of intent—of what both parties would like to see happen—the definitive Purchase Agreement is binding. In fact, the definitive Purchase Agreement is just that. It *defines* the purchase, detailing the Term Sheet provisions described in the previous chapter and adding the provisions elaborated on below.

- Parties

- Structure

- Purchase Price

- Seller's employment requirements, including covenant not to compete, duties and length of term

- Pre-Closing Covenants and Conduct of Business

- Seller's Representations and Warranties
    This important section is explained in more detail below. This section provides the new owner with an owner's manual for his new company. Because the seller, through the representations

and warranties, states that "this is how things are" it does create liability on the part of the seller.

- Buyer's Representations and Warranties

  This section includes items such as the Buyer's Authorization to Enter Into the Transaction, the statement that the purchase does not contravene any other agreements such as lending or financing agreements between the buyer and third parties. It also spells out the responsibility to pay investment banking fees, if any. Along with the seller's representations and warranties, this section determines the length of the document.

- Closing Conditions

  This section documents the responsibility to deliver lists, schedules, odometer certificates, leases, and similar information prior to or at closing.

- Indemnification

  This section tells the buyer that if things aren't as the seller says they are, how the buyer is to be made whole. It is perhaps unnecessary to state that the buyer is made whole through the seller acting as an insurance company for that buyer. For this reason, this section is the object of serious negotiation by attorneys for the seller and the buyer. It sets the "baskets" (deductibles) that must be exceeded before the buyer can make a claim for indemnification. It also contains caps (or limits) on how much the seller will have to pay.

- Survivorship Periods

  Just how long will the representations and warranties that you make to the buyer continue after the closing? You certainly don't want them to last forever. It is seemingly insignificant sections like this that are subject to serious negotiation, give and take, and compromise. You may think your deal lawyers are just running up the billable hours negotiating intricate contractual provisions that will never see the light of day. But these provisions are potentially the difference between keeping or repaying the purchase price. Your lawyers earn their money here. Really.

- Termination

   The termination of the Definitive Purchase Agreement is an issue only if the closing on the deal and the signing are not simultaneous. In most transactions the Definitive Purchase Agreement is signed at the same time that the closing takes place.

- Post-Closing Covenants

   These are covenants that deal with actions the seller promises to take or not take after the closing of the deal.

Once signed, the Definitive Purchase Agreement commits you to selling and it commits the buyer to paying millions of dollars for a business it likely knew nothing about a few months before.

REPRESENTATIONS AND WARRANTIES

The buyer will insist upon assurances, in the form of Indemnifications, Representations and Warranties, as well as other contractual promises and guarantees, that everything is exactly as represented. If these "reps and warranties" are overly broad making their future performance unlikely, you will be committed to adjusting the purchase price. In other words, if non-compliance is discovered post-closing, you will be required to indemnify the buyer for any damages it suffers.

In my experience, sellers do not enjoy repaying money to buyers. So let's look at representations and warranties a little more closely.

Working through the representations and warranties is also where the lawyers earn their money. All attorneys can nit-pick and argue sticky and difficult points. You want to hire the ones that can resolve the difficult points **and** keep the deal moving forward. This normally requires *both sides* to hire experienced (at least a dozen years in the M&A trenches) attorneys to negotiate key terms. A young and inexperienced attorney representing the buyer can effectively bring the process to a halt. Why? The greatest fear of any attorney is making a mistake. Inexperience prompts these attorneys to argue, with great inflexibility, every point, major and minor. In this situation, it is the investment banker's job to intervene and to circumvent the negotiations on non-vital points.

Representations and warranties are contractual promises you make to the buyer (if the buyer has its way) about almost every aspect of your business. Or (if your lawyers have their way) they are the promises you make about as few areas of your business as absolutely necessary to get the deal done. Examples of representations and warranties are:

- Organization, Qualification and Corporate Power

- Capitalization

- Noncontravention

- Authorization of Transaction

- Title to Assets

- Subsidiaries

- Financial Statements

- Events Subsequent to Closing

- Undisclosed Liabilities

- Legal Compliance

- Tax Matters

- Real Property

- Intellectual Property

- Tangible Assets

- Inventory

- Contracts

- Notes and Accounts Receivable

- Powers of Attorney

- Insurance

- Litigation

- Product Warranty

- Product Liability

- Employees

- Employee Benefits

- Guaranties

- Environmental, Health and Safety Matters

- Certain Business Relationships with Seller

- Brokers' Fees

- Disclosure

If it seems like a pretty straightforward list, it is. But let's look at just how complex two of the items on this list (Authority and Leased Property) can be as crafted by the buyer's attorneys.

Authority. Each Seller has full individual, corporate or limited liability company power and authority to execute and deliver this Agreement and Seller Ancillary Documents and to perform its obligations hereunder and thereunder and to consummate the transactions contemplated hereby and thereby. The execution and delivery of this Agreement and Seller Ancillary Documents by each Seller and the performance by each Seller of its obligations hereunder and thereunder and the consummation of the transactions provided for herein and therein have been duly and validly authorized by all necessary individual, corporate or limited liability company action on the part of each Seller. The stockholders or members of each Seller other than the Individual Owners, and the Individual Owners individually, has approved the execution, delivery and performance of this Agreement and Seller Ancillary Documents and the consummation of the transactions contemplated hereby and thereby. This Agreement has been, and Seller Ancillary Documents shall be as of the Closing Date, duly executed and delivered by each Seller and do or shall, as the case may be, constitute the legal, valid and binding agreements of each Seller, enforceable against each Seller in accordance with their respective terms, subject to applicable bankruptcy, insolvency and other similar Laws affecting the enforceability of creditors' rights generally, general equitable principles and the discretion of courts in granting equitable remedies.

Leased Real Property

(a)   Schedule 1.4(a) sets forth a true and correct list of all leases, subleases, licenses, concessions or other agreements (written or oral) and all amendments thereto pursuant to which any Seller holds the Leased Real Property, in each case reflecting the name of the lessor, the lease term and the basic annual rent, and reflecting whether consent is required for the assignment of any such instrument. Each Seller has delivered to Buyer true and correct copies of all matters listed on Schedule 1.4(a).

(b)   Each Seller has a valid leasehold interest in its Leased Real Property and a valid leasehold interest in the Leased Real Property will be assigned to Buyer at Closing, free and clear of all Liens other than Permitted Liens. No Seller is in breach of or default under and no event has occurred which would, with notice or passage of time or both, constitute a breach of or a default under or permit termination, modification or acceleration of any provision of any such lease.

(c)   There are no disputes, oral agreements, or forbearance agreements in effect as to the Leased Real Property. No Seller has assigned, transferred, conveyed, mortgaged, deeded in trust, or encumbered any interest in any leasehold or subleasehold under the Leased Real Property. To the Knowledge of each Seller, all facilities leased or subleased under any lease are supplied with utilities and other services to the extent reasonably necessary for the present operation of the Business.

(d)   To the Knowledge of each Seller, the present use by each Seller of the Leased Real Property is in compliance with all applicable zoning ordinances (or authorized variances granted therefrom) and other applicable Laws, and there does not exist any notice of any uncorrected violation of any housing, building, safety, fire or other ordinance or applicable governmental regulation applicable to any Seller with respect to the Leased Real Property. Except for assessments not yet due and payable, no Seller is liable for any unpaid assessments, nor to the best of each Seller's Knowledge, for any public improvements, as lessee of any Leased Real Property, nor has Seller received any written notice from any appropriate Governmental Entity of its intention to make any public improvement for which Seller will be assessed directly or by reason of a leasehold interest.

(e)   The Leased Real Property listed on *Schedule 1.4(a)* constitutes all the Leased Real Property used in the Business.

MAINTAINING MOMENTUM

Remember the steam locomotive metaphor? By this point in the sale process, that locomotive is carrying a full load of cargo: lawyers negotiating the definitive purchase agreement, the buyer reconsidering financing options, due diligence issues raising their ugly heads and requiring negotiation, and so on. In the middle of all this, you have a business to run. Momentum must be maintained. As I mentioned earlier, a deal is not a real deal unless it has been derailed—in the ditch—at least five times. What gets the train back on track and keeps it there is momentum. A critical attribute of a successful Transaction Team is its ability to maintain momentum. Your Team cannot allow the buyer's lawyers, accountants and investment bankers to slow down this train. (This is the key reason for making absolutely certain that your pre-sale due diligence has addressed any problems long before the buyer begins his investigation.)

Maintaining momentum also applies to your company. It is critical that you keep your business generating ever-greater cash flow while your advisors sweep aside obstacles on the tracks. Work with your original Exit Planning Advisor and perhaps your regular advisors to maintain company performance.

Finally, maintaining momentum also applies to you. You must keep the business moving forward without allowing the ups and downs of the deal to distract you.

MAINTAINING CONFIDENTIALITY

Finally, we reach the topic so near and dear to every business owner's heart: confidentiality. Every owner is justifiably concerned that news of his decision to sell his company might, through the pre-sale due diligence process, be divulged to key employees, customers or others. Uncertainty about how to prevent untimely disclosure often prevents an owner from moving forward.

Confidentiality can be maintained, however, provided you and your Transaction Team take proper measures to preserve it. In my experience, leaks generally come from the sellers themselves or from potential buyers. Situations, of course, vary. But complete security can be maintained for some time if your CPA firm collects all financial information, and your law firm obtains all legal and contractual information necessary for due diligence. If confidentiality is to be maintained, tell your CFO (and others who may be called upon to assemble legal information and records) that the company is simply performing a legal audit to make certain its legal and contractual documentation is as organized and supportable as its financial information and documentation.

CLOSING THE DEAL AND BEYOND

The check is **not** in the mail. With a good Transaction Team on board, it should be *in your pocket*. You are almost, but not quite, ready to proceed to the final chapter—Life After The Sale. The sale process does not end at closing. There are a number of events that will take place—some within 30 to 120 days and some within 24 to 36 months.

In the short term, you can expect a price adjustment to be made. These adjustments are a result of the buyer's *post-closing* audit of items on your balance sheet such as net worth, working capital and accounts receivable.

Yes, the buyer audits your books after the sale. How smoothly this audit proceeds is directly related to how carefully and thoroughly you and your advisors undertook due diligence prior to the sale. This audit is not primarily a fishing expedition for fraud (although the buyer's accountant will be watching for it); rather the audit is done because business value is a fluid asset. The value of inventory, cash on hand and accounts receivable change on a daily basis. Or, if you've been paying yourself or your wife a little extra, the EBITDA value will be adjusted.

Longer-term issues include: releases of escrow, indemnification, survival period, payments on holdback notes and earn-outs. You and your transaction attorney will have discussed these items during the negotiation of the definitive purchase agreement. All your efforts to disclose everything during due diligence and all of your attorney's efforts during negotiations should pay off at this point. You should be protected from any significant negative price adjustments. After the deal closes, you are ready to go on with "Life After The Sale."

SECTION FIVE

ADJUSTING POST-SALE EXPECTATIONS

I f you are not ready to sell or you can't envision your life without the business, and want to read nothing else, I ask that you read this part of the book.

This section contains interviews with real owners sharing their stories with you (and hopefully thousands of others!). They have agreed to share their stories for one reason: at one time they were in your position. They, too, owned successful businesses. They, too, wondered if life after the sale could be as satisfying, challenging and as fulfilling as life as an owner. They faced the uncertainties of the sale process itself: issues of confidentiality, finding the right advisors, getting enough money, dealing with employees and more.

A swirl of uncertainty can create indecision at a time when firm decisions based on a sound understanding of goals and process is essential. These owners share their journey in the hope that they can clear up some uncertainty, show you the process described in this book and prove that there really is a road map that leads to a new, dynamic and fulfilling life after the sale.

12

WHAT DO I DO AFTER I HAVE SOLD MY BUSINESS?
FORMER OWNERS SPEAK OUT ABOUT LIFE AFTER THE SALE

In this final chapter, we recount the stories of several Baby Boomers who have left their companies—by negotiated sale, controlled auction or organized liquidation. Each of these owners provides current owners some guidance about the experience before, during and after the sale.

A MAN WITH A LOT OF OPTIONS
HAROLD BADE

When Harold Bade tells the story of the sale of his company, you may wonder if he has found a second career as Kevin Short's publicist. Harold's story is one of the best illustrations of the value of the investment banker, the value of the controlled auction and how an owner's objectives direct the process that I've ever seen.

—John Brown

Harold Bade was the sole owner of ASP Enterprises, Inc., a Midwestern distributor of erosion control and drainage systems. ASP had three offices in two states, 23 employees and had annual revenues in the $10 million to $20 million range. When Kevin Short met Harold in March of 2006, Harold was a 63-year-old survivor of a serious heart problem, a subsequent coma and lengthy hospital stay. His banker had suggested that Harold and Kevin meet to look at an offer to buy his company that he had received from one of his main suppliers. Since Harold had decided to slow down, he was seriously considering the offer.

Before Kevin even looked at the numbers, he asked Harold what he wanted and needed from the sale of his company. Having already met with his financial planner, Harold knew the amount he needed to fund his retirement. His goal was to retire without any adverse affect on his family's lifestyle.

Harold also wanted to sell to a company that would keep his employees and treat them well. He preferred a buyer who would retain the corporate culture he had worked 30 years to create.

The buyer Harold was considering met all of those requirements, but Kevin was concerned that the offer was below what the market would bear and that, with only one buyer at the table, Harold's negotiating strength would be seriously compromised.

"I had an idea of what my company was worth," Harold explains. "My CPA had estimated its value so I was focused on price. After an hour with Kevin, I realized just how many negotiable issues other than price were on the table."

"Specifically," Kevin recalls, "I showed Harold that, because the offer did not include the assumption of his debt, the **net** purchase price was about $2.6 million less than he'd thought. Further, the offer required Harold to carry back about a third of the purchase price in a promissory note and a large percentage of the buyer's payments were subject to Harold's company meeting various contingencies."

Harold retained Kevin after that meeting and Kevin put Harold's company on the market in April 2006. Only seven months later Harold sold the company.

The short time frame was possible for several reasons. First, the vice president of ASP had kept meticulous corporate records and books. She was the only employee to know of Harold's sale plans and was able to provide the buyer what it asked for quickly and efficiently. Not only were there no land mines hidden in Harold's records, but the fact that the records were easily accessible and well organized allowed Kevin to keep the pace of the deal moving quickly.

The second less tangible, but no less important, reason that Harold enjoyed a short time frame between going to market and leaving the closing table was that Harold was a mature and objective seller. He knew what he had to sell and he knew what he wanted. "Because Harold knew his priorities and *because he had communicated them clearly to me,* we were able to keep the deal moving," says Kevin. "Finally, Harold kept control of his emotions. As I mentioned in Chapter 9, this is not an easy task for all owners."

"The third reason that we were able to move quickly to a sale," remembers Kevin, "was that Harold's company was profitable and large enough to attract significant market attention. Consequently, its size allowed us to demand a higher multiple." Harold adds that, "Capital gains taxes were low and companies like mine were fetching high prices." "Armed with squeaky-clean records, Harold's maturity, and a well-performing, good size company, we were able to move quickly to take full advantage of the favorable Merger & Acquisition environment," Kevin concludes.

Harold's insight about the robust health of M&A activity in his industry proved dead on. Within eight weeks, 11 legitimate prospective buyers had submitted Term Sheets. Rather than sign with any one of them, (and subject Harold to any type of stop shop agreement) Kevin continued negotiating with each buyer.

As negotiations progressed, buyers left the table when they could not meet the better offers of their competitors. With so many buyers at the table, Harold was in the catbird's seat. If a buyer asked for something Harold was not willing to give, Kevin simply moved on to the next buyer.

Four prospective buyers eventually submitted signed Purchase Agreements for Harold's review. Harold chose the buyer who best met his financial and personal objectives and left the closing table with no debt, and $2 million more than the original offer in his pocket.

"I'm not in the business of selling companies," Harold notes. "Kevin's firm took a huge load off my shoulders. I didn't have to stumble around or rely on trial and error in the biggest financial deal of my life."

"Harold had a great company to sell, and he knew what he wanted. His objectives were so clear that they gave me a reference point in all subsequent negotiations," says Kevin.

Asked what surprised him most about the entire process, Harold talks about confidentiality. "I'm still amazed that while better than 50 percent of the prospective buyers were in my industry, not a whisper got back to my employees until the day I closed."

Today, Harold runs the company he sold free from the burdens of ownership. He is nearing the end of his one-year employment agreement. "With the new owner assuming a hands-off role in another city, I'm free to do what I've always done with one or two exceptions. The checks I sign use someone else's money and I'm training someone to take my place if I decide to retire at the end of the year."

When asked exactly what he plans to do at year's end, Harold again is the man with all the options. He can renegotiate his employment agreement and stay on or he can retire. If he retires, Harold plans to do a lot of fishing. He adds, "I might do a little traveling and some volunteer work."

One of the reasons that the controlled auction is such a successful sale method is that it gives an owner options and options (more than one offer) give an owner considerable negotiating strength. In Harold's case, options also give him peace of mind about his range of retirement choices.

GIVING BACK WHILE GETTING OUT
WAYNE BERGER

"If I run out of money by the time I'm 80, I'll get a job." So says the always-candid Wayne Berger, another Baby Boomer who launched into life after the sale with renewed vigor. I interviewed Wayne not only because he was a successful seller who has obviously adjusted well to life after a sale, but also because he structured his sale so that his favorite charities would benefit as well.

—John Brown

Today, Wayne Berger is a 56-year-old sailor, husband, father, philanthropist and investor. All occupations he enjoys and can now devote himself to without the distraction of owning a multi-million dollar company.

In 1977, Wayne started the first office of Berger & Co., a staffing company providing computer consulting services to businesses. Berger & Co. offered high-end consulting to clients needing software or hardware business solutions. Starting in Houston, Berger eventually opened offices in Ft. Lauderdale, Denver, Dallas and Salt Lake City.

Over the years, Wayne sold equity positions to several key employees. "As we grew, and especially during the last ten years, we were approached numerous times by buyers or suitors seeking a merger. None of these offers hit at the right time. I'd discuss the possibility of selling out or merging with one of my partners and we'd decide to ride the roller coaster just a little longer. The company kept getting bigger and along with that, our multiples improved."

So what finally prompted Wayne to agree to a sale at age 46? "Doing the same thing every day was getting old. I wanted to do something new and different and the buyer I chose (one of six) presented that new and different opportunity." Berger's buyer, Career Horizons, wanted Berger to do, on a national level, what he done at a regional level. That challenge appealed to Berger.

After interviewing a number of investment banking firms, Wayne chose a Denver based firm to represent him. "All were qualified. I chose the one that I thought I could work with because they were both flexible and creative. I wasn't interested in those who were locked into their own methodology."

Most advisors not trained in Exit Planning generally assume that owners using the controlled auction process will choose the highest bidder in the controlled auction. Not so with most owners and not so with Berger. Wayne chose the bidder whose offer reflected market value, but also the one that he felt would deal with this staff and clients the way he had—fairly and honestly. It also offered the unique challenge that Berger was seeking.

Berger makes the story of his decision to sell seem quite spontaneous but, as his attorney, I happen to know that his decision involved careful planning. Several years prior to selling, Berger anticipated the impact that state income taxes would have on his sale proceeds. Since he had offices in three states, (Colorado, Texas and Utah) he chose to live in the state with no income tax. Few owners consider this tax minimization technique and fewer still execute it. In Wayne's case, however, he had legitimate business interests in Texas. Unmarried at the time, he was able to move without uprooting a family. This approach ultimately saved Wayne millions of dollars.

Wayne also was planning—well in advance of any negotiations to sell his company—to commit a significant portion of his sale proceeds to charity. He created Charitable Remainder Trusts, transferring millions of dollars of value (in the form of his company's stock) so that, upon the ultimate sale, no taxes would be levied on the stock owned and sold by the Charitable Trust.

Today, Wayne (now the trustee) enjoys the income distributed by the trust during his lifetime and knows that upon his death the trust's funds will be distributed to the charity of his choice. This type of planning is particularly time-sensitive. If you are interested in both giving to charity and avoiding taxes, talk to your planning advisors *now* to initiate the necessary analysis and planning.

Berger's sale process—from offer to closing—lasted less than one year. He then jumped right into a three-year employment agreement. Within a month of his sale, however, one of the unsuccessful bidders in Berger's controlled auction purchased Career Horizons. "That was just not a good match for me. Once I completed two of the three years of my employment agreement, we negotiated a deal that satisfied my desire to leave (and the earn outs I had agreed to) and met the new owner's goals as well."

By the time Wayne left, he was more than ready to spend time on the things, people and causes he loved but had not had enough time for when running Berger & Co. As an owner, Wayne had always been active in charities—primarily those helping children or focusing on education. "I feel that is where I can get the best return on my charitable investments," Berger explains. Selling his business freed Wayne to serve on the boards of the charities that interested him. "When I arrived in Denver, I knew no one. I placed an ad in the newspaper and Denver treated me well. I've always felt that I owed something back to this community."

Wayne purchased a home in Ft. Lauderdale complete with a three-bedroom trawler to take his family wherever the spirit moves them. He has invested in several IT ventures, real estate and even a nursing home. He has considered the idea of re-entering the business world in a more active way, but he just has not found anything "exciting enough" to entice him back to work every day. "I've thought about everything from becoming a CEO of a non-profit to becoming a boat broker." The determining factor for Wayne is: if he's not excited about it, he won't do it.

And why should he? He and his family are financially secure. They are seeing the world from the deck of a trawler and when in port, enjoy a beautiful home. Wayne is in touch with his former partners and stays current with trends in his previous industry. He's a great example of a Boomer former owner: enjoying life, active in his community but never quite out of the game. When Wayne tells me that he just doesn't know what he wants to be when he grows up, I suspect that there are chapters yet to be written.

IMAGINING THE WORST-CASE SCENARIO
DAVID F. DRISCOLL

In this story, we describe an owner who built a successful company, but, before he could sell, factors outside his control made the company unsellable. I hope his story helps you think about what can happen if market changes strip your company of its value. I hope, too, that this story will inspire you to take time to think about life beyond ownership.

—John Brown

In 1979, Dave Driscoll was 24 years old. He'd worked in banking through college and then for an envelope company for about two years after graduation. Wanting more independence, he decided to open his own shop as an envelope broker. "I didn't buy any printing equipment until 1980 when I realized that there wasn't enough money to be made in brokering." He loved creating relationships with customers, putting together deals, and producing a product.

When he started, Driscoll's goal was to offer customers personal service and a high value product. He formed personal relationships with his customers and serviced their accounts. As he added equipment, he offered envelopes printed on higher-tech machinery than did many of his competitors.

This formula worked for Driscoll as his company, Ambassador Envelope (the name it assumed in 1989), experienced steady growth through the late '80s, despite the fact that, "Starting in the mid-'80s, our margins started to compress because the industry had overbuilt volume, and our market started to take some hits," observes Driscoll.

On the supply side, some of the large paper companies that had purchased numerous envelope companies began to spin them off in the mid-80s. In turn, the buyers, saddled with debt, lowered prices to increase their volume. Also contributing to the volume glut were tax laws of the 1970s and '80s that allowed owners to claim investment tax credits on new equipment and then take higher write-offs in future years. "Given the choice of paying taxes or buying equipment, most companies bought the equipment and took advantage of the accelerated depreciation," explains Driscoll.

"On the demand side in the 1980s, we were starting to see the affects of increasing postal rates and more widespread use of the fax machine," he says. "As a result, at the beginning of the 1990s, too many of us were chasing too few orders." Driscoll responded to this challenge by acquiring an envelope company and the intellectual property of another, both in his market. "On the day we announced the acquisition, another company announced its closing." In one day, he'd seen the number of local competitors cut by 25 percent.

Through the 1990s, Driscoll continued to focus on his strength: personal service and value over price. This formula worked through the infancy of e-mail because the economy was good and the credit card mailing industry was gearing up. Remember the days when finding four credit card pre-approvals in the mailbox every day was not unusual? Driscoll was one of the manufacturers making those envelopes. By 2001, "we were running machines six days a week. We would not keep up with the demand."

Driscoll was supplying envelopes not just to credit card companies, but also to St. Louis' largest financial institutions. At the height of the frenzy, Driscoll's company was doing $18 million in sales and employed 185 people. "It was not a problem to net 15 percent on sales," he recalls.

After five years into the boom, the only thing left on Driscoll's "To Do" list was to build his own building. "I'd moved the company six times since 1979 and I was tired of the disruption and of paying the huge costs of leasehold improvements." In 1997, he started building and by January of 1998 took occupancy.

It was also during this boom time that Driscoll was approached by and turned down a serious buyer. "I was 42 at the time, making $2 million a year. I'd experienced nothing but growth and couldn't imagine a serious downturn. I remember telling my wife one evening when we were walking through our neighborhood that if things were only 50 percent as good as they were at the time, we'd still be okay."

While he could imagine a 50 percent drop in earnings, Driscoll could not imagine what might happen if the bottom fell out of his market. He also could not imagine how he would define himself without his company. "This company had fulfilled all of my dreams," Driscoll says. "I simply could not see what my life would be without it."

Only three months after taking occupancy of the new building, the St. Louis market began to change. St. Louis's largest financial player, AG Edwards, decided to bring some of their printing in-house. Several other financial firms did the same as they outsourced their statement processing to large data houses (like ADP and Moore Wallace). These companies received electronic data from the financial firms, processed and mailed customer statements and stock trade confirmations.

Weeks later the largest direct mailer in the state declared bankruptcy. "In one year, they'd order 520 million envelopes. That was a $2.6 million hit to my sales numbers."

The trend persisted over the next few years. "We had provided envelopes to Boatmen's Bancshares, one of the state's largest banks (and its branches in nine other states) until it was bought by NationsBank in 1997. Mercantile Bank was acquired by USBank, and Magna Bank was acquired by Union Planters (Regions Bank). In each case the acquiring companies had access to envelopes in their home cities, and we couldn't compete with the added freight costs."

Driscoll continues, "We did a lot of business with General American Life until they were acquired by Metropolitan Life Insurance Company. St. Louis County Water Company was acquired by American Water Company of New Jersey, National General Insurance moved its headquarters to Winston-Salem and Southwestern Bell left for San Antonio." Each one of these transactions and relocations created a permanent loss of recurring sales for Ambassador.

Then September 11, 2001. On its heels was a recession and, more specifically for the envelope industry, the Anthrax scare. "Sales plummeted and things got a lot worse than just 50 percent." E-mail correspondence was coming on strong, and all manufacturers were suffering. To remedy the pain, out-of-state competitors started hunting in Driscoll's territory. One very large wholesale manufacturer hungry for more volume completely changed its business model to include competing in the consumer direct marketplace. "That alone devalued our market by 25 percent," he says.

At that point, Driscoll decided to dig in and scale back his operations to match the reduced demand. "It was tough for everyone. Sales people who had made lots of money during the good times didn't want to work as hard as they needed to find new accounts and to meet increasing customer demands. They complained that they just weren't having fun any more."

While Driscoll may not have been having fun either, he decided to concentrate on running the store. Consistent with his original business plan, he spent money on pre-press IT to improve value to the customer. He sold machines and laid off workers in an effort to re-size. He instituted new manufacturing management techniques and reduced delivery times to days (rather than weeks). His on-time rate improved to 98 percent and, "customers loved us. The company was running better than it ever had," Driscoll remembers. "I put lots of money back into it convinced that I could turn things around."

And for a while, he did. "I brought sales back from an $8 million low point to $10 million but it wasn't enough to keep us above water."

Bruised by the market and by employees who, "were no shows when I needed them," Driscoll looked again at selling. "I had a lot of industry contacts so I put out some feelers. Even though I had a great reputation and had staged a recovery, everyone in the industry was in the same boat. They just couldn't pay enough and my EBITDA wasn't high enough."

At that point, Driscoll approached a former competitor, now working as an investment banker. "He suggested that I try to right the ship and then sell. I thought about it for a while, and decided instead to pull the plug. After years of fighting to 'right the ship,' I was emotionally drained."

Driscoll's options were to declare bankruptcy or to pursue an orderly liquidation. "I got all the information about both but I just couldn't go through with a bankruptcy. I knew that if I did, the attorneys would get more than the creditors."

At that point, Driscoll held about $8.5 million in debt, with $5.5 in the building alone. He presented his liquidation plan to his secured creditors. When it was accepted in late 2006, "I paid my senior secured creditor in full, negotiated to agreement with my junior secured creditor, paid all employees for accrued payroll and PTO (Personal Time Off) and a percentage to my unsecured creditors. For me, it was the right thing to do."

Today, Driscoll has already put in place the framework (eight employees, 6,000 square feet of office space, the intellectual property that he purchased from Ambassador, and a simplified business plan) for a new company. "I'll offer the personalized sales that I enjoy but, this time, there's a twist based on one of the frustrations I had when I was trying to reorganize Ambassador. I kept hearing that we were just a 'one trick pony' and that customers wanted multiple products from one supplier. This time around I'm going to offer more than just envelopes (in fact about 65,000 products), and I'm not going to make huge capital investments in heavy machinery."

Today Driscoll has no illusions about what can happen during a downturn. "I know now that when times are good and someone makes you an offer for your company, they do so because they see the potential. Let them go after that potential and cash out!"

Driscoll also tells owners to set aside their emotions. "If the offer comes before you are ready, you will find something else to do. In the meantime, start working on yourself—rather than spending all of your energy on your company."

He advises owners to be careful not to follow their customers' lead 100 percent of the time. "As they demand more and more from you and you respond by making the capital commitments in building and equipment to support those demands, at the end of the day, they can leave you high and dry. You've got to take time to pause, to take stock of where you are, and of where you are going," says Driscoll. "As hard as it may be to imagine, business is cyclical and times are not always good. You can't sell your way out of everything."

Driscoll, a Boomer owner, has moved on, albeit not via a sale. He's found a way to do what he loves (sell a valuable product in the context of personal customer relationships) and to do what he knows best—run a company.

WALKING AWAY ... ALL THE WAY TO THE BANK
REGIS HILLOW

When counseling sellers, I constantly remind them that they must be emotionally ready to walk away from the table at any time. Regis Hillow is perhaps the best example of an owner who used the "walk" to achieve the sale price he desired. That ability, combined with his confidence in his instincts, made Regis a fierce competitor, a successful businessman and the kind of seller who gives acquisition guys nightmares.

—Kevin Short

In 1991, Regis Hillow was a medical supply salesman making the rounds in St. Louis, Missouri's hospitals and clinics. He didn't need a statistical analysis to see that the chronically overflowing needle disposal containers in every hospital presented a real risk to health care workers. "My idea was to replace those disposable containers with reusable ones that we'd exchange when the containers were half-full." Needle stick injuries, once frequent in St. Louis hospitals, dropped to zero. "In

14 years of doing business, not one needle stick was ever associated with our containers," recalls Hillow.

From providing usable "sharps" containers and pick up, Hillow's company, Medical Systems, Inc., expanded into serving the medical waste needs of physician offices (including dental offices, nursing homes and clinics) and hospital red bag (non-sharp medical waste) pick up. Medical Systems grew steadily and profitably as it saturated the market. "By the time I sold, we were servicing all of the region's 42 hospitals and 2,000 other facilities as well," Hillow says.

Over time, Hillow watched the number of his competitors shrink nearly as dramatically as his business expanded. "When I started, there were eight of us in the market. By 1999, there were only two of us left."

Not only did Hillow drive competitors out of the marketplace, the largest player in the medical waste disposal industry, Stericycle, could not break in. Stericycle was not able to pick up one sharps account in a St. Louis hospital.

When asked to account for what was happening in his market, Hillow is blunt. "I never let up. I treated every day in business like Day One." Hillow describes his mindset this way, "Each time my assistant announced a call from a customer, before I picked up the phone I imagined that he was calling to cancel. I always did whatever it took to maintain my relationship with my customers. Periodically, we'd even clean our customers' biohazard rooms to project our high standards and level of service."

Hillow admits to operating out of the same fear that drives some athletic competitors: a fear of losing. "Like an athlete, I drove myself and my company hard to keep from losing a customer." In fourteen years, he never lost a major customer.

Not surprisingly, Hillow's company had attracted Stericycle's attention. In 1999, Stericycle approached Hillow with an offer to buy Medical Systems. "They offered me about $6 million, a good offer, and my accountant negotiated the deal." Several days before closing, however, the buyer's representatives told Hillow that its Board had made about $4 million available for the acquisition. "They did exactly what any smart buyer would do," Hillow remembers. "They found a reason to drop the price near closing and expected me to accept the new price rather than look for a new buyer." Instead, Hillow rejected their revised offer and went back to work.

*Regis and I had not yet formally met in 1999 so I cannot take credit for counseling him, as I do all my clients, to maintain, at all times, a willingness to walk away from the deal. Hillow was not only willing to walk, he was **able** to walk first because he had time on his side: In 1999, Regis was only 39 years old. Second, his company was profitable and all its momentum was positive. Regis was riding a rocket and without good reason, wasn't ready to jump off.*

—K.S.

As the M&A market recovered from its 2001 slump, Hillow began to think again about selling. As he saw it, he could take the company to the next level—expansion into other cities—or he could sell. He decided to explore both options and in 2004, contacted Kevin Short. "I decided to interview Kevin because I knew who he was, I had heard good things about him and his name was in the local business journal all the time for closing deals." Hillow chose Short to represent him in the same way he chooses all his advisors, "I knew he was a guy I could work with and who could do the job."

After discussing Hillow's options during an early strategy session, Short and Hillow decided to split roles. Hillow would pursue expansion and Short would contact Stericycle with an offer to buy. "Their reaction? Laughter," recalls Short. "They could not believe that the David, who only five years ago slammed the door was now ready to take on their Goliath." To prove the seriousness of their offer, Short provided information that Hillow could financially back up his offer, or at least was too formidable to be run off.

"For the next few weeks," Short remembers, "I took Stericycle's calls and answered the question 'How much does Hillow want for his company?' with the response Regis and I had agreed upon, 'Medical Systems is not for sale.'" This exchange went on for weeks until Short presented Stericycle a number based on what he and Hillow had estimated the company's worth to be in five years; five years into a vigorous expansion plan. "Regis is willing to sell for $20 million," Short explained. This time there was no laughter at the other end of the line. "They may have questioned my mother's heritage but there was certainly no laughter," Short recalls.

While $20 million would have satisfied all of Hillow's financial needs and desires for the rest of his life, so too would the counter-offers Stericycle made over the next few months. "Fulfilling my financial needs wasn't really my goal," Hillow explains. "When I started my company, my goal was not to go bankrupt. Later, I wanted financial security and to take some chips off the table, but, ultimately, what I was looking for was a signal that the buyer was paying me what my company was worth to them—not a penny less."

"Most owners have a particular number in mind when they enter the process," Short explains. "Regis did not. This may have helped him to maintain that emotional readiness to walk unless the deal met his requirements."

Over the course of the next few months, Short and Stericycle agreed on a number. The signal that Hillow was looking for came when Stericycle asked Hillow to guarantee that his company, under new ownership, would be able to meet the previous year's sales numbers. When Hillow agreed, Stericycle let Hillow know that if Medical Systems fell short, Hillow, personally, would owe Stericycle $4 for every $1 deficiency. That arrangement seemed fair to Hillow, "As long as for every dollar Medical Systems earned above the previous year's numbers, Stericycle paid me something."

"When their M&A guy started to sweat," Hillow recounts, "I knew. I knew I had achieved what I wanted. We had finally agreed on a price that really represented what my company was worth to this Billion Dollar Goliath."

Hillow closed on the sale of Medical Systems to Stericycle in March of 2005—just about one year after retaining Short.

Today, Hillow's longest-term goal is, "to lose 10 pounds and improve my short game. I play golf and I manage my portfolio. I'm happy hanging out. I can't understand anyone in my position using the word 'bored' to describe not working every day."

Hillow has no interest in getting involved in another company or showing up every day for work. If he did, it wouldn't be in the same industry. "I respect Stericycle and plan to honor my covenant not to compete. I can't even play on a softball team for one of Stericycle's competitors," Hillow jokes.

Hillow does some casual business consulting for friends interested in his insight and experience. When asked about what to expect after the sale, Hillow says, "Expect a huge mindset change. It takes about 18 months to get comfortable going from a regular, hefty paycheck to no paycheck at all." He advises those new to the post-sale life to, "Put the cash away for six to twelve months. Don't go crazy, just maintain. I've seen too many guys buy too much and end up back at work."

Wise advice from a man who has walked the walk . . . all the way to the bank.

THE ART OF CREATING A SUCCESSFUL "PLAN B"
MAEVE McGRATH AND JETTE BRAUN

In my law practice, I worked with owners to create Exit Plans suited to their unique goals. Often this meant creating a plan to transfer the company to key employees. All too often, owners and I learned that the key employees either didn't want the responsibility of ownership or didn't want to pay for ownership. Subsequently, we initiated "Plan B." Here we see how two owners used their "Plan B" to orchestrate a great exit and move on to new lives.

The Exit Planning attorney in this story, Elizabeth Mower, was an associate in my law firm and now works with Exit Planning Advisors at Business Enterprise Institute.

—John Brown

In 1985, Jette Braun and Maeve McGrath formed a partnership, McGrath & Braun, to provide corporate art consulting services to the Colorado market. "We'd met and worked together for several years as consultants for an art gallery," explains Maeve. "When the owners of that gallery began to have their own difficulties, we decided to go into business for ourselves," Jette adds.

Maeve and Jette concentrated their marketing efforts on professional firms: law firms, insurance, investment, financial, real estate and energy companies. "We used a number of techniques to find out what buildings were going up, who was designing them and who would occupy them," explains Maeve, the partner who assumed most of the networking and marketing responsibilities.

"Once we were hired," Jette adds, "we would meet with both the architects and designers to review floor plans and finishes in order to understand their design concepts for the space. Only then did we meet with the client, usually the CEO (or someone with similar level of responsibility), to establish a style and direction for the artwork."

"These were people who knew everything about their industry," Maeve says, "but when it came to art, they were a little out of their element. Jette and I always tried to make the process of buying art unthreatening, fun and interesting."

Making the process fun was just one aspect of McGrath & Braun's competitive edge. Jette had developed relationships with a large number of artists and Maeve had developed systems that delivered the art in a cost-efficient and timely way. This partnership of product and process led to continuous growth through the 1980s and 1990s.

In the early 2000s, Maeve and Jette decided to take some time to look at the business and its future direction. "We could expand beyond our niche or stay within it. To help us decide, we hired a business consultant," recalls Jette. At the end of that decision process, Maeve and Jette decided to stay within their niche but to seek out larger projects.

They were on that track when they met with their Exit Planning attorney, Elizabeth Mower, in 2004. "Our goal was to create a plan to sell the company to our key employees," says Maeve. "We were turning 60 and really didn't want to work for the rest of our lives," explains Jette. "We had two employees who had been with us for several years and to whom we'd turned over numerous networking and client contacts," Maeve adds. "We assumed that they'd be our successors and were consciously grooming them to take over."

The plan Jette and Maeve developed used a portion of the employees' compensation to pay Maeve and Jette for their ownership interest. "We had been over-compensating these employees for several years so we thought they'd be willing to shift some of that excess compensation into payments for the company," remembers Jette.

They were wrong. When Maeve and Jette first presented the plan to their employees, the first reaction was no reaction. "They asked us to table the discussion for the time being," recalls Maeve. They argued that events in their personal lives did not leave adequate time to discuss a buy out. "We were willing to wait as we were in the middle of a huge project," Jette adds.

In retrospect, it appears that personal issues provided a smoke screen so that the employees could organize their own departure. "While the two of us were focused on that major project, the two of them had rented space and created marketing materials to launch their new company," says Maeve.

The two key employees (one of whom was on maternity leave) asked for a meeting during the first week of 2006 and, as the first order of business, presented their letters of immediate resignation. "We had a hunch that one of them might be looking elsewhere, but we were stunned that they were making plans in tandem," recalls Jette.

The feeling of shock evaporated only two days later when Jette and Maeve started receiving calls from their contacts and clients asking about the announcements they had received from the two former key employees. "At that point, we became completely re-energized. While leaving the company was in the back of our minds, we focused exclusively on making our company as successful as it could be," Maeve says.

Regrouping and reenergizing characterized their efforts for the next year. "We renewed relationships with all of the people we had turned over to our key employees," recalls Maeve. At the same time, Maeve and Jette were talking to industry contacts about their eventual desire to exit. "Our word of mouth efforts interested two or three possible buyers but nothing developed," Jette says. "One of the potential buyers," Maeve recalls "had recently given birth to twins and after much soul searching decided to focus her energy on her children instead of on a business."

So, the two hired a local business broker to market and sell their company. "Our instructions were clear," says Maeve. "We would negotiate terms (covenants not to compete, promissory notes, working for the buyer after the sale) but we would not negotiate on price," Jette explains.

The broker attracted several serious buyers, all of whom Jette and Maeve met. "There was a fatal flaw with each of the first three," Jette remembers. One woman thought she could run the company from her base nearly 200 miles away from Denver. Another was a couple with grandiose plans to build the company, but who planned to pay, not in cash, but in the form of a share of that future growth. The third candidate was a newly married couple who expected Maeve and Jette to work with the wife for 30 days before the couple would commit to a purchase. "When our broker refused their request suggesting that in one month she could learn enough to set up a competing company," Maeve recalls, "they decided they were not interested after all."

"When we met the fourth buyer, we recognized that this couple would be our buyer," says Maeve. In fact, this prospective buyer did submit a Letter of Intent only to withdraw it several days later. This was only the first bump on the road to closing. After this same buyer resubmitted its Letter of Intent, negotiations proceeded on the purchase contract.

After meeting the prospective buyers, Maeve's and Jette's broker controlled all the negotiations. He strongly suggested that Jette and Maeve forbid a meeting between one of their key employees and the buyer. "Had the buyer met our employee—who had a salary agenda of her own—the deal may have collapsed," Jette says.

As negotiations progressed, the buyer was dealing exclusively with the broker and attorneys for two reasons. First, as would most transaction intermediaries, the broker wanted to keep Maeve and Jette separated from the day-to-day deal negotiations. Especially in situations in which the former owners will work for the new owners, it is best to negotiate through the transaction intermediary. Second, Maeve had reached a point when she remembers telling Jette, "I am through selling this business. It is up to them to buy it."

These buyers did purchase McGrath & Braun in June of 2007. Maeve and Jette describe the process of selling to a third party as "surprisingly quick and amazingly smooth." They will work for the new owners for at least one year as the new owners execute their plans to market the company's services nationally and internationally.

"It is great fun to be working for someone with such incredible energy and vision," says Maeve. "Our buyers have both art and marketing backgrounds, and are committed to making this company a powerhouse in our industry."

Jette notes that, "It is incredibly liberating to do what we love everyday without the responsibility of ownership. We are having the time of our lives."

Not only have they shed the burden of ownership, Maeve and Jette have taken on a project they never would have as owners. "Shortly before the sale, Maeve and I were approached by a former client to work on a resort property in California," says Jette. "We were able to accept the job because, serendipitously, California was not included in our Covenant Not to Compete, but also because we were free from the daily responsibilities of running a company," Maeve explains. "Today," Jette says, "we are having a great time traveling together and combining business with seeing family."

Repotted into a new life as valuable employees, Maeve and Jette look forward to another transition into a "retirement" full of travel, visiting grandchildren and possibly building vacation homes. These are activities that Maeve and Jette enjoyed in the years prior to sale because they had made a conscious decision to enjoy life while they built their company. "Soon we'll have more time to enjoy the things we love," says Jette, "but in the meantime, we are thrilled to be working for owners who are able and willing to maximize the company's potential."

LIFE IS GOOD
CARL AND BARBARA MITCHELL

Baby Boomers Carl and Barbara Mitchell sold their successful company at ages 61 and 59, respectively. We include their story not only because it encapsulates many of the themes of this book, (creating a valuable business, running the company with an eye on the exit, and using skilled advisors in the sale transaction) but also because Carl and Barbara provide a great example of how to create a fulfilling life after the sale.

—Kevin Short

In 1985, Carl Mitchell and his wife, Barbara, started CM Systems, Inc. in the basement of their home. Carl had "retired" from a then Big Eight accounting firm to try his hand at consulting but, "to keep the kids fed, I became a dealer of software designed for the construction industry," he explains. CM Systems added training and support services to the software programs and the home-based business was launched.

The software program that CM Systems sold, installed and supported proved to be so popular that Carl was soon unable to handle all aspects of the company alone. "I love sales. I love meeting people and solving problems but I knew, intuitively I guess, that if I was ever to sell this company, I could not be the lead salesman," Carl says. "Somebody else—somebody willing to stay with a new owner after closing—would have to be the one generating the lion's share of our sales."

With that goal in mind, Carl hired a newly minted graduate of a master's degree program and taught him what he knew about sales. Carl sent this new employee to sales training programs and this "rookie matured into a great salesperson," recalls Carl.

Carl's marketing and sales strategies paid off as the company grew to about 250 customers, yet Carl was not satisfied. "We were busy and we were making money but I knew that to sell the company when I was ready, I needed a bigger company to sell. I needed more customers, more value."

Rather than grow organically through its own sales efforts, CM Systems instead purchased another company's book of business, "about 200 to 250 more customers," Carl remembers. Growth through acquisition met Carl and Barbara's goal of speedier growth. "That acquisition worked so well that a few years later, we purchased another 60 customers from another source," Carl says.

By 2003, Carl's growth strategy resulted in a customer list of around 600 customers paying annual support fees. "We were still selling software systems (that cost between $12,000 and $15,000 each) and we never had one returned."

Carl recalls, "I was running an all-cash business and loving the challenge. Originally, I was the Jack-of-all-trades but eventually I became a conductor, or figurehead. As it evolved, my job became keeping everything and everyone running smoothly."

Meanwhile, Barbara had become more active in the company over the years and gently reminded Carl about his promises to leave before they were too old to enjoy their retirement. "We'd had a couple of offers in the late 1990s but I wasn't ready to sell," says Carl. "We were also approached by Kevin Short's firm through a letter probing our interest in buying another company in our industry. We were not interested but I did keep Kevin's name in the back of my mind."

By 2005, Carl was seriously thinking about selling. "My wife is a very persuasive person who made a good argument for getting out while we were still young enough to travel and to do the things we'd put off while running the company. Second, the daily grind was wearing me down. Third, I was concerned that the taxes I'd pay on the sale would be exorbitant if Congress raised the capital gains tax rate." These three considerations, ones faced in varying degrees by most owners, prompted Carl to make a sale plan.

Carl's sale objectives had always been to sell stock (not assets) and to make a clean break from the company. "I was not willing to finance a buyer and I didn't want to work for one either," says Carl. In September of 2005 after putting out a few feelers in his industry, Carl was ready to sign up with a national business broker. "There was a lot of pressure to sign but before I did, I called Kevin's firm," Carl recalls. "We met and I knew that it was a fit."

"I suspected that the sale of my company would require professional expertise," explains Carl, "and I was right. Over the next year, Kevin's experience and expertise kept the sale on track to closing."

Kevin found that while Carl lacked a formal written exit strategy, he had created a complete one in his head. First, he had set clear exit objectives: (1) Carl knew when he wanted to leave (soon!); (2) he knew how much he wanted to sell for (full value); and (3) he knew to whom he wanted to sell (a third party). Carl had also set his ancillary goals: an all-stock deal and no post-closing work for the new owner. Carl knew what his company was worth and had installed numerous Value Drivers to improve its price and marketability (motivated key employees, repeatable systems and solid operational policies).

"When Carl and I met," recalls Kevin, "he knew what he wanted and he had the vehicle (a valuable company with meticulously kept records) to take him there. My job was to find a well-financed buyer and to close the deal."

At first, Kevin's marketing efforts attracted three qualified buyers but as the due diligence process progressed, each one faded away. One buyer's financing dried up, while a complex accounting issue spooked the others. "After a great deal of thought, Carl had listed on his balance sheet an asset that significantly affected the sale price," Kevin explains. "Carl's reasoning was rock-solid but we learned how buyers could interpret the placement of this asset differently."

"The negotiations about an accounting issue surprised me," Carl recalls. "That and the number of pages in the final contract!"

Going back to the market, Kevin was more sensitive to how buyers might react to the accounting issue and attracted another serious buyer to the table. "What started as a controlled auction (multiple suitors bidding simultaneously for the company) became a negotiated sale with one buyer," says Kevin.

"Kevin did a great job guiding this buyer to the closing table but he also helped deal with my key employee/salesman who was initially interested in buying my company," Carl remembers.

"Carl's situation in which a key employee expresses an interest in buying is not unusual," explains Kevin. "There is often a key employee who, while interested in buying, simply cannot come up with the cash. It is my job to help the owner handle this highly-emotional situation in a way that keeps the key person on board *and* motivated to work for a new owner."

"In our case, once our employee understood that he couldn't afford the company," recalls Carl, "we negotiated a new employment agreement and covenant not to compete that benefited both of us as well as the new owner."

The day of closing was not without its own drama. The buyer's banker was slow to wire the funds, giving his advisors time to think once again about the accounting issue. "Not only was I confident that we'd cast this asset correctly," remembers Kevin, "I knew that we'd given the buyer adequate protection from any possible negative ramifications in the Warranties and Representations." Carl adds, "Kevin had limited my exposure to less than 13 percent of the purchase price and had negotiated a shorter period of exposure in the Warranties and Representations. In the end, the buyer got the protection he wanted and I limited my exposure."

After closing, Carl and Barbara worked 50 to 60 hours for the new owner to smooth the transition and packed their bags for New Zealand. There, they joined other volunteers to build a Habitat for Humanity home for an indigenous family. "It was a wonderful experience and we'd like to do more of that," says Carl.

Bungee jumping into a gorge and diving the Great Barrier Reef might also fall into many former owners' definition of "wonderful experiences." After meeting with their financial advisor, Carl and Barbara have budgeted for annual trips to see and volunteer in other parts of the world.

"I really thought that after I left the company, I'd be lonely. I thought I'd miss the daily excitement but that has not been the case," explains Carl. With no plans to return to work, Carl and Barbara say only that, "Life is good."

These are two owners who are using their own good life to make life good for others as well.

OLD FRIENDS AND NEW OPPORTUNITIES
DAVE AND LINDA VISGER

I have known Dave Visger since high school and Linda for over 30 years. I've had a front row seat watching them create a successful company, sell using a negotiated sale, spend six or so years trying out a life of leisure and then return to business to create another successful company. These two owners come to mind when people ask me for examples of Baby Boomers who have successfully sold, and just as successfully, created a new life full of more enjoyable challenges.

—John Brown

Dave and Linda Visger started their Florida-based company, Ross Office System Supply, Inc. (ROSS) in 1979. While selling office supplies to businesses, they established their competitive edge in linking their company directly to their customers. In those pre-Internet, pre-superstore days, ROSS put personal computers or dumb terminals in their customers' offices. Customers used those computers to place supply orders and ROSS provided next-day delivery. Using this system, customers could eliminate supply rooms and supply management personnel positions, while retaining complete price control and accountability.

This concept was so successful that by the early 1990s, the company, with annual revenues of about $10 million, employed nearly 70 people.

Also by the early 1990s, the office supply landscape was changing. "Staples, OfficeMax and other superstores were entering the retail market. We knew that it was just a matter of time before the same model would cross over into the commercial market," observes Linda.

Dave and Linda had been keeping an eye on industry developments and in response, had acquired five or six smaller companies over the years. Their goal was to grow to the size necessary to attract the attention of a large industry buyer. "We also knew that when it comes to valuation multiples, size matters," Dave adds.

Early in 1994, one of the larger industry players approached Dave through a golf buddy. "On the back of a napkin at the 19th hole, he made me an offer I couldn't refuse," Dave recalls.

Both Dave and Linda agreed that the time was right to sell and that this offer was the right one for them. Linda explains, "The buyer was willing to pay 90 percent cash up front, the balance after one year and wanted us to work for them for three years." Linda and Dave immediately entered negotiations with this buyer.

Although an advocate of the controlled auction process, I could hardly argue with the Visgers' choice of buyers. The terms were generous: the offer reflected the company's value in the marketplace and the proceeds would allow Dave and Linda to have a full and financially secure retirement. And, at age 47 and 45 respectively, Dave and Linda faced a long retirement!

Second, the buyer was a professional. The company had orchestrated numerous acquisitions so there were no surprises or unusual terms. The Visgers' law firm was similarly experienced and Linda says, "We were amazed by how easy it all was. In 30 days we had sold the company."

Like all sellers, the Visgers were concerned about confidentiality during the sale process. Unlike many sellers, however, their sale process was so abbreviated that they had little time to be overly anxious. Linda remembers that, "The cat was out of the bag only at the eleventh hour when our sales and distribution guys had to sign the buyer's covenants not to compete." The damage that "land mine" (as Kevin Short calls these events) was able to inflict was minimal because Dave and Linda were easily able to demonstrate that the employees would enjoy better benefits and opportunities for advancement under the new ownership. The fact that Dave and Linda were staying on with the new owner only strengthened their argument.

Dave and Linda began their three-year employment contracts, but after one year, realized that they really were not needed anymore. They were bored. They had transitioned the company and the buyer agreed that they could go without penalty.

My friends began spending six months each year at their northern Michigan home (on a golf course) and six months in Florida (on a golf course). They were taking classes, golfing, and enjoying the break that they'd never had the time to take. I, of course, was still working.

For the next five to six years, I worked hard while Dave fine-tuned his golf game. Knowing him as I do, however, I was not surprised when he told me that he and Linda were thinking about buying a franchise in Naples, Florida. Linda explains, "After a while, we missed the stimulation and action of running a company. We looked at various opportunities taking our time to find one that met our criteria." In 2002, they bought a Garage Tek franchise because, Dave says, "It looked fun, interesting, financially promising and it fit our skill set." That may have been the moment I realized that owners, provided they have financial security and reasonably good health, can undertake several new ventures after they sell.

Dave and Linda quickly put to work the expertise gained from nearly 25 years of starting, running and leaving a successful company. "By buying a franchise, we skipped the start-up and could jump right in," says Linda. "The franchisor already had marketing processes, product development and operational systems in place." The Naples franchise proved such a good fit that the Visgers purchased another six months later.

Linda is quick to point out that this second go 'round is quite different from the first. "We are so lucky that, this time, we don't have to depend on the income to live on. With our nest egg tucked safely away, we can focus on and enjoy the growth process." Dave adds, "When we started ROSS, we had nothing to lose because we *had* nothing. This time, we only have a small amount at risk so we can really enjoy making the company grow."

The Visgers' experience is not atypical. For many owners the sale of a business brings financial freedom and choices—related both to how they spend that money and what they do with their time. Many devote part of their time and a portion of their assets to new, usually smaller and more controllable, businesses. They put back into service the skills and experiences gained from years of ownership. This time, the stress that once seemed integral to ownership no longer exists. Owners do what they know and love, and do not do whatever it is that they don't enjoy—all without significant financial risk.

In Dave and Linda's case, they have chosen to return to active involvement in a company. Many former owners choose a more passive role, investing money or expertise in a company without putting in time at the office.

Never ones to take passive roles, Dave and Linda have recently purchased another franchise, this one in the direct mail business. "Garage Tek uses lots of direct mail advertising and we understand that business. It just seemed like the logical thing to do," explains Linda. "Owning a company (or two, or three)" adds Dave, "has always provided us a good return on our investment."

When asked how long they plan to keep these franchises, the Visgers agree, "As long as we are having fun doing what we are doing." They insist that when the time comes to launch in a new direction, they'll know. Given their track record, I'm inclined to agree.

PREACHING WHAT
HE PRACTICED
EDWARD K. WEKESSER

When business consultant Ed Wekesser hangs huge yellow sticky notes on the walls crowded with bullet points clarifying my company's goals, I am tempted to believe that Ed resides in the "ideal world" while I must operate in the "real world." What I know, however, is that Ed now preaches, as a consultant, what he once practiced as a successful business owner.

—John Brown

In 1986, Ed Wekesser and two partners launched Customer Insight Company, Inc. (CIC) to serve the database marketing analysis needs of the banking industry. CIC created software that enabled banks to efficiently analyze financial data in the PC, rather than mainframe, environment.

Wekesser remembers that he and his co-owners had one goal before they even opened the doors: grow the company and sell it. "At the time, we did not know the exact dollar amount we would need from a sale to retire but our focus was always to grow as quickly as possible so that we could sell as quickly as possible."

In an industry where rough and tumble competition is the rule rather than the exception, Wekesser and his partners thrived. "Competitors, disguised as interested buyers approached us numerous times over the years. We never really paid much attention first because we saw through the ruse (as a great way to root out competitive information) and second, because none were willing to pay the price we required."

For eight years, CIC grew in revenues, market share and number of employees. "By 1994, we employed between 110 and 115 people, and were doing about $13 million in revenue," Wekesser recalls. When asked how they fostered such phenomenal growth in just eight years, he highlights two causes. First, CIC had a great management team working relentlessly to achieve clearly defined goals. "The incentive plan that we set up for senior management helped all of us to maintain our focus." Second, "We had a first class product and strong organizational processes," says Wekesser.

Wekesser and his partners used the dollar amount that they would need from a sale as the basis for the incentive plan. Under this plan, as the managers built the company, they would share (in an increasing percentage) in the proceeds. "From that moment forward, this dynamite team was riveted on reaching that goal," explains Wekesser.

So riveted that the team took them far enough to see the finish line. At that point, Wekesser and his co-owners recognized that only an infusion of capital could fund their robust growth, and brought in a venture capital investor.

"One beneficial by-product of linking our sale goal to the senior management incentive plan," says Wekesser, "was that each senior manager realized that, in order to achieve that goal, he or she would need to keep quiet about our plans. Any worry I might have had about confidentiality disappeared. Ironically, by revealing our plans to our top people, we were able to keep our sale plans quiet."

Only two years later, a serious buyer approached Wekesser and his partners with an initial offer that, while intriguing, fell well below their stated threshold. The issue the owners now confronted was whether to conduct negotiations with this one buyer or hire an investment banker to orchestrate a controlled auction. "I favored the controlled auction strategy and had chosen an investment banker who I thought could bring us better terms. My partners instead preferred to negotiate with the buyer at the table; ultimately, that is what we did."

During the nearly 12 months of negotiations, Wekesser and his partners spent little time on the day to-day negotiations. "The President of the company handled most of the issues only bringing us in as necessary." Even so, Wekesser's one-word description of the process is "Brutal." "Our buyer was a Fortune 500 company with a high-powered Chicago law firm which put every detail under the microscope," he elaborates.

In just under one year, negotiations ended in a closing and Wekesser left the company. "I knew long before the sale that the only owner likely to be retained after a sale was the one who made the software tick," he explains. "In fact, that owner did stay for a couple of years on favorable terms."

Wekesser had no specific expectations for life after the sale. He admits, "I was not very well prepared for that period." Wekesser's wife may not have had specific expectations, but she voiced a general one within days of closing. "I was sitting at the kitchen table reading the newspaper at about 11 o'clock one morning when she announced, 'You know, I don't do lunches.' I did not know exactly what she meant but I knew she was telling me something important." Within weeks, he had set up his home office, was playing a lot of golf and, unexpectedly, was embroiled in a lawsuit.

"Within months of completing the sale, a third party accused us of stealing their software code," Wekesser recalls. "Knowing that we had not, I initially didn't take the suit seriously. I assumed that everything would be cleared up at the first hearing before a magistrate." At that hearing, Wekesser realized the plaintiff had its own version of events. He also understood that if the suit was successful, every dollar that CIC's buyer had paid could go back to the buyer. "That's when things got very serious."

As the discovery process progressed, the huge importance of the small details of a sale contract became evident. "In a nutshell, we would not have to pay for any post-closing lawsuits (based on pre-closing activities) unless we were found to have done something illegal." That was a relief but the suit weighed heavily on Wekesser until the suit was resolved nine months later.

Finally, Wekesser had the time to enjoy life after the sale. "I played a lot of golf, continued an active role in my church and did some traveling." It was on one of those trips that he found a new investment opportunity. "It looked great at the outset but didn't develop as I hoped," Wekesser explains. "As I look back on it, I see that my 'entrepreneurial itch' prevented me from digging as deep as I should have."

From that experience, Wekesser learned that more than being back in the game, what he really missed was working with entrepreneurs. "I like people who get things done." That understanding led him to formally establish his consulting business. "At first, owners would ask for my opinion about a specific problem. It wasn't long before I set up a consulting business."

Today, Wekesser acts as a consultant to business owners sharing the expertise he gained from running and selling a successful company. The advice he gives owners considering a sale covers the periods before, during and after the sale. "First, set clear goals before beginning the sale process. Second, find the best expert advice you can to guide you through the growth and sale process. And finally, talk to other owners about life after the sale."

I couldn't have said it better myself.

—J.B.

MAKING THE GAME LOOK EASY
DOUG AND LAURIE WILLERDING

In my Exit Planning books, articles and seminars, I have always advocated that owners should start planning their exits the day they start their companies. Without benefit of any of my advice, Kevin Short's clients, Doug and Laurie Willerding, figured out what it took me years to learn and reaped all the rewards.

—John Brown

In 1974, Doug and Laurie Willerding started Willerding Welding Company, Inc., a welding fabrication company. Doug, a gifted welder, and Laurie, a natural business woman, married the following year and, "The game was on," says investment banker, Kevin Short.

Kevin uses the word "game" for two reasons. First Laurie describes the years of hard work and sacrifice (necessary to build a successful business) as "having a lot of fun with my best friend." Second, every game has rules and a defined goal. "Unlike most owners I know," says Kevin, "Doug and Laurie established both their rules and their goal at the outset. Their rule was to build the company carefully yet aggressively." Their goal was to sell and retire when they were still young, and healthy enough, to enjoy their freedom.

"We were young and we made some mistakes but we knew how we wanted to run our company," Laurie explains. To the Willerdings, this meant taking only calculated risks and being cautious when taking on debt. "Our strategy was to take advantage of the busy times by working hard to make money to pay down debt. When the slow times came along, and they always did, the debt load was not insupportable."

As the years went on, this formula worked so well that the Willerdings were able to finance their expansions and to avoid debt completely. When the Willerdings last expanded their building (a 38,000 square foot addition) they did not take out a loan. "We actually got ahead of the game by expanding our buildings beyond current needs so we were prepared for future opportunities," Laurie recalls.

As the company grew, Doug and Laurie were approached by two well-known companies advertising themselves as business brokers. "We learned the hard way that these outfits were not what they advertised," Laurie remembers. "Their method was to get owners excited about the prospect of selling, charge thousands of dollars for a business valuation and then disappear." Neither "broker" ever marketed the company for sale.

Laurie pauses here to advise other owners to steer clear of these brokers by asking for references. "Make sure the broker has a history of sales and take names," she suggests.

Burned twice by "experts" in the Mergers & Acquisition market, Doug and Laurie did not approach the subject of selling again until they were in their attorney's office preparing their estate plan. Their attorney asked them about their business plans and learned that the Willerdings were ready to sell "anytime." They just hadn't found the right way to go about doing it.

That attorney recommended that the Willerdings meet with Kevin Short. "During our first meeting," Laurie recalls, "I knew that this would be a completely different experience. We left that meeting with a thumbnail valuation, a predicted sale price, and an understanding of the sale process."

The Willerdings may have learned a lot during that meeting but so did Kevin. "In addition to my introduction to how the Willerdings conducted themselves and their business," Kevin recalls, "I discovered that Doug and Laurie knew exactly how much money they'd need to retire." Laurie had managed their personal and corporate finances for 30 years so forecasting their retirement needs was not difficult for her.

Kevin also learned that confidentiality during the sale was extremely important to both Doug and Laurie. "The Willerdings are private people by nature and wanted the sale process to be private as well," Kevin explains. "Only after the sale did I learn that even Laurie's mother did not know of the sale until it closed!" Laurie feels strongly that if employees catch whiff of a sale, they will start looking for new jobs. She also believes that the very word "sale" prompts customers, suppliers and competitors to assume that there must be some underlying trouble. While this was not the case for the Willerdings, the rumor mill can take on a life of its own.

The Willerdings' absolute insistence on confidentiality and the size of their company presented Kevin with two challenges. The first meant that Kevin could visit their plant only once (and then only under the guise of an insurance advisor) and that he could not market the company to its customers, suppliers or competitors. During the marketing process, Kevin's firm allowed fewer than five interested parties into the Willerdings' plant.

The second challenge was that the Willerdings' company was in the gray area between a sale to an individual and a sale to a large industry player or Private Equity Group. The price tag on the Willerdings' 40-employee company was simply not large enough to attract the attention of the large players. On the other hand, it was rich enough to deter all but the most creative individual buyer. For that reason, Kevin told the Willerdings that the process might take as long as 12 months to complete.

"I immediately converted Kevin's 12-month estimate into an 18-month time frame so I was not surprised when it took 18 months," says Laurie. The Willerdings did have the patience to wait for the right buyer—an individual who put together a cash package comprised of his own funds, bank and Small Business Administration loans.

At ages 52 and 50, Doug and Laurie left the closing table having achieved their goal: they were still young, and healthy enough, to enjoy the part of their lives that they had worked toward since their early twenties.

Since they sold their company in April of 2006, Doug and Laurie have had the time to enjoy the things they love most. That list is a long one so it takes Laurie a moment to decide what activities are at the top. "Doug builds what he wants when he wants. I have my home office in part of Doug's workshop. In it are my computers, a fireplace and our dogs." Most of all, the Willerdings enjoy being home. "We used to have to leave town to get away from it all. Now, we can be away from it all in our own home."

Have they adjusted to life after the sale? Laurie can hardly believe the question. "After working together through all the challenges of running and building a business, this part of life is a piece of cake."

AFTERWORD

Whether your company is small or large, selling it to a third party is the biggest challenge—and opportunity—of your business life. I urge you to grab hold of this opportunity. Refuse the role of bystander or bit player. Instead, take center stage as an active and full participant in the sale process and you will add value and minimize uncertainty and risk.

In this book, my goal was to show you the decisions you need to make in order to cash out and move on. I hope I've shown you how your involvement can be not only proactive, but can actually add value to your company.

Had my father written this book, the title would not have been "Cash Out—Move On." He could not cash out: the business wasn't prepared to be sold, there was no plan, no advisors, no idea of business value, no sense of Value Drivers and their importance, and the M&A world barely existed. Plus, his vision of life after the sale was very different than ours.

Moving on for him and for others in his generation had a different meaning than it does for today's Boomers. We are healthier, wealthier, better educated, and, most importantly, our outlook is far different. We are more optimistic and we want to continue to lead full lives. Rather than retire, we plan to move on to the next adventure and challenge.

Make the sale of your business your greatest victory: for yourself, your family, your company and your employees. It is the springboard for the rest of your life. As a Boomer, you likely want more from the business than just "top dollar." As the title of this book states, you want more than just money. If you are like most owners we know, you want freedom to do the things you want. Use the sale of your business to give you the freedom you want to find out exactly what "more" means to you.

Good luck. You now know what needs to be done. If I can help in any way, please contact me at the address below. If you'd like additional insights, visit our Web site (www.BEIBooks.com) to request a free subscription to our e-mail newsletter, **The Exit Planning Review™**.

John Brown
President, Business Enterprise Institute, Inc.
jbrown@exitplanning.com

DECISION CHECKLIST APPENDIX

The following Decision Checklists are designed to help you understand how to get from where you are now (thinking about a sale) to where you want to go (a successful, fulfilling life after the sale).

The first set of charts is designed for those owners who anticipate a sale in one to two years. You'll see a summary of the decisions to be made during those two years followed by a specific list of actions that must be taken to support those decisions.

The second set of charts helps those owners who won't be ready for a sale for three years or more. Again, we've provided a summary of actions or decisions that need to be made, followed by a more detailed list of actions that you must take (with the help of your advisors) to achieve your goals.

DECISION CHECKLISTS

TODAY

Read this Book to:

1. Learn what the sale process is all about both from experienced Exit Planning Advisors and owners who have gone through it.

2. Learn what to look for in an Exit Planning Advisor.

3. Learn how to decide when you can/should exit your company.

When you finish this book, you will set your goal to leave in less than 2 years or in 3+ years.

TARGET DEPARTURE: 1–2 YEARS
DAY 1–60

Day 1–30

☐ Establish preliminary Exit Objectives (in writing).

☐ Select an experienced Exit Planning Advisor.

☐ Get marketability and pricing assessment.

☐ Prepare yourself for life after the sale.

Day 31–60

☐ Select transaction intermediary (investment banker or business broker).

☐ Select balance of Deal Team.

☐ Begin tax planning.

☐ Begin Legal Audit/pre-sale due diligence.*

☐ Review and enhance Value Drivers.

☐ Provide family and business security.

☐ Make confidentiality decisions.

☐ Prepare employees.

Note: This will cost money and it depends on a transaction intermediary's assessment that a sale is likely.

TARGET DEPARTURE: 1–2 YEARS
DAY 61–YEAR 2

Day 61–90

☐ Make ownership transfers (if applicable).

☐ Implement incentive plans/stay bonuses.

Day 91–120

☐ Market company to potential target buyers.

Day 121–365

☐ Negotiate Letter of Intent.

Year 2

☐ Review/update estate plan to ensure its consistency with expected sale proceeds.

☐ Reassess marketability of company to ensure that expected sale proceeds meet financial security needs.

The detailed checklist below provides specific activities or decisions (and chapter references) that support each item on the previous list.

TARGET DEPARTURE: 1–2 YEARS
DAY 1– DAY 30

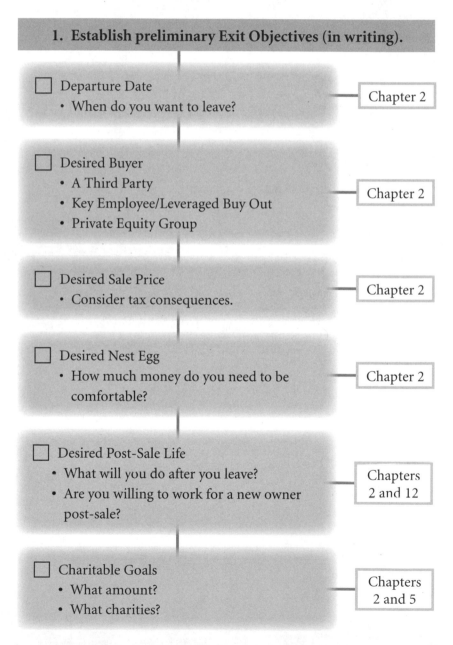

1. Establish preliminary Exit Objectives (in writing).

☐ Departure Date
  • When do you want to leave?

Chapter 2

☐ Desired Buyer
  • A Third Party
  • Key Employee/Leveraged Buy Out
  • Private Equity Group

Chapter 2

☐ Desired Sale Price
  • Consider tax consequences.

Chapter 2

☐ Desired Nest Egg
  • How much money do you need to be comfortable?

Chapter 2

☐ Desired Post-Sale Life
  • What will you do after you leave?
  • Are you willing to work for a new owner post-sale?

Chapters 2 and 12

☐ Charitable Goals
  • What amount?
  • What charities?

Chapters 2 and 5

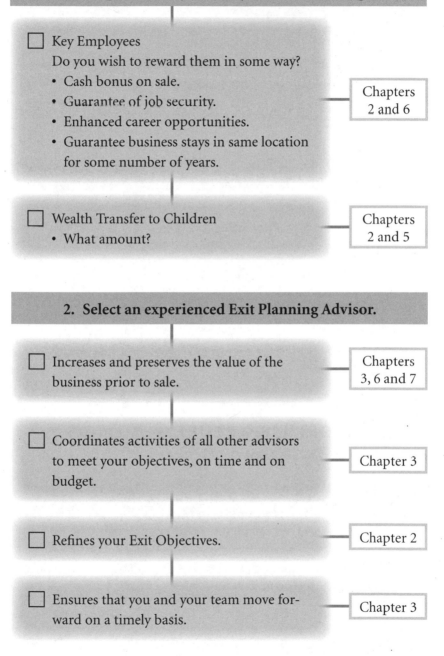

1. Establish preliminary Exit Objectives (in writing), con't.

☐ Key Employees
Do you wish to reward them in some way?
- Cash bonus on sale.
- Guarantee of job security.
- Enhanced career opportunities.
- Guarantee business stays in same location for some number of years.

Chapters 2 and 6

☐ Wealth Transfer to Children
- What amount?

Chapters 2 and 5

2. Select an experienced Exit Planning Advisor.

☐ Increases and preserves the value of the business prior to sale.

Chapters 3, 6 and 7

☐ Coordinates activities of all other advisors to meet your objectives, on time and on budget.

Chapter 3

☐ Refines your Exit Objectives.

Chapter 2

☐ Ensures that you and your team move forward on a timely basis.

Chapter 3

3. Get marketability and pricing assessment.

☐ Interview an investment banker to secure valuation and identify range of likely value of your company based on deal activity and industry sector.

> Chapters 3 and 4

4. Prepare yourself for life after the sale.

☐ Read about what other owners have done after selling.

> Chapter 12

☐ Take some time off to:
  • probe your own post-sale objectives;
  • evaluate how your company runs without you at the helm.

> Chapters 2 and 12

TARGET DEPARTURE: 1–2 YEARS
DAY 31– DAY 60

1. Select transaction intermediary (investment banker/business broker).

☐ Assess the "extrinsic" factor of the deal—the status of the M&A market for your industry.

> Chapters 3 and 8

☐ Assess company's Value Drivers.

> Chapters 3, 6 and 7

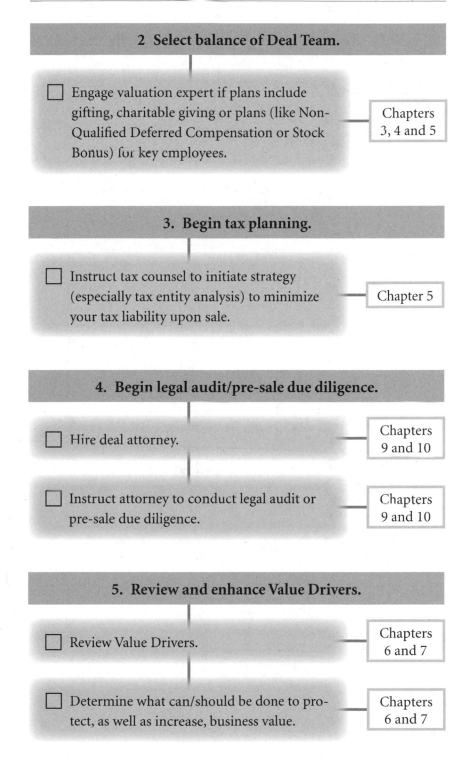

2 Select balance of Deal Team.

☐ Engage valuation expert if plans include gifting, charitable giving or plans (like Non-Qualified Deferred Compensation or Stock Bonus) for key employees.

Chapters 3, 4 and 5

3. Begin tax planning.

☐ Instruct tax counsel to initiate strategy (especially tax entity analysis) to minimize your tax liability upon sale.

Chapter 5

4. Begin legal audit/pre-sale due diligence.

☐ Hire deal attorney.

Chapters 9 and 10

☐ Instruct attorney to conduct legal audit or pre-sale due diligence.

Chapters 9 and 10

5. Review and enhance Value Drivers.

☐ Review Value Drivers.

Chapters 6 and 7

☐ Determine what can/should be done to protect, as well as increase, business value.

Chapters 6 and 7

6. Provide family and business security.

☐ Review estate plan and business continuity arrangements to make sure family is protected in case of your death/disability.

Chapter 3

7. Make confidentiality decisions.

☐ Create and execute non-disclosure agreement.

Chapters 6 and 10

☐ Determine circulation of non-disclosure agreement.

Chapters 6 and 10

8. Prepare employees.

☐ Inform necessary employees of your desire to organize and collect documents for "legal audit."

Chapters 3 and 8

TARGET DEPARTURE: 1–2 YEARS
DAY 61–DAY 90

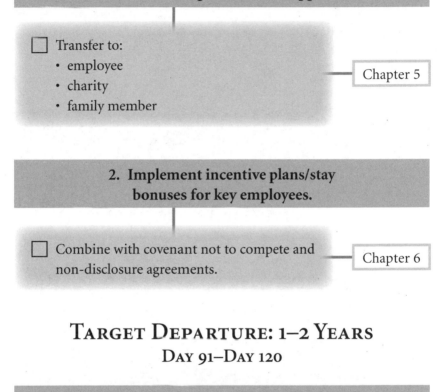

1. Make ownership transfers (if applicable).

☐ Transfer to:
  • employee
  • charity
  • family member

Chapter 5

2. Implement incentive plans/stay bonuses for key employees.

☐ Combine with covenant not to compete and non-disclosure agreements.

Chapter 6

TARGET DEPARTURE: 1–2 YEARS
DAY 91–DAY 120

1. Market company to potential target buyers.

☐ Assist transaction intermediary by providing company information.

Chapters 3 and 9

☐ Keep focus on running the company.

Chapters 3 and 9

☐ Review Deal Book (if applicable) for accuracy and completeness.

Chapters 3 and 9

TARGET DEPARTURE: 1–2 YEARS
DAY 121–DAY 365

1. Negotiate Letter of Intent.

☐ Reconfirm all offers meet *all* of your objectives. ── Chapter 10

☐ Keep focus on running the company. ── Chapter 9

TARGET DEPARTURE: 1–2 YEARS
YEAR TWO

1. Review/update estate plan to ensure its consistency with expected sale proceeds.

☐ Meet with estate planning counsel to revise estate plan consistent with (presumably) increased value of company.

2. Reassess marketability of company to ensure that expected sale proceeds meet financial security needs.

☐ Meet with financial advisor.

TARGET DEPARTURE: 3+ YEARS
DAY 1–365

Day 1–30

☐ Select lead Exit Planning Advisor.

☐ Select valuation specialist.

☐ Analyze financial needs.

☐ Prepare yourself for life after the sale.

Day 31–60

☐ Engage planning attorney.

☐ Engage estate planning attorney.

☐ Increase business value via focus on Value Drivers.

Day 61–90

☐ Engage tax counsel.

☐ Engage business consultant (as necessary).

Day 91–120

☐ Determine preferred tax strategy for sale.

☐ Begin implementing gifting and charitable decisions.

☐ Review/revise estate plan.

Day 121–365

☐ Begin key employee incentive planning.

☐ Protect business assets.

☐ Implement/refine Value Drivers.

☐ Implement strategic business plan.

TARGET DEPARTURE: 3+ YEARS
YEARS 2 AND 3

Year 2
- [ ] Revalue business.
- [ ] Meet with entire planning team.
- [ ] Revisit www.BEIBooks.com for planning and sale resources.

Year 3
- [ ] Repeat Year Two activities.

The detailed checklist below provides specific activities or decisions (and chapter references) that support each item on the previous list.

TARGET DEPARTURE: 3+ YEARS
DAY 1–DAY 30

1. Select lead Exit Planning Advisor to facilitate planning process and sale process.

- [ ] This person will make sure all advisors work together to meet your Exit Objectives. — Chapter 3

- [ ] This person can help recommend other specialized advisors. — Chapter 3

- [ ] If you are willing to sell immediately for the "right price," this advisor should contact a transaction intermediary to secure a market assessment of value. — Chapter 3

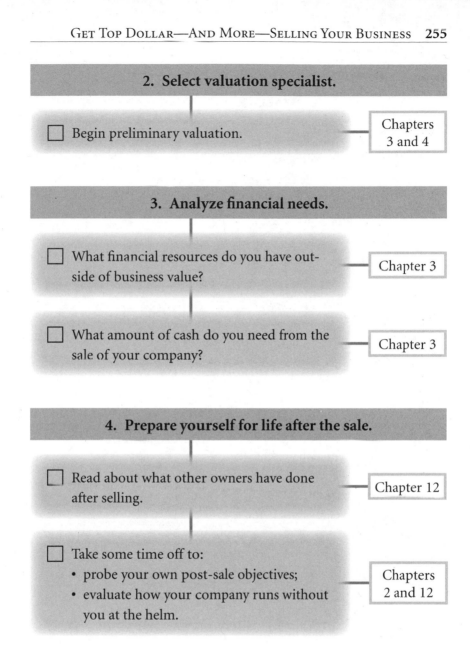

2. Select valuation specialist.

☐ Begin preliminary valuation.

Chapters
3 and 4

3. Analyze financial needs.

☐ What financial resources do you have outside of business value?

Chapter 3

☐ What amount of cash do you need from the sale of your company?

Chapter 3

4. Prepare yourself for life after the sale.

☐ Read about what other owners have done after selling.

Chapter 12

☐ Take some time off to:
 • probe your own post-sale objectives;
 • evaluate how your company runs without you at the helm.

Chapters
2 and 12

TARGET DEPARTURE: 3+ YEARS
DAY 31–DAY 60

1. Engage planning attorney.

☐ Create key employee incentive plans.
- Stay Bonus Plans
- Stock Bonus or Non-Qualified Deferred Compensation Plans

Chapter 6

☐ Protect value.
- Covenants Not to Compete
- Trade Secrecy Protection
- Non-Disclosure Agreements

Chapter 6

☐ Enhance/Install Value Drivers
- Motivate management team.
- Diversify customer base.
- Install systems that sustain growth.
- Upgrade facility appearance.
- Install realistic growth strategy.
- Grow cash flow, profitability and revenues.
- Establish presence in attractive business sector.
- Protect proprietary technology.
- Grow through acquisition.

Chapters 6 and 7

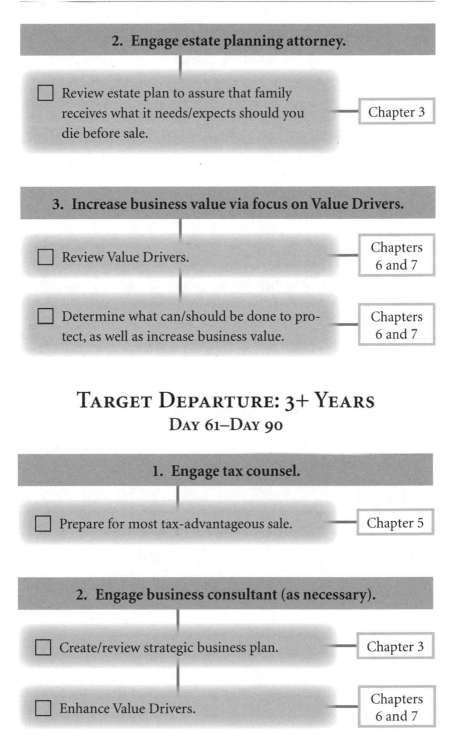

2. Engage estate planning attorney.

☐ Review estate plan to assure that family receives what it needs/expects should you die before sale.

Chapter 3

3. Increase business value via focus on Value Drivers.

☐ Review Value Drivers.

Chapters 6 and 7

☐ Determine what can/should be done to protect, as well as increase business value.

Chapters 6 and 7

Target Departure: 3+ Years
Day 61–Day 90

1. Engage tax counsel.

☐ Prepare for most tax-advantageous sale.

Chapter 5

2. Engage business consultant (as necessary).

☐ Create/review strategic business plan.

Chapter 3

☐ Enhance Value Drivers.

Chapters 6 and 7

TARGET DEPARTURE: 3+ YEARS
DAY 91–DAY 120

1. Determine preferred tax strategy for sale.

☐ Identify entity choice. — Chapter 5

☐ Select tax counsel. — Chapter 3

2. Begin implementing gifting and charitable decisions.

☐ Work with financial, tax and legal advisors. — Chapter 5

3. Review/revise estate plan.

☐ Meet with estate planning attorney and insurance advisors. — Chapter 3

TARGET DEPARTURE: 3+ YEARS
DAY 121–DAY 365

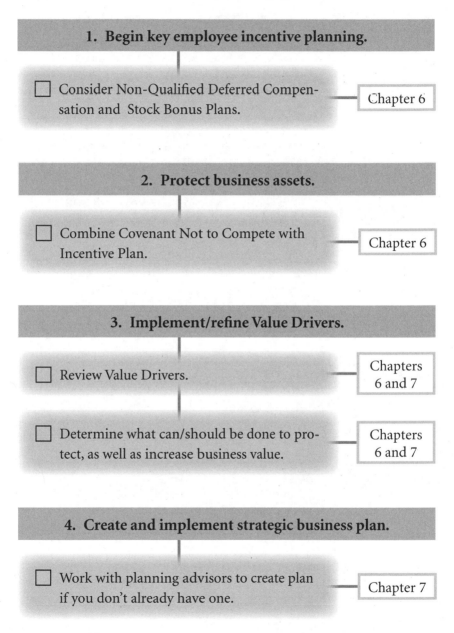

1. Begin key employee incentive planning.

☐ Consider Non-Qualified Deferred Compensation and Stock Bonus Plans. | Chapter 6 |

2. Protect business assets.

☐ Combine Covenant Not to Compete with Incentive Plan. | Chapter 6 |

3. Implement/refine Value Drivers.

☐ Review Value Drivers. | Chapters 6 and 7 |

☐ Determine what can/should be done to protect, as well as increase business value. | Chapters 6 and 7 |

4. Create and implement strategic business plan.

☐ Work with planning advisors to create plan if you don't already have one. | Chapter 7 |

TARGET DEPARTURE: 3+ YEARS
YEAR TWO

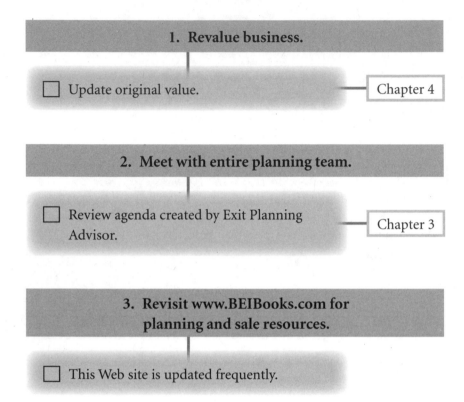

1. Revalue business.

☐ Update original value.

Chapter 4

2. Meet with entire planning team.

☐ Review agenda created by Exit Planning Advisor.

Chapter 3

3. Revisit www.BEIBooks.com for planning and sale resources.

☐ This Web site is updated frequently.

TARGET DEPARTURE: 3+ YEARS
YEAR THREE
REPEAT OF YEAR TWO

1. Revalue business.

☐ Update original value.   Chapter 4

2. Meet with entire planning team.

☐ Review agenda created by Exit Planning Advisor.   Chapter 3

3. Revisit www.BEIBooks.com for planning and sale resources.

☐ This Web site is updated frequently.

APPENDIX TO CHAPTER 3
FINDING, HIRING AND USING
THE MOST SUITABLE ADVISORS

When it is time for you to add advisors to either your Planning or Deal Teams, we hope that you will use this Appendix to help you understand what those advisors should be doing for you and what experience and expertise they need to have *before* joining one of your teams.

TEAM PLAYERS

We have divided the business life of the owner into three Phases:

- Phase I: Pre-Sale

- Phase II: The Sale

- Phase III: Post-Sale

You will require different advisors depending upon where you are in the process. The following chart will help you determine which advisors you need and when you need them.

Advisor	Phase I: Pre-Sale The Planning Team	Phase II: The Sale The Deal Team	Phase III: Post-Sale
Certified Public Accountant	X	X	X
Exit Planning Advisor	X	X	X
Business/Tax Attorney	X		
Estate Planning Attorney	X		X
M&A Attorney		X	
Business Consultant	X	X	
Financial/Insurance Advisor	X	X	X
Transaction Intermediary (Investment Banker/Business Broker)		X	
Business Appraiser	X		

This chart gives you a good idea of the type of advisors you will need as you move through each phase of the sale process. Keep in mind, however, that it is somewhat fluid. For example, your financial advisor or business attorney may be your primary Exit Planning Advisor. If he or she is also an estate planning attorney, as I was, your chart will look a little different. Also, in some deals, the M&A attorney takes the lead in negotiations, while in others (usually larger deals) the investment banker runs the show.

PHASE I: PRE-SALE

THE PLANNING TEAM

During Phase I, you should work with planning-oriented advisors to prepare you and your business for sale. They should work together to help you evaluate, clarify and prioritize your exit goals related to:

- When you want to sell your company;

- How much money you want from the sale; and

- Who you want to succeed you (insider or third party).

The Planning Team includes:

Exit Planning Advisor
- Creates owner's comprehensive Exit Plan.
- Assembles the Planning and Deal Teams.
- Facilitates and guides Teams based on owner's objectives.
- Preserves, protects and promotes the value of the company.

CPA
- Conducts income tax analysis.
- Designs and implements tax-efficient strategies.
- Prepares reviewed financial statements or certified audit (depending on company size).
- Provides valuation support to transaction intermediary.

Business Planning Attorney
- Documents the business continuity plan.*

- Conducts pre-sale due diligence.
- If not experienced in M&A, recommends M&A attorney.

Estate Planning Attorney
- Creates owner's Estate Plan.

Business Consultant
- Increases the value of the company.

Financial/Insurance Advisor
- Determines/analyzes owner's financial goals.
- Projects owner's post-closing financial needs.
- Ensures that owner's family's financial needs are met should owner die before sale is complete.*
- Provides insurance funding and investment services as appropriate.

> *It may sound morbid or pessimistic, but more than one owner has died during the weeks and months preceding a sale. It is your attorney's job (and your financial advisor's job) to implement simple steps to protect your business and your family should the unexpected happen to you.

Transaction Intermediary
- Estimates likely sale price and marketability of company.

Business Appraiser
- Necessary only if owner desires pre-sale transfers

EXIT PLANNING ADVISOR

Creates owner's comprehensive Exit Plan. From the day you retain your Exit Planning Advisor, this person should be working with you to create a comprehensive Exit Plan. The Seven Step Exit Planning Process™ that I developed over years of practice includes the following steps.

Step One—Setting Exit Objectives
Each business owner's unique objectives drive the creation of his or her Exit Plan. Step One articulates and tests owner objectives so that

the comprehensive Exit Plan focuses on achieving those goals. Key exit objectives of any Exit Plan include: (1) the owner's desired departure date, (2) the value that the owner wants or needs from the business, and (3) the individuals or entities to whom the owner wants to sell/transfer the business. Since you are reading this book, we assume that one of your Exit Objectives is to sell to a third party.

In addition to these primary exit objectives, owners also may have other secondary objectives. For example, some owners wish to transfer value to children or to charity. In this case, they must determine how much they can transfer without jeopardizing their own security. Other owners may set a departure date, but want (or may need) to work for several more years for the new owner.

Step Two—Determining Valuation and Cash Flow

Step Two determines what owners *have*—how much the business is worth and how much cash flow the business can generate. The current value and projected cash flow are used to determine the paths and planning tools available to reach the owner's objectives. In a sale to a third party, your transaction intermediary will perform the valuation.

Those owners who want to transfer value to children or to charity will, for two reasons, need a certified valuation specialist to value their companies. First, should the IRS question a valuation performed for either purpose (passing business value to children or to charity), a certified, credentialed business appraiser will carry far more weight. Second, the IRS does not consider the sales and marketability assessment performed by your transaction intermediary to be an appropriate measure (for tax purposes) of valuing a gift to charity or to children. Either type of gift should be made as far in advance of a sale as possible.

Step Three—Preserving, Protecting and Promoting Value

The elements that build the value of a business or protect the value the owner has worked so hard to create are called Value Drivers. In Step Three, owners and their advisors identify which Value Drivers are important to meeting the owner's overall exit objectives and devise specific steps to maximize the impact of the Value Drivers. These specific steps: 1) tax planning strategies, 2) preserving value, and 3) creating Value Drivers are all discussed in chapter 5, 6 and 7.

Step Four—Converting Business Value to Cash

During Step Four, owners, like you, who want to sell their businesses to a third party work with their advisors to identify ways to do so in the manner that results in the most beneficial sale price and terms. Not all business owners go through Step Four—those who don't either retain their ownership long-term or skip to Step Five.

Step Five—Selling the Business Over Time

If you are reading this book, we assume your intent is to sell to a third party so you would ignore this step. Step Five includes a detailed plan to transfer the business to insiders (children, key employees or co-owners). Careful planning in Step Five allows the owner to both receive the desired value from the business, and to minimize risk, while using the resources of the business should the purchaser have little or no personal capital. Owners who are not yet ready to contemplate a sale to a third party may consider transferring some ownership to others (such as a key employee or child) using tax-sensitive tools particular to this step.

Step Six—Contingency Planning for the Business

Step Six prepares the owner for the contingencies that affect the business and its owners. A complete Exit Plan incorporates potential challenges, such as death or permanent disability of an owner, so that the owner's objectives can still be achieved if circumstances change. Again, your Planning Team is charged with making sure arrangements are in place so that your family receives their due (Step Seven) if you don't live long enough to sell your business.

Step Seven—Wealth Preservation Planning

The sale of a business generates cash for owners, their families and the IRS. During Step Seven, owners and their advisors create a plan that not only preserves wealth, but minimizes taxes using both lifetime and estate planning tools.

Assembles the Planning and Deal Teams. Because your Exit Planning Advisor understands the scope and the details of the entire exit process, he or she can help you to choose the members of your Planning and Deal Teams. As you review the various types of advisors needed, you'll see how one advisor can perform a lot of the legwork such as finding, initially interviewing, and checking references. That advisor then presents his or her findings to you for your review and ultimate selection.

Facilitates and guides team based on owner's objectives. Every owner reading this is thinking, "Using all of these advisors has got to be incredibly expensive." It is. If your advisors are efficient and work together, they are more than worth the expense. Remember, you, your company, and likely your regular advisors, are not experienced and skilled in developing intrinsic value, understanding the M&A cycles and promoting the company's value throughout the sale process. You need outside specialists. What you don't need is duplicative work, delay, and unnecessary communication. Using at least one advisor skilled in facilitating these processes reduces delay, increases effective communication, and coordinates each step of the value building and sale processes.

Preserves, protects and promotes the value of your company. Once you make your decision to sell to a third party, your attention turns to building your company's value. In Chapters 6 and 7, we discuss the factors that buyers look for in the companies they consider buying. We call these factors Value Drivers. Your Exit Planning Advisor is instrumental in designing Value Drivers based on your objectives and facilitating their implementation.

Certified Public Accountant

Income tax analysis. As part of the initial planning process, a CPA may help you develop your personal financial Exit Objectives and help plan to *minimize income tax consequences* of the sale. You need to know—before you begin the sale process—what the various possible tax results will be when you sell the business. (See Chapter 5 for a general tax overview.)

Designs and implements tax-efficient strategies. Once identified, your CPA will help you design and implement the most tax efficient strategies for selling your company.

Prepares reviewed financial statements or certified audit (depending on company size). For the reasons discussed in Chapter 4, you will likely need a certified audit performed by an independent accounting firm. While in smaller deals it may be possible that a potential buyer would require only reviewed financial statements, even these are typically prepared by an independent accounting firm. While reviewed financial statements or audits are expensive, *audits will make you money* because the would-be buyer can rely upon them. Audited financial statements also reduce the buyer's risk of basing the buying decision on incorrect financial information. With increased buyer confidence and decreased risk comes a greater willingness to pay more money. Audited financials also enable your investment banker to depend on the numbers.

You will need to determine (often with the help of your transaction intermediary) whether your current CPA firm is able to perform the audit. If not, the audit firm you choose should be experienced in audits, pre-deal income tax planning designed to minimize tax consequences, and should have participated in the sale of at least five to ten businesses of a comparable size

Provides valuation support to transaction intermediary. Your CPA will provide needed financial information and support to the transaction team as needed.

Business Planning Attorney

Typically, your transaction attorney is not the same person as your planning attorney.

Documents the business continuity plan. A continuity plan for both the company and the owner's family is a critical part of an owner's comprehensive Exit Plan. Unexpected illness, disability and death can happen to any owner, but financial disaster should not. It is your estate planning attorney and Exit Planning Advisor's job to draft the documents necessary to safeguard your family and your company.

Conducts pre-sale due diligence. Skilled business attorneys often perform much of the pre-sale due diligence as part of their ongoing representation. They understand that it is better to locate—and eradicate—the skeletons in your company's closet *before* a potential seller does. They also understand that speed is critical once the sale process begins. If those skeletons don't kill a sale, they will, at a minimum, cause delay. For that reason, your advisors' efforts to organize and clean up your records will serve you well during the sale.

Recommends a Merger & Acquisition attorney. If your business attorney is not a Merger & Acquisition attorney (and most are not), he or she may be able to recommend a reputable one in your community. If not, ask your other advisors for recommendations.

ESTATE PLANNING ATTORNEY

Creates owner's estate plan. The best time to give assets to your children and thereby avoid estate taxes is probably now—before a higher value is placed on your business as a consequence of the sale process. There are a variety of techniques that, when used in advance of a sale, can sidestep estate taxes on millions of dollars of gifts. (Please see Chapter 5 for a more complete discussion.) It is important to begin working early in the process with your attorney to minimize taxes of all types upon the sale of your business.

BUSINESS CONSULTANT

Increases the value of your company. It is not uncommon for an owner's Exit Planning Advisor to recommend that the owner retain a business consultant to help create and enhance the Value Drivers that increase the value of the company. Consultants can be invaluable in setting up Key Employee Incentive Plans (both short term and long term) and operating systems that improve the sustainability of cash flows. They also can help you create a plan to diversify your customer base (if necessary). Finally, they are uniquely suited to help an owner create a realistic growth strategy.

FINANCIAL/INSURANCE ADVISOR

Many articles recently have been written in financial planning journals about the need and opportunity for financial advisors to help their business owner clients exit their businesses. I know. I've written some of them. If you work with an experienced financial/insurance advisor, that person is a valuable addition to your Planning Team.

Determines/analyzes financial goals. After helping you determine what amount of cash you will need to move on, your financial advisor can help you determine what sum of money you need *from the sale of your business* to attain financial security.

Projects owner's post-closing financial needs. Expect your financial/insurance advisor to project your post-closing financial needs and coordinate changes to your estate plan to account for the changed circumstances brought about by the sale of your business.

Ensures that family's financial needs are met should owner die before sale is complete. The process of selling your business can last a year or even two before you receive full payment for your company. As your spouse may occasionally remind you, you are not getting any younger. Add to that the stress of the deal process and what happened to one of my clients may not surprise you. Two days prior to his closing, he died of a heart attack while riding his stationary bike.

Don't let the possibility that you could die before closing deter you from proceeding with a sale. Instead, let it encourage you to take the steps necessary to insulate and protect your family and business from the financial impact of your untimely demise.

Provides insurance funding and investment services as appropriate. Owners typically underestimate the value of their companies during the years before a sale. They purchase insurance to replace the loss of themselves or of a key employee based on that value. As the sale date approaches, however, your advisors are able to establish a more accurate value. Your financial/insurance advisor can work with you to make the appropriate adjustments to your insurance coverage.

TRANSACTION INTERMEDIARY: INVESTMENT BANKER OR BUSINESS BROKER

Investment Banker. Over the years, investment bankers have convinced me of the indispensable role they play in the sale of middle-market companies. Early in my career, I thought that using an investment banker in a deal worth less than $5 million was as efficient as using a brick to kill a fly when a flyswatter would suffice. Especially in cases when owners had already been approached by buyers I thought, "Why use an investment banker? The lion's share of his job—finding a buyer—is already done!"

As I grew more experienced representing owners, I began to appreciate not only the many roles investment bankers play in the third-party sale process, but also how an experienced banker is worth his or her weight in gold. In the Introduction, I compared the direct relationship between the skill of the surgeon and positive outcomes to the skill of an Exit Planning Advisor and successful business exits. The same analogy holds true with investment bankers: the more experienced your investment banker, the better your chances for a good transaction outcome.

Good investment bankers act as the owner's primary transaction advisor, directing much of the sale process. They become involved in Phase I (Pre-Sale) of the sale process because their job begins much earlier than locating a buyer and negotiating a sale. Let's look at what an investment banker does during Phase I.

Estimates a likely sale price for the company.

When you first meet with an investment banker, he or she will look at your financial statements. Knowing the status of the Merger & Acquisition market, as well as the activity in your industry sector, the banker will give you an idea of the *saleability and marketability of a company like yours*. Only after you engage the banker will he or she look closely at your company's financials, Value Drivers and any unique characteristics (perhaps its customer base, geographic location or unique product or service) to estimate *your company's value*.

Business Broker. Owners retain a business broker in place of an investment banker when their companies are worth less than a few million dollars. This doesn't necessarily mean those companies won't sell for cash, or largely cash; it does mean few investment bankers are interested in representing a business below a value of $5 million to $10 million.

Depending on the broker's experience, they are active in deals ranging in value from a few hundred thousand dollars to several million dollars. Among brokers, there is a much broader variation in experience, skill and ability than you will find in investment bankers. Often, the business broker's only licensing requirement is a realtor's license (investment bankers don't require more). Consequently, almost anyone can hold himself out as a business broker. Nevertheless, there are many respected business brokers who are well-qualified to help smaller businesses: 1) determine marketability and a likely sale price range during Phase I of the process; 2) explain to you the sale process for your particular company; and 3) conduct the negotiated sale process described in Chapter 9. At the upper end of experience and expertise, brokers also will conduct controlled auctions.

Investment Banker or Business Broker?   Let's pause here to talk

about the type of transaction intermediary that you use to sell your company. Your choice primarily depends on the size of your company. Based on our experience in working with companies in the mid-market, we see a Transaction Intermediary Threshold of about $5 million and often higher. Those companies below $5 million in value are typically sold using a business broker, while those above $5 million in value are sold using investment bankers.

Just as the Value Threshold (the threshold that separates those companies that can be sold via controlled auction from those that will typically be sold using a negotiated sale and require the owner to carry back a portion of the purchase price) is approximate and constantly shifting depending on market conditions in your industry, so too does the Intermediary Threshold change. (Please refer to Chapter 4 for more information about the Value Threshold.)

The Intermediary Threshold is the business value that separates those companies that are sold using services of an investment banker from those sold using the services of a business broker.

Today's Intermediary Threshold is around $5 million. Therefore, if your company is worth at least $5 million, we recommend that you hire an investment banker who works with owners in the middle market ($5 million to $150 million). Owners of companies in the gray area (value hovering around $5 million) find that there are business brokers who, through experience, are skilled handling sales in this range. Joining their ranks are financially-oriented advisors such as CPAs who have M&A experience or training. As you should do with all of your advisors, check references and carefully interview them to determine their ability with selling companies like yours.

Investment banker Kevin Short provided four important observations about the challenges owners of companies below the Intermdiary Threshold face as they hire business brokers.

1. A deal worth less than $5 million is no easier to negotiate than a deal worth more than $5 million. In fact, it is more difficult for the reasons we mentioned in our discussion of Value Threshold in Chapter 4 (lack of management team, dependence on the owner, weak financial systems, creative bookkeeping and lack of value drivers). Well-financed buyers understand these deficiencies and are not willing to devote the time necessary to address them in return for the minimal impact on their bottom lines.

2. It is harder to attract a buyer to a deal worth less than $5 million because few individuals have enough cash to finance the purchase and well-heeled institutional type buyers (such as Private Equity Groups) steer clear of smaller companies. A seller in this situation has several choices. First, with adequate planning and time, he or she can sell to key employees, if they exist and have the money. Second, he or she could sell to family members, again, if they are willing and able to pay the sale price. Third, he or she can sell to an interested competitor. Or, his or her broker can look for an entrepreneurial buyer. This is the individual, usually a second- or third-tier manager who wants to be an entrepreneur. Unfortunately, this typically 40- to 55-year-old executive is not easy to find. Usually, owners have to wait until this type of buyer approaches them.

3.   All-cash deals in the less than $5 million range are understandably rare. If you locate the entrepreneurial buyer we just described, remember that he or she does not have deep pockets. He or she will bring some cash to the table, but will have to finance the bulk of the purchase price. As a bank considers the size of its loan, it will note that this buyer has never run a company and therefore has no track record. As I'm sure you've surmised, you, as the seller, will be required to finance a portion of the price in order to close the deal.

4.   Entrepreneurial buyers are represented by attorneys and accountants. This means that the due diligence process in a smaller deal is just as thorough as the due diligence in a larger deal. The buyer's accountants will pour over your financial records. The buyer's attorneys will write the Warranties and Representations in the Purchase Agreement so that if any of your financial representations prove incorrect, you will be required to return cash to the buyer after closing.

Sellers of smaller companies then, are between a rock and a hard place. On the one hand they need skilled transaction intermediaries as much as, if not more than, sellers of larger companies. On the other hand, in the transaction marketplace, investment bankers and business brokers charge based on the size of a deal. Few investment bankers will take on a client unless he or she can expect at least $250,000 in fees (about 5 percent of a company worth $5 million). For that fee, he or she brings expertise, contacts and a great deal of transaction experience to the table. You need to weigh the benefits of using an investment banker in a smaller-sized deal (assuming you can find one interested in taking you on as a client) against the proportionally larger fee.

Business brokers work with owners on deals in the $1 to $4 million range. The problem is that while there are a number of business brokers in most metropolitan areas, there are few successful ones. We are not impugning the integrity or work ethic of business brokers here. Instead, we are pointing out a simple reality: in return for a fee of approximately $5,000 to $150,000 the business broker will have to find a buyer who is as well hidden as a needle in a haystack. The broker will have to work with less reliable financial records and across the table from skilled buyer representatives. In short, brokers are often asked to perform a more difficult job, for less money, than an investment banker. This is not a recipe for a long and lucrative career.

Over the years, Kevin has been approached by a number of owners of smaller companies who want the expertise of the investment banker as they enter the biggest transaction of their lives. "They are in a difficult position," Kevin explains. "Usually through experience, they understand that it will be hard for them to find a buyer, but harder still to close the deal. They also appreciate that without the assistance of a skilled advisor, they are likely to sell for little more than book value. In these cases, in return for a set fee, I will negotiate the sale—often, but not always, with a buyer they have already chosen. The fee is a larger percentage of their sale price (than it is with a mid-size company) but in return, I, most importantly, *close the deal*. As an added bonus, I close for more money than they could have gotten on their own."

BUSINESS APPRAISER

Owners who intend to sell to a third party retain the services of a business appraiser or Certified Valuation Analyst when their Exit Objectives include transferring wealth to family members or to charity. In these cases, the mechanisms used to make these transfers (usually some kind of trust) must be in place before the sale process begins.

Owners who plan to transfer their companies to insiders (family members or key employees) also will often retain appraisers. In insider transfers, it is best to establish a low value for the company to enable buyers with little cash to make the purchase and decrease the seller's risk of not being paid. (If you are interested in the techniques used in insider sales, I suggest that you read my first book, **The Completely Revised How To Run Your Business So You Can Leave It In Style**.)

> To determine if you have the right advisors on your Planning Team, ask yourself, "Have my advisors been helpful to date in suggesting planning concepts and techniques to help ensure a smooth, tax-efficient transfer. Or have they been silent?"

PHASE II: THE SALE

As the sale process begins, the makeup of your team changes. You will transition from a Planning Team to a Deal Team. In doing so, the specialized services of the M&A attorney and the transaction intermediary that you chose during Phase I will swing into high gear. Your Exit Planning Advisor will continue to monitor the progress of these new advisors to make sure that your Exit Objectives are met.

Exit Planning Advisor
- Provides continuity during the sale process.
- Analyzes buyers' offers in light of owner's goals.

CPA
- Provides financial information to transaction intermediary.
- Implements plans to minimize owner's tax liability.

M&A Attorney
- Directs the due diligence process.
- Negotiates the purchase agreement.

Transaction Intermediary
- Directs the controlled auction.
- Markets company, negotiates and closes the deal.

EXIT PLANNING ADVISOR

Provides continuity throughout the sale process. As the member of your team who is active in all three phases of the sale process, your Exit Planning Advisor is uniquely suited to protect and address your Exit Objectives. Your Exit Planning Advisor will make certain that all of your non-financial goals (such as transferring wealth to children) are not ignored during the push to get the deal done.

Analyzes buyers' offers in light of owner's goals. It is worth noting here that the goals you set in Phase I of the sale process provide invaluable instruction to your transaction intermediary in Phase II. Your Exit Planning Advisor will make sure your transaction intermediary is aware of your goals so that every offer (and every deal term) is examined in light of your goals (when you want to leave, if you want to work for the new owner, how much cash you need at closing, and what kind of successor you want).

CERTIFIED PUBLIC ACCOUNTANT

Provides financial information to transaction intermediary. Based on its long-term representation of you and your company, your CPA firm can provide your transaction intermediary an important historical perspective. It can explain, for example, how expenses were historically allocated and why.

Implements plans to minimize owner's tax liability. From the outset, it has been your CPA's role to minimize your tax liability. It is during the sale process that your CPA makes sure the deal is structured so you pay no more than the required amount of tax.

MERGER & ACQUISITION ATTORNEY

Also known as "transaction attorneys," these lawyers represent you and your company during the sale process.

Directs the due diligence process   We describe the due diligence process in Chapters 9 and 11, but here's the short version. Due diligence is the process during which a prospective buyer asks for and examines the details of *everything* that affects the operation of your company. The buyer examines your financial and legal documentation, your contracts and your internal procedures. At some point, the buyer will speak with your employees and possibly your customers. The buyer will probe every nook and every cranny—both above and under the ground—and inspect your facility.

Negotiates the purchase agreement. With your investment banker, (or, in smaller deals, on his or her own) the M&A attorney negotiates the provisions of the binding purchase agreement; particularly the numerous representations and warranties that you will be required to make. Deals "go into the ditch" with clocklike regularity over the reasonability of these "reps and warranties." Your attorney will earn his or her keep by skillfully negotiating to minimize the scope and duration of the warranties and representations you will have to make. Some typical warranties and representations are described in Chapter 11.

TRANSACTION INTERMEDIARY

Directs the controlled auction.   If your company meets the Value Threshold, your investment banker will orchestrate a controlled auction (the sale process in which there is more than one buyer bidding for your company). For a complete description of that process and the investment banker's role in it, please see Chapter 9.

If your company falls short of the Value Threshold, your business broker will work with your attorney to complete the sale of your company using the negotiated sale process. Please see Chapter 9 for a description of the negotiated sale process.

Negotiates deal terms and conditions.   In a nutshell, the investment banker in a larger deal or the business broker and your attorney in a smaller deal, will negotiate every term and condition of the sale. Again, please see Chapters 10 and 11 for a more complete discussion of all the terms and conditions contained in the sale of a business.

PHASE III: POST SALE

Exit Planning Advisor
- Coordinates activities of all advisors.
- Helps owner to move on.

CPA
- Prepares tax returns.
- Offers advice on tax-efficient investment strategies.

Estate Planning Attorney
- Adjusts estate plan, as necessary, to meet owner's goals.

Financial/Insurance Advisor
- Allocates and invests sale proceeds.

Exit Planning Advisor

Coordinates activities of all advisors. Once you complete the sale of your company, your Exit Planning Advisor will help coordinate the activities of your other advisors. Your advisors will assist you in more personal endeavors (preparing your personal tax returns, helping you analyze investment vehicles, etc.) than they did when you were running your company.

Helps owner to move on. Your Exit Planning Advisor can help guide you through the process of moving on to this new phase of your life. He or she has helped several owners analyze the numerous options available to the successful seller and can share these experiences with you.

Certified Public Accountant

Completes personal tax returns. Your CPA will likely continue to prepare your personal and any trust returns (trusts that you may have created as part of your Exit Plan).

Offers advice on investment strategies. CPAs are often a reliable, unbiased source of information about possible investment strategies.

Estate Planning Attorney

Adjusts estate plan, as necessary, to meet owner's goals. Having consummated what was likely the largest financial transaction of your life, you may wish to adjust your estate plan in ways that you had not anticipated. Some owners decide that they don't want their children to inherit "too much." Others put restrictions on when and how their children will inherit their money. Still others decide that they would like to become philanthropists. Your estate planning attorney can help you understand your options.

Financial/Insurance Advisor

Allocates and invests sale proceeds. Your financial advisor will help you allocate and invest the mountains of cash you will receive at closing in a way that will protect your newfound financial security.

WHAT SKILL SETS DO ADVISORS NEED?

Advisors on both your Planning and Deal Teams share several characteristics. First and foremost, each should be deeply and thoroughly trained and experienced in his or her specific field. Second, each must be willing to work cooperatively with the others while never forgetting his or her primary allegiance to you. Third, all should be "battle-scarred" from the successful completion of many deals. You need advisors with both *professional* experience and *deal* experience.

As you review the lists below, keep in mind that one of your advisors must be trained, experienced and skilled as an Exit Planner. Visit our Web site (www.BEIBooks.com) for a list of advisors who are skilled in Exit Planning. These advisors are Members of Business Enterprise Institute and understand the ins and outs of Exit Planning.

One final note: as you read through each professional's checklist, remember that asking your existing advisors and colleagues for references and checking those references is another great way to locate advisors. These checklists will provide some guidance as you interview prospective members of your Exit Planning and Deal Teams.

CERTIFIED PUBLIC ACCOUNTANT

The CPA or CPA firm that you choose to help you in the sale process should have experience in the following areas:

- Projecting Cash Flow

- Business Valuation (Including Minority Discounts)

- Reducing Business Value in Order to Increase Owner Return

- Analyzing Company Marketability

- Creating Financial Models to Project Future Growth

- Tax Planning Related to Business Sales

- Valuation for Buy/Sell Purposes

- Preparing Audited or Reviewed Financial Statements

- Debt Management
- Capitalization

BUSINESS ATTORNEY

Your business attorney should have experience in:

- Analyzing Risk Implications of Various Sale Scenarios
- Analyzing Risk Implications of Various Tax Scenarios
- Non-Qualified Deferred Compensation Planning
- Equity- and Stock-Based Incentive Plans
- Buy/Sell Agreements
- Shareholder Agreements
- Stay Bonus Agreements
- Employment Agreements
- Non-Compete Agreements
- Fiscal Year End Meetings
- Legal Audits and Due Diligence
- Negotiating Purchase Agreements
- Preparing All Transaction-Related Documents
- Business Entity: Choice, Protection, Revising and Creating Multiples
- Understanding: ESOPs, CRTs, Off-Shore Trusts

ESTATE PLANNING ATTORNEY

Your estate planning attorney should have experience in:

- Using Charitable Remainder Trusts
- Designing Estate Plans to Transfer Wealth (Pre-Sale) to Children

- Using Sophisticated Wealth Transfer Vehicles such as:
  - Grantor Retained Annuity Trusts
  - Intentionally Defective Grantor Trusts
  - Family Limited Partnerships
  - Limited Liability Companies
  - Charitable Remainder Uni-Trusts
  - Charitable Income/Estate Tax Planning

MERGER & ACQUISITION ATTORNEY

Your Merger & Acquisition attorney should be:

- Tax-Knowledgeable with respect to deals—or have that knowledge available.

- Well-Experienced—Lead Attorney in:
  - At least 50 deals.
  - The same size range and similar industry as your company.

FINANCIAL/INSURANCE ADVISOR

Your financial or insurance advisor should have:

- Technical resources and capabilities to prepare financial needs projections. This includes computer modeling capability.

- "People skills" and experience based on having helped five or more owners through the Exit Planning Process. Lack of experience in this area is not fatal if one of your other advisors has it.

- Financial advisory and investment experience representing at least a dozen clients with your level of expected investment wealth.

- Ability to recommend specific products appropriate for owner's family income needs.

BUSINESS CONSULTANT

"Business consultants come from a wide variety of backgrounds so, to choose the one who can help you with your project, match the expertise you need with the expertise of the consultant," says business consultant, Paula Cope. "For example, if owning her own business is the only experience that a consultant brings to the table, you probably should look for someone with expertise that you do not already have. Depending on your project, you should find a consultant who may have owned a business but who also has other 'tools' in his or her toolbox."

"Many well-qualified consultants have other certifications as well," Cope adds. "They may be certified in various management or communication courses (Myers-Briggs, LIFO® or Predictive Index®), in facilitation techniques or in specific large-scale methodologies such as Future Search or Appreciative Inquiry. Some consultants will also have a master's degree in business administration, organization development, human resource management, organizational psychology or finance."

INVESTMENT BANKER

Look for an investment banker with the following skills and experience:

- Served as lead banker on at least 25 deals of the size and complexity of yours. (This is fairly easy to determine as most investment bankers post lists of successful transactions on their Web sites.)

- Has a supporting team consisting of associate bankers, financial analysts and accountants. The associate bankers conduct research, help prepare the company for market and sometimes make the initial contact with potential buyers. Performing these more basic tasks frees up your investment banker to negotiate with your best potential buyers. The financial analysts vet and prepare all the assembled financial data so that they tell a story of growth to potential buyers. Accountants probe the reliability of your data before the accountants on the buyer's side begin their dissection.

- Possesses an appropriate educational background. This varies but usually includes a CPA designation, an MBA degree, or both.

- Enjoys great references from former clients who had businesses in your company's size range.

- Elicits from you a positive "gut reaction." This is a good indicator of people skills and negotiation skills.

Business Broker/Transaction Intermediary

Look for a broker with:

- Good references from respected advisors in your community and from the broker's former clients.

- Experience completing at least a dozen deals of the size and complexity of yours. (Check the broker's Web site for a list of completed transactions.)

Getting The Most Value For Your Dollar

The owners we've worked with want to remain in the driver's seat throughout the sale of their companies. Overall, the best way to do that is to provide accurate and timely information, to be available whenever needed, and to keep your attention focused on maintaining the business.

What else can you do? If you understand how each advisor charges, you can make sure both you and each of your advisors is working at maximum efficiency.

Certified Public Accountant

The best way to control the cost of the activities your accountant will undertake is to maintain organized accounting records from the outset.

To control an accountant's actions, you need an understanding of exactly what he or she is to do. The two of you then can discuss the pros and cons of various courses of action with you making the final choice.

Accounting costs generally are not significant, provided previous record keeping has been good and income and expenses have not been excessively manipulated in past years in an effort to minimize income taxation. Recording inventory accurately and consistently is extremely important, as the following fictional owner learned the hard way.

Vince Diamond owned a successful plumbing parts company in Detroit, Michigan. For years, Vince had understated his inventory in an effort to reduce his profits, thus reducing his tax liability. Vince provided the doctored numbers to his accountant who year after year, used those numbers to prepare the company's tax returns.

At Vince's 60th birthday party, his youngest son (who Vince had always hoped would take over the business) announced his plans to attend medical school. Vince's employees had neither the money nor the will to take over the company so Vince decided to investigate the option of selling his company.

During Vince's first meeting with a business broker, the broker questioned Vince's stated inventory of $250,000. "How can you possibly support annual sales of $2.5 million with an inventory this small?" Vince then admitted how, unbeknownst to his accountant, he had cleverly "saved hundreds of thousands" in taxes over the years by understating his inventory.

"Well," his broker began, "now you face a difficult choice. We can correct your inventory numbers so that your EBITDA will support a $10 million sale price." "Great! Let's do it!" Vince replied. "If we do," the broker cautioned, "the IRS can, and probably will, charge you with tax fraud."

Vince then asked, "What happens if we let the numbers stand?" The broker replied, "In that case, I have good news and bad news. The good news is: you don't go to jail." Taken aback, Vince asked, "Then what is the bad news?" The broker replied, "The bad news is that without correcting the numbers, your company's EBITDA is too low to support a $10 million price. In fact, no buyer will want to risk buying a company with unsupportable numbers."

Dejected, Vince left the broker's office. He ran the company for eight more years until he had enough money in the bank to support himself in his retirement. At the end of those eight years, Vince liquidated what he could and closed the doors.

BUSINESS ATTORNEY

I am assuming that you have established a relationship with your business attorney and are comfortable with his or her expertise, the way he or she bills and the time he or she spends. If not, this would be a good time to change attorneys or review and revise the ground rules.

As a business owner myself, I hate hourly billing structures. It rewards professionals for inefficiency. I much prefer to know the cost for the entire project. Your business attorney may be able to do this. All you need to do is ask.

MERGER & ACQUISITION ATTORNEY

Controlling costs charged on an hourly basis—the basis upon which these professionals charge—is no easy feat. These attorneys aren't cheap—expect to pay between $300 and $500 per hour. But before you blow your cool about blowing all that money, know that these senior attorneys will not spend as much time on your deal as you might think. Less experienced (and less expensive) attorneys in the firm will perform much of the due diligence, document drafting and negotiation of less crucial deal points.

There are, however, a few techniques that can help you control costs.

First, secure an estimate of fees up front—in writing. Understand what this estimate includes and what factors will affect it.

Second, get a list of hourly rates for all firm members. Ask which attorneys will be working on your deal. Not only will you see how using less experienced attorneys to perform simpler tasks saves you money, but this list also will prove helpful later as you review your invoices.

Third, find out how the firm bills time. For example, does it bill in tenths of an hour or in quarters? (The smaller the increment, the more accurately it reflects time spent.) What kind of time is charged and is there a difference in rate? For example, does the attorney charge for driving or flying to a meeting, and if so, at what rate? Some attorneys bill less for travel time than for drafting complex documents.

Fourth, tell your attorney what kind of information you want to see reflected in your invoices. Some owners want the date the service was performed, the amount of time spent and a description of the services performed. Others want that information as well as the name of the person performing the task and the dollar amount of each task. Decide what level of detail meets your needs.

Fifth, and most importantly, find out how you or members of your company can facilitate your attorney's efforts (for example, assembling documents for due diligence). You want to make sure your attorney gets answers when he or she needs them from the person best qualified to give them. Repeated requests not only cost money, they impede the progress of your deal. Those delays may derail the deal itself.

Sixth, it bears repeating: communication is critical. Make yourself available, be organized and supply all information promptly.

BUSINESS CONSULTANT

Business consultant Paula Cope tells owners that, "Consultants typically charge on a fee for service basis and should offer daily and hourly rates based on time and materials. A top-flight consultant will charge in the same range as an experienced attorney or senior accounting partner. Some consultants work on retainers or on a flat fee per project basis, known as 'fixed price.' An experienced consultant should be able to quote a price for any project the business owner requests, provide written contracts for review and signature, and be able to furnish proof of professional liability insurance before any work commences."

FINANCIAL/INSURANCE ADVISOR

Many financial advisors work on a commission basis only. Controlling this type of advisor is as easy as controlling your spending. But many advisors, especially those trained in Exit Planning, charge fees for planning and fees for managing assets. It is this type of advisor who is most valuable to you. Their industry is highly regulated and their fees are disclosed before or as they begin their representation.

BUSINESS BROKER

First, remember Rule Number One: All Fees Are Negotiable. Business brokers tend to charge on a flat percentage basis depending on the size of the transaction. The average fee is about 10 percent, but can be as low as 8 percent or as high as 12 percent.

INVESTMENT BANKER

Investment bankers typically work on a commission basis sometimes known as a "success fee." Most charge a monthly retainer, partly to cover some of their expenses, but mostly to evidence your commitment to selling your business. The money paid is non-refundable and usually does not exceed $10,000 per month for six months.

In the past, investment bankers used a sliding commission scale so that the percentage they collected decreased as the sale price increased. Many advisors find that formula to be antiquated and believe that the ideal fee structure is one designed to motivate the investment banker to get top dollar for your business.

I suggest that you use the likely sale price determined by your investment banker as the base value for fee setting purposes.

Let's say that your sale price estimate is $27 million. You may agree to pay the investment banker 2 percent of the sale price up to $27 million. Now, the motivator: You also agree to pay 5 percent of the sale price from $27 million to $30 million and 10 percent over $30 million. This fee arrangement financially motivates the investment banker to work as hard as possible to extract every dollar possible from the buyer's jealously guarded pocketbook. If your business sells for $34 million, the investment banker makes twice as much as if it had sold for $27 million. Quite an incentive for the investment banker!

Selling for more is good for the investment banker and good for you. You want to align your interest with that of the banker. Contrast that with a flat or even decreasing fee schedule and you will see why, as a seller, you should put the investment banker's interests in exact alignment with yours.

If you sell your business under any formula that relates decreasing commission percentages to increasing sale prices, your investment banker will only make an additional $100,000 or so in commissions (on a sale price of $34 million).

Can you not imagine, under these circumstances, that an investment banker might be motivated to take the easier path of selling for only $27 million? To earn only $100,000 more, it might take twice the time, effort and skill to negotiate the last few millions of deal value above the $27 million.

Investment bankers, (and if you can find a business broker willing to work on this fee basis) using a fee schedule that rewards superior results, are obviously motivated to sell your business for as much as they possibly can. So there's very little controlling to be done. What you must do is clearly describe all of your objectives before and after the engagement commences. Otherwise, business brokers and investment bankers tend to focus on your financial objectives to the exclusion of your other Exit Objectives. After all, that's how they get paid. Your other objectives, such as transferring wealth to children or charity, are actually impediments to the process. (Making sure these other objectives are met is the job of the Exit Planning Advisor on your Advisor Team.)

Additionally, like your interaction with your transaction attorney, your investment banker or business broker will be more efficient if he or she has easy access to you or someone in your company for prompt answers to questions.

GLOSSARY

A

Acquisition: The process by which the stock or assets of one corporation come to be owned by another entity. The transaction may take the form of a purchase of stock, purchase of assets, assumption of liabilities, reorganization, or merger.

Acquisition Agreement (Purchase Agreement): A legally binding contract for the sale of the stock or assets of a company.

Add Backs: The concept of restating financial statements to reflect the "true" profitability of the company.

Adjusted Basis: The initial basis, plus all additional expenditures, minus the accumulated depreciation and all other direct charges.

Agent: A party authorized to act for either the buyer or the seller in the sale of a business. An agent arranges and negotiates transactions for a fee.

Allocation of Purchase Price: Assignment of the purchase price to individual tangible and intangible assets. Where a premium has been paid over the historical costs of acquired assets, acquirers often either "step-up" the value of tangible assets or apply a part of the purchase price to tangibles.

B

Basis: The historic cost of an asset.

Basket: A minimum threshold of claims that must be reached before any liability is triggered. Buyers seeking post-closing purchase price adjustments typically cannot make claims unless and until their total aggregate damages reach a specified dollar amount.

Book Value: Net Worth. Assets minus liabilities, as recorded on a company's balance sheet.

Brokerage Agreement: An agreement between a professional intermediary and client that fully describes the terms under which the intermediary will develop and implement a strategy to sell the client's business.

Break Up Value: The value of a company's assets if sold separately, as in liquidation.

Broker (Intermediary, Investment Banker): An agent who acts for either the buyer or the seller in arranging a transaction. An intermediary is involved in searching for appropriate merger candidates, as well as negotiating and structuring the deal. An intermediary acts as a financial advisor to his or her client.

Buy/Sell (Purchase Agreement): A legally binding contract for the sale of the stock or assets of a company.

C

C Corporation: A corporation that is subject to "double taxation." In other words, it has not elected S corporation status. The taxable income of a C corporation is subject to tax at the corporate level as income while the dividends continue to be taxed at the shareholder level. In a sale of assets, the gain from the sale is taxed at the corporate level and a second tax is imposed on the proceeds of the sale, usually as a dividend, when those proceeds are distributed to the shareholders.

Capital Gains: Profits from the sale of capital assets. The gain for tax purposes is based on the gross consideration received less the basis of the ownership.

Capital Structure: A company's net worth plus its long-term debt, as recorded on its balance sheet. The capital structure is the "foundation" on which a company is built.

Capitalization Rate: A rate (expressed as a multiple) applied to a company's earnings that reflects both perceived risks and anticipated earnings growth.

Cash Flow: The excess of all cash sources less all cash uses. Often defined as a company's cash profit plus all non-cash expenses. "Free cash flow" is defined as cash flow less all capital expenditures.

Cash Transaction: A transaction that is purely completed with cash.

Closing: The consummation of a transaction, when the conditions of a change in ownership are fulfilled and funds are transferred. A closing generally occurs simultaneously with the execution of a purchase agreement, though not always. A purchase agreement may be executed with a closing to follow, pending certain conditions being met.

Covenant not to compete: A covenant not to compete is found in most purchase agreements, whereby the seller agrees not to compete with the business being sold. To enforce non-compete clauses, courts have demanded that they be specific in activity, place and time. Acquirers often seek to allocate a portion of the purchase price to a "covenant not to compete," especially in circumstances where they are paying more than the net worth of a company's assets.

Covenants: In a letter of intent or purchase contract, an agreement to perform or abstain from performing certain actions. Covenants can apply to either party of a transaction, both before and after a closing. A typical pre-closing buyer covenant would be to maintain the confidentiality of all negotiations. A typical post-closing seller covenant would be to not compete in the same business for five years.

D

Depreciation: An accounting convention reporting (on the Income Statement) the decline in useful value of a fixed asset due to wear and tear from use and the passage of time.

Discounted Cash Flow: The prospective future cash flows of a company discounted back to today's dollars.

E

Earnings Before Interest, Tax, Depreciation and Amortization (EBITDA): A metric used to measure a company's profitability.

Earn-outs: Additional payments made to sellers contingent on their meeting certain performance goals in the future. Earn-out payments are generally predicated on meeting certain sales or profit levels. Thus, the seller "earns out" a portion of the purchase price.

Escrow: A "Holdback" of a portion of the purchase consideration pending fulfillment of certain conditions. Generally, in acquisition matters, buyers demand that a portion of the purchase price be deposited in an escrow account for a certain period pending the outcome of contingent liabilities, such as collection of receivables.

Exclusive Agreement: Provides the intermediary with the exclusive right to offer a company for sale. The intermediary will receive a fee in any transaction that occurs during the term of the agreement, whether the intermediary introduced the buyer or not.

F

Fair Market Value: The value at which an informed buyer will buy and an informed seller will sell, neither under any compulsion to do so.

G

GAAP: General Accepted Accounting Principles. Accepted accounting norms and conditions, as established by the Financial Accounting Standards Board (FASB).

Goodwill: An intangible asset, representing the excess of the cost of assets over their carried or market value. Goodwill is usually created by purchasing assets at a value higher than fair market value. Goodwill is essentially "air;" it represents nothing tangible, only the perceived value of the acquired company's name, reputation and anticipated stream of earnings.

H

Holdback: The retention of a portion of the purchase consideration pending the outcome or fulfillment of certain conditions.

Hurdle Date: During the "stop-shop" period (set in a Letter of Intent) the seller requires the buyer to prove his or her continued interest (and progress toward closing) by establishing periodic performance dates. Each of these performance dates is called a hurdle date. For example, the buyer may have to provide proof of financing two weeks after signing the LOI, a draft of the Purchase Agreement after four weeks and completion of the environmental studies after six weeks.

I

Internal Rate of Return (*IRR*): The compounded rate of return on an investment in an acquisition, including interest, dividends and capital gains, expressed in a per annum basis. The customary IRR expected by a senior lender is 12 to 18 percent; the IRR commanded by equity investors in acquisitions ranges from 20 to 40 percent.

Intermediary Threshold: The business value that separates those companies that are typically sold using the services of an investment banker from those sold using the services of a business broker.

L

Letter of Intent: A non-binding, written summary of the buyer's and seller's mutual understanding of the price and terms of an acquisition in the process of being negotiated. Since letters of intent involving public companies must be openly disclosed, transactions involving public companies often go right to contract, skipping the letter of intent stage.

Leveraged buyout: A purchase of a company, using borrowed funds. The acquired company's assets serve as security for the loans taken out by the acquiring firm.

Liabilities: Obligations that a company has toward third parties.

Liquidation: The dissolution of a company through the sale of its assets. The cash from the sale is used to first satisfy creditors with any remaining cash distributed to shareholders.

M

Management Buyout: A leveraged buyout in which all or part of a management teams buys the company.

Merger: A combination of two businesses into one. In a merger, Corporation A combines with and disappears into Corporation B.

Misrepresentation: False or misleading information provided to a party in making an offer or contract.

Multiple: The multiplier of EBITDA (earnings before interest, taxes, depreciation, and amortization) used to estimate enterprise value.

P

Payback Period: The time required by a buyer to recoup his original investment in a company through its earnings. Generally, acquirers demand payback periods of between five to seven years, taking into account the time value of money.

Price to Earnings Ratio (*P/E Ratio*): A ratio or multiple derived by dividing the total consideration paid in an acquisition by the acquired company's earnings (either current or projected). P/E ratios are generated for comparative reasons, to test the relative cost of an acquisition versus other similar deals.

Principal: One of the parties in a transaction. As generally used in this book, a principal is one who will hold significant ownership in an acquired company. A principal is often represented by an agent.

R

Recapture of Depreciation and Tax Credits: The amount of gain resulting from the disposition of property that represents the recovery of depreciation expense (and tax credits) previously deducted or credited on the seller's income tax returns.

Recourse: An agreement by a seller to make a buyer whole on the value of any assets that prove to not be worth their stated value. Recourse arrangements generally apply to the collection of receivables or the obsolescence of inventory.

Retrading: The negotiating over money and issues (such as warranties and representations) that happens after the Term Sheet is signed but prior to closing.

S

S Corporation: In general, an S Corporation does not pay income taxes. Instead, the corporation's income or losses are divided among and passed through to its shareholders. This is why an S Corporation is referred to as a "pass-through" tax entity. The shareholders report the income or loss on their own individual income tax returns. There are eligibility and qualification requirements imposed by the IRS that must be met and maintained.

Seller's Promissory Notes (*Take Back*): A note held by the seller to help finance an acquisition. Generally, seller's notes are unsecured obligations, though they can be secured by a lien (usually junior) on the assets or the stock of the company.

Senior Debt: Secured debt that has the highest preference to assets in liquidation.

Shareholder loans: Loans given to the corporation via shareholders.

Statutory Merger: One corporation completely absorbs another; it is a continuation of two (or more) companies into one new corporation. All shareholders of the previous companies become shareholders of the new company. These mergers are generally governed by state statutes.

Stepped-Up Basis: The result of increasing the basis of an asset from its historic, depreciated cost to one determined by an acquirer's cost or fair market value.

T

Take-Over: Acquiring a controlling interest in a target company, often without the consent of the target company's management.

Target Company: A company that has been selected by a potential acquirer as an attractive candidate.

V

Value Threshold: A term coined by John Brown to describe the minimum business value necessary for an all-cash or (nearly all-cash) sale.

Vertical Integration: The acquisition of companies engaged in either earlier or later stages of production or marketing. The acquisition of either a supplier or a customer would be a "vertical" acquisition.

W

Working Capital: The excess of current assets less current liabilities.

INDEX

A

adjacent industry or
adjacencies 149, 155
adjustment to sale price 148
advisors,
Exit Planning 33–36, 39, 53, 62, 63,
84, 202, 244, 247–248, 253, 254,
264–269, 278–281, 291
Deal Team 34–37, 118, 172–173, 200,
203, 244, 264
Transaction 34–37, 172, 195, 202
assets,
purchase of 174, 184
attorney
business planning 253, 256, 264–266,
270-271, 283, 288
estate planning 253, 257, 264, 266,
280-281, 283-284
M&A or transaction 151, 264, 271,
279–280, 284, 288-289
audits, 99–100, 159, 166
post-closing 203–204

B

Baby Boomers xiii–xix, 8, 49
demographics xiv–xv, 104
longevity xvii–xviii
succession plans xiv, 116, 241
Bade, Harold 4, 18, 117, 207–210
basket 197, 293
Berger, Wayne 4, 6, 210–213
Braun, Jette 4, 222–226
break-up fee 188–189

business appraiser 264, 266, 277
business broker 36, 39, 46, 52, 264,
273–277, 286, 289–290, 291, 294
business consultant 91, 253, 257, 264,
266, 271, 284–285, 289
Business Enterprise Institute, Inc. xx, 33,
106, 222, 242, 282
business plans, 95
strategic 95–99, 253, 259
business sector, attractive 102, 108, 256

C

C Corporation 33, 58–63, 184–185, 294
CRT 63–68, 212, 283
capital gains rate 121, 123–124, 228
affect on M&A market 123–125
caps 197
cash flow 45–46, 91, 94–95, 100,
101–108, 202, 256, 267, 282, 295
Certified Valuation Analyst 277
Charitable Remainder Trust 63–68,
212, 283
Clayton Capital Partners xx, 105, 113,
137
closing 146, 148, 160, 164, 295
conditions 197
date 191
confidentiality 15–16, 163, 203, 210,
232, 239, 244
Confidentiality Agreements 157,
171–172, 176
consulting agreements 186, 189–190
contingencies 172, 191

REQUEST FORM

☐ Please send me _____ copy/ies of *Cash Out Move On: Get Top Dollar—And More—Selling Your Business.* ($24.95 each for paperback; $34.95 each for hard cover) Please call for volume discount information.

☐ Please send me _____ copy/ies of *The Completely Revised How To Run Your Business So You Can Leave It In Style.* ($24.95 each for paperback) Please call for volume discount information.

☐ Please send me _____ copy/ies of *The Completely Revised How To Run Your Business So You Can Leave It In Style Companion Workbook* ($14.95 each).

☐ Please send me a free subscription to The Exit Planning Review™, BEI's electronic newsletter. My e-mail address is:

_____.

☐ Please send me more information about upcoming Exit Planning Seminars:
    ☐ In my area
    ☐ Anywhere

☐ I am an advisor and I want more information about how BEI can support my efforts to help my clients get top dollar selling their businesses.

Company Name: _____

Name: _____

Address: _____

City: _____ State: _____ Zip: _____

Telephone: (_____) _____

E-mail Address: _____

FAX ORDERS: (303) 853-4979

PHONE ORDERS: Toll Free (888) 206-3009

POSTAL ORDERS: Business Enterprise Institute, Inc.
741 Corporate Circle, Suite J
Golden, CO 80401 USA

ONLINE ORDERS: www.BEIBooks.com

SALES TAX: Please add 7.6 percent for books shipped to Colorado
addresses.

SHIPPING: $4.50 for the first book, $2 for each add'l book; $4.50 for
the first workbook, $2 for each add'l workbook

PAYMENT:

- Check enclosed

- Credit Card
  - VISA
  - MasterCard
  - AmEx
  - Discover

Card number: _____

Exp date: _____

Name on card: _____